The Lovell Haggadah

ILLUMINATIONS, TRANSLATION, AND COMMENTARY BY
MATTHEW L. BERKOWITZ

Nirtzah Editions, LLC

מכון שכטר למדעי היהדות
SCHECHTER INSTITUTE OF JEWISH STUDIES

Schechter Institute of Jewish Studies

The Lovell Haggadah

Project Management: Rabbi Matthew L. Berkowitz, Nirtzah Editions, LLC, Boca Raton
Production Supervision: Yair Medina, Jerusalem Fine Art Prints, Jerusalem
Editing: Prof. David Golinkin, Rabbi Miriam C. Berkowitz, Prof. Moshe Benovitz,
Prof. Steven Brown, Dr. Shula Laderman, and Fern Allen
Printing and Binding: Printiv, Jerusalem
Haggadah Design: Irit Harel, Rabbi Matthew L. Berkowitz, Yair Medina
Hatikvah Calligraphy: Izzy Pludwinski, Jerusalem

ISBN 978–965–7105–51–1

FIRST PRINTING © 2008
The Schechter Institute of Jewish Studies and Nirtzah Editions, LLC
Produced and Printed in Jerusalem, Israel

The publishers gratefully acknowledge the kind permissions of the following copyright holders:

Doubleday, a division of Random House, Inc. for the quote from Avivah Gottlieb Zornberg, *The Particulars of Rapture,* Copyright © 2001

Marc Gold, of Gold's Horseradish, Inc., for allowing the replication of the Gold's Horseradish label in Plate 17

Rabbi Prof. David Golinkin for sharing portions from his essay, "*Pesaḥ Potpourri:* On the Origin and Development of Some Lesser-Known *Pesaḥ* Customs," in Golinkin, *Insight Israel: The View from Schechter,* Second Series, Schechter Institute of Jewish Studies, Copyright © 2006

Farrar, Straus & Giroux, Inc. and Prof. Susannah Heschel for excerpts from Abraham Joshua Heschel, *Moral Grandeur and Spiritual Audacity,* Copyright © 1996 Sylvia Heschel, Introduction Copyright © 1996 Susannah Heschel

Nogah Hareuveni *z"l,* for photographing the Israeli landscape which inspired the painting of *Eretz Yisrael.* Original photograph of *Bik'at Beit Netofa* in the Galilee appears in *Tree and Shrub in Our Biblical Heritage,* Neot Kedumim Ltd., Copyright © 1984, p. 10

HarperCollins Publishers, Prof. Arnold Eisen, and Prof. Edward Greenstein for excerpts from Michael Strassfeld and Betsy Platkin Teutsch (illus.), *The Jewish Holidays: A Guide and Commentary,* Text Copyright © 1985 Michael Strassfeld, Illustrations Copyright © 1985 Betsy Platkin Teutsch

Henry Holt and Company, for the quote from Isabel Allende in Jay Allison and Dan Gediman, eds., *This I Believe,* Copyright © 2006

Jewish Lights Publishing for the poem by Sheila Peltz Weinberg in *The Women's Seder Sourcebook: Rituals and Readings for Use at the Seder,* Copyright © 2003

Library of The Jewish Theological Seminary and Prof. David Kraemer, for use of the image from *The Prague Haggadah: 1526,* Fol. 3r

Perseus Books and Michael Walzer, Institute for Advanced Studies, Princeton, NJ, for excerpts from his book, *Exodus and Revolution,* Basic Books, Copyright © 1985

Schocken Books and David Biale, for the excerpt from Ilana Pardes' essay, "Imagining the Birth of Ancient Israel: National Metaphors in the Bible," in *The Cultures of the Jews,* Copyright © 2002

Rabbi Prof. Ismar Schorsch, for his excerpts from *Canon Without Closure,* Aviv Press, Copyright © 2007

Dedicated with love
to
Jac Lovell, who was born on Pesaḥ
and
Paul "Pesaḥ" Calick
by their children,
Dedee and Stephen J. Lovell

Marvelous and beautiful is life in the body,
but more marvelous and more beautiful is life in a word . . .
When a good man dies, his soul becomes a word and lives on in God's book.

Abraham Joshua Heschel

בס"ד

To Jacob,

לשנה הבאה בירושלים —
Next year in Jerusalem —

בברכה,
In blessing,
Matt B_____

Dear Jacob,
    On this first Seder of 2013,
we feel blessed to tell, ask,
and hear the story of Passover.
We sincerely hope that you
will read and study this Hagaddah,
and someday use it in your
own Seder!
        We love you,
        Bubbe and Zayde

Table of Contents

Foreword

Appreciation is at the heart of the Jewish people. In Hebrew, we are called יהודים (*Yehudim*). The name is derived from יהודה (*Yehudah*). As Leah gives birth to her fourth son, she declares," 'This time I will thank the Lord.' Therefore, she named him יהודה" (Genesis 29:35). Rabbi Yoḥanan teaches, "From the beginning of time, no one ever thanked God until Leah did" (*BT Berakhot 7b*). And so, in the appreciative spirit of Leah, as this haggadah is born, there are many I wish to acknowledge.

Upon ordination from The Jewish Theological Seminary, I was fortunate to be hired as JTS's first rabbinic fellow. Charged with creating a substantive program of adult learning, I began tailoring classes to individuals, couples, and small groups, showing the potential for creativity and passion in text study. Two of my first students were Dedee and Stephen J. Lovell. For two years, I studied with the Lovells at their home in Sands Point: "Prayer," "The Philosophy of Abraham Joshua Heschel," and "The Archaeology of the Passover Haggadah." We have continued to learn long-distance for the past six years. Their love of learning inspires me in turn to seek, to question, and to study.

No rabbi could ask for more precious and devoted students. Our learning together is like an exchange between colleagues, based on the *havruta* model. Both Dedee and Stephen consistently share insights into the text that previously eluded me in my own readings. I am inspired and moved by the love and respect they show each other. It is a love that knows no bounds and only deepens with the passage of time. They are wholly (and "holy") present in all that they do for family, friends, and community. More than that, their lives are immersed in Torah, *hesed*, and their ever-growing family. They lovingly and enthusiastically participated in the first JTS Israel Mission, opened their home to my study groups, celebrated in the opening of my exhibit at Yeshiva University Museum, graciously hosted me for a scholar-in-residence program at their home congregation of Temple Beth Sholom in Roslyn, New York, and together we share a deep love for The Jewish Theological Seminary and The Schechter Institute of Jewish Studies.

Toward the conclusion of our study of the haggadah, Dedee and Stephen requested to see my art portfolio. Seated at their kitchen table overlooking the north shore of Long Island, they asked if I would consider creating a new family haggadah. Stephen proudly handed me an early edition of Mordechai Kaplan's *New Haggadah*, their well-used and bruised companion for many a family seder. A thick piece of electrical tape held the binding and all its contents together, and wine stains could be seen throughout. Dedee wanted to retain Kaplan's keen focus on moral and ethical imperatives. However, she and Stephen were ready for a contemporary text, accessible and egalitarian, to encourage discussion around the seder table. Memories of their two fathers sparked a creative idea. Dedee's father, Paul Calick, was named *Pesaḥ* in Hebrew, and Stephen's father Jac Lovell, *Yaakov Ben Moshe HaLevi*, was born on *Pesaḥ*, April 15, 1902. What could be a greater tribute to the memory of two beloved fathers with such a deep connection to Passover than to create a haggadah in their honor?

As we moved into the final stages of this project, I expressed my hope and desire to title this work *The Lovell Haggadah*. In their usual soft-spoken, thoughtful, and humble way, Stephen and Dedee modestly resisted. On September 30, 2007, I authored a letter to convince them of my position. I cited four reasons, including the tradition to acknowledge patrons of illuminated manuscripts; the fact that the values expressed throughout the haggadah are the qualities they cherish as a family; the wish to create a multi-generational conversation *l'dor va dor* within the family; and the Talmudic teaching *gadol ha'm'aseh min ha'oseh*, "greater is the one who causes others to do than the one who does" (*BT Bava Batra 9a*).

Each person who holds this haggadah in their hands, lives through a unique seder night, derives inspiration from the artwork, adopts some of the creative ideas, considers a question they have never thought of before, or looks at the text from a new perspective, has the Lovell family to thank. Words cannot express my personal gratitude for their loving support, inspiration, guidance, and patience.

Another moment in my life also planted the seeds of this work, poignantly recalling the verse, "One who sows in sorrow will reap in joy" (Psalms 126:5). I had long wished to author a haggadah, but thought it would wait until the sunset of my career. In the winter of 1995–1996, my friend, roommate, and rabbinical school classmate Matthew Eisenfeld and I were students together at The Schechter Institute of Jewish Studies in Jerusalem. He was working on a haggadah in anticipation of his parents and sister coming to spend Passover in Israel. That dream came to an end as two Palestinian terrorists boarded a bus in the heart of the city. Just as Matt *z"l* was setting out for Jordan, on a journey of cultural exploration, his life was ended, abruptly and much too soon. In his creativity, passion for Jewish learning, and seriousness of purpose, Matt *z"l* inspired my own journey. I resolved then to create a work infused with the learning Matt *z"l* loved so dearly and animated by the colors with which he illumined his own life and the lives of others. In partnering with The Schechter Institute of Jewish Studies in the publication of this work, we celebrate Matt's life and honor his memory.

Many other people shared of their talents and encouragement in various ways.

I am deeply obliged to all those at The Jewish Theological Seminary who have supported my endeavors. Were it not for the vision and leadership of Chancellor Emeritus Prof. Ismar Schorsch, I would not have become a rabbinic fellow in the JTS KOLLOT: Voices of Learning Program and would never have met Dedee and Stephen Lovell. Rabbi Carol Davidson, Vice Chancellor of Institutional Advancement, has been a constant source of encouragement in my teaching and in this project. Rabbi Jerry Schwarzbard of the Rare Book Room, was instrumental in assembling a number of medieval *haggadot* for my perusal at the early stages of this project. Jerry was generous with his time, and he is a wealth of knowledge in the area of Rare Books. Locally, my colleagues in the JTS Florida Office have been enthusiastic in seeing this project take shape.

The Moss Haggadah inspired my understanding of the power of art to illuminate sacred text. I am indebted to its creator, David Moss, for kindling my own potential.

Richard Levy, patron of *The Moss Haggadah* and collector of Judaica, has repeatedly opened his home and heart, allowing me to teach about his collection of illuminated *ketubbot* and *ḥanukiot*. In addition, Richard's extensive book collection provided background material for some of the illuminations. Arthur Jaffe and his exceptional staff at *The Arthur and Mata Jaffe Collection: Books as Aesthetic Objects*, at Florida Atlantic University, have also offered ideas for format and design.

I am further indebted to the skillful reading and editing of Prof. Steven Brown, former Dean of The Davidson School of Education at The Jewish Theological Seminary. Over the past few years, I have had the privilege of leading *sedarim* with Steve Brown. His energy, brilliance, and insights all inspired me to think more creatively and to include more family activities before and during the seder.

Rabbi David Golinkin, President of The Schechter Institute of Jewish Studies, enthusiastically accepted this book for publication. He and his colleagues Prof. Moshe Benovitz, Professor of Talmud, and Dr. Shula Laderman, Lecturer in Jewish Art, offered scholarly critiques and trenchant editorial suggestions. During my years as a rabbinical student, David and Moshe cultivated my love of Torah learning. I made the acquaintance of Shula Laderman during the 2005 JTS Israel Mission in which she led the group on a tour of The Israel Museum. All three possess overwhelming breadth and depth of knowledge, and their valuable contributions fine-tuned this work.

No thanks would be complete without singling out Yair Medina of Jerusalem Fine Art Prints, who oversaw production of *The Lovell Haggadah* and its companion, the limited edition portfolio *Passover Landscapes: Illuminations on the Exodus.* Yair is a dreamer— creative, kind, and hard-working. From the beginning, he understood and embraced the project, and engaged a talented book designer, Irit Harel.

I thank my parents, Rita and David Berkowitz for their constant love and for nourishing my Jewish identity and artistic abilities.

My wife, Rabbi Miriam Carey Knight Berkowitz, has been my muse. She sparked my career in Jewish art by suggesting that I design our *ketubbah.* She has always encouraged me to make time for painting. She has edited and re-edited this work countless times and composed many of the discussion questions.

Our son, Adir Pinḥas, made frequent visits to my studio to check on the latest painting. Adir is like the wise son; his questions and critiques continually helped to sharpen my own thinking. Adir was born days after I completed the writing of *Megillat Esther;* our daughter Rachel Naama's birth coincided with the completion of the limited edition portfolio *Passover Landscapes: Illuminations on the Exodus.* Her happy nature, wide smile, and precociousness have brought joy to our home, and I am glad she could share in the culmination of this project. Just prior to finishing *The Lovell Haggadah,* we were blessed with the birth of Shira Lilach— affectionately called "trade edition" by her siblings. May her zestful cry yield to a lifelong song of joy.

Above all, I thank God for the many blessings that have enabled me to reach this day.

Rabbi Matthew L. Berkowitz
18 Tevet 5768, *Parashat Shemot*
Boca Raton, Florida
Jerusalem, Israel

The Unique Approach of *The Lovell Haggadah*

The Lovell Haggadah, in its translation, questions, artwork, and essays, encourages a tapestry of responses in its retelling of the *Pesaḥ* story.

Liturgy

Only when we are attuned to sensitivities of language and expanding the spectrum of voices in the interpretation of sacred text can we hope for a complete redemption. For example, women were just as much a part of *yetziat mitzrayim* as the men. The rabbis teach regarding women, *af hen hayu b'oto ha'nes*, "women too were part of this miracle" (*BT Pesaḥim 108b*). Every attempt has been made to render the translation as inclusive, modern, and egalitarian as possible, while remaining loyal to the original Hebrew.

Furthermore, while this haggadah retains the traditional Hebrew liturgy, it does so with a questioning consciousness. While some questions and comments deepen the reader's understanding of the traditional text, others seek to challenge those same teachings. Far from considering this approach to sacred text disrespectful, the tradition demands wrestling. It is for this reason that the Kotzker Rebbe offers a wonderful interpretation of the verse *"lo ta'asun ken la'Adonai Eloheikhem,"* "that one should not do likewise to the Lord your God" (Deuteronomy 12:4). While the context of the verse is with respect to idolatry, the Kotzker Rebbe translates the verse literally, "you will not make a 'yes' to the Lord, your God." In other words, do not simply be a "yes-man" to God. Seek, ask, compare, challenge, and make the Torah your own; find its relevance to your generation, surroundings, and life experience.

Artwork

One of the goals of *The Lovell Haggadah* is to open the doorway to interpretation through art. Just as Rashi, Ibn Ezra, Radak and other classical commentators open our hearts and minds to new ways of seeing old verses, so too does art have the potential to broaden our exegetical vision. Each of the twenty-seven illuminations is an archaeological dig, demonstrating the ability of art to interpret sacred text. Collectively, we have underappreciated the power of art to inspire hearts and minds to Judaism. However, like music, it is one of the common denominators that one can begin to appreciate with little background. Art tells its own story. Let the animated colors, iconography, and text lend themselves to new *midrash* around the table. Interpret with your own eyes before reading the extensive explanations found in the *Appendix*. Seder leaders may read through this section each year and select several illuminations as centerpieces for conversation during the evening.

Discussion

Discussion questions are suggested along the evening's path to spark the imagination and creativity of participants around the table. Spontaneous conversation is welcome; indeed this is the essential *mitzvah* of *Pesaḥ*, *v'higadeta l'vinkha*, "and you will tell it to your child" (Exodus 13:8). Embellishing the story is precisely what the five sages in *B'nei Berak* were doing all night long.

Creative engagement sparks discussion. Prior preparation enhances the quality of dialogue around the table. Accordingly, the *halakhah* prescribes that we spend the thirty days before *Pesaḥ* preparing ourselves spiritually and otherwise for the seder.

Here are a few suggestions to nurture conversation:

- The leader of the seder may author questions connected to each of the themes throughout the haggadah and vary them from year to year.

- Give guests some Passover homework as the festival approaches. Assign one section of the seder to each guest and encourage them to bring something new and creative.

- Have children create their own seder plates.

- Get white painters' caps and in the tradition of Prof. Steven Brown, paint each step of the seder on a different cap—as the seder progresses repeatedly sing the various steps of the seder and change caps.

- Ask your guests to author their own "Four Questions."

- Choose a historical or literary figure that made the theme of freedom central to their life. Place cards with these names under each person's plate prior to the seder and when you arrive at *b'khol dor va'dor*, "in every generation" (page 108), have participants lift their plates and role-play the person they received, while answering the question, "what does freedom mean to me?"

- Begin the seder with a *kavannah* (meditation) or *D'var Torah* (word of Torah)—ideally something that reflects on the year that has passed and expresses hopes for the year to come.

Reading Well

The fifteen steps of the seder are said to mirror the steps leading up to the inner court of the Temple in Jerusalem. And just as these steps represent an elevation of one's spiritual self as one approaches the inner sanctum, so too does the progression of the seder urge us to raise ourselves higher and higher. To this end, *The Lovell Haggadah* identifies an essential quality or idea associated with each step of the journey. The notion behind this is to give pause to the seder participant. In the introduction to his book *Daybreak: Thoughts on the Prejudices of Morality* (1886), Friedrich Nietzsche writes of the importance of this approach to reading. He decries the hurried pace of life and suggests that we pay more attention to the art of philology, the study of words:

> For philology is that venerable art which demands of its votaries one thing above all: to go aside, to take time, to become still, to become slow—it is a goldsmith's art and connoisseurship of the word which has nothing but delicate, cautious work to do and achieves nothing if it does not achieve it *lento* [slowly]. But, for precisely this reason, it is more necessary than ever today, by precisely this means does it entice us and enchant us the most, in the midst of an age of "work," that is to say, of hurry, of indecent and perspiring haste, which wants to "get everything done" at once, including every old or new book: this

art does not so easily get anything done, it teaches to read well, that is, to read slowly, deeply, looking cautiously before and aft, with reservations, with doors left open, with delicate eyes and fingers.

Unknowingly, Nietzsche expresses what it is to read a text Jewishly. To survey a sacred text, especially the haggadah, in a cursory or superficial way is to do injustice to the text and to ourselves. We are robbed of the many layers of meaning; even worse, one sacrifices the potential for personal transformation. Instead of racing through the seder, cultivate a more thoughtful sense of the evening's ritual and purpose. Move thoughtfully and deliberately from one step of the seder to the next.

Pesaḥ Lento: What's In a Name?

The Book of Samuel observes, *k'shmo ken hu,* "one's name reflects one's essence" (I Samuel 25:25). What is the meaning of the word *Pesaḥ (pey-samech-ḥet),* and how does it illuminate our observance of the seder ritual? Exegetical sources yield three distinct yet complementary interpretations.

Partnership

The most common definition of *Pesaḥ* is "passing over," "skipping over," or "springing over." Numerous classical commentators, including the eleventh-century exegete Rabbi Shlomo Yitzḥaki (Rashi, 1040–1105, France) have explained the Hebrew *Pesaḥ* as "pass over," based on Exodus 12:13. Naḥum Sarna elaborates, "It was through the influence of the Latin Vulgate version that 'pass over' became the predominant English rendering . . ."

Rabbi Samson Raphael Hirsch (1808–1888, Germany) delves deeper into this perspective on *Pesaḥ.* He argues that *Pesaḥ (pey-samech-ḥet)* is related to the word *pesiah (pey-samech-ayin),* meaning "to step." While *pesiah* denotes a continuity of action, an uninterrupted stepping motion, Hirsch argues that the replacement of the Hebrew letter *ayin* by the letter *ḥet* indicates "a restriction, a hindrance of the idea which is expressed by the *ayin* in the root." Accordingly, *pasaḥ al* (Exodus 12:27) means "to step haltingly over something." Hirsch further hones the definition of *Pesaḥ*: the word reflects God's deliberate and thoughtful action of "stepping haltingly over Israelite homes," noting carefully which homes belonged to Israelites and which to Egyptians.

The Israelites are enjoined to take an active and deliberate role in their redemption: to slaughter the Paschal Lamb, gather hyssop, and smear the blood of the lamb on the doorpost. They must participate in their own salvation. This idea is reinforced by Rashi's commentary on Exodus 12:13, which teaches that "the blood [of the Paschal Lamb] will be a sign *for you*"—specifying "for you and not for others. From here it is derived that the Israelites placed the blood on the inside of the doorway and not on the outside." What then is the goal of this ritual if not to serve as a sign to God? Rashi explains: "God said, 'I will set my eye to see that you are occupied with my commandment and then I will pass over you.'" According to this definition, it is insufficient for the Israelites to remain passive as God unleashes the final plague (Death of the Firstborn) on the Egyptians. Redemption will not come solely from the work of God.

Hirsch spells this out even more clearly: "Israel was to make itself deserving so that the destruction that befell the Egyptian houses should pass over their heads." They were to eat and enjoy their *Pesaḥ* offering with conscious acknowledgment of God's role and a confidence "that the danger which hovered over their heads also, would not affect them." Hence, at its most basic level, *Pesaḥ* suggests *partnership* between human beings and God. Redemption crystallizes through the acts of humans and God together.

Protection

A second and even more compelling definition of *Pesaḥ* reveals itself elsewhere in the *Tanakh*. Isaiah 31:5 teaches, "Like the birds that fly, even so will the Lord of Hosts shield Jerusalem, shielding and saving, protecting (*pasoaḥ*) and rescuing." According to this reading, as the Angel of Death is unleashed, it is insufficient for God to merely "pass over" the Israelite homes. God actively protects every Israelite home from the threat of annihilation.

This interpretation dovetails well with one of the traditional names given to the seder evening, *leyl shimurim*, "the night of protection." Like a vigilant guard surveying the perimeter of a home, God watches over the Israelites, observing and shielding. One of the metaphors employed in Exodus, in the verse from Isaiah, and elsewhere in *Tanakh* is that of a bird protecting its young:

> "You have seen what I did to the Egyptians, how I bore you on eagles' wings and brought you to me" (Exodus 19:4). How is the eagle different from all other birds? All other birds carry their young between their feet, because they are afraid of birds flying above them. But the eagle is afraid only of man, who might shoot an arrow at him. Therefore the eagle carries the young upon its wings, reasoning, 'I would rather have an arrow lodge in me than in my young.' (*Mekhilta*, ed. Horovitz-Rabin, pp. 207–208).

Isaiah's promise that God will again shield and save, protect and rescue Jerusalem, sheds light on God's earlier protection of the Israelites on the eve of the Exodus. The gesture is an expression of divine love, an overwhelming act of God's care. *Pesaḥ* interpreted as "protection" suggests a more active role for God in delivering these former slaves.

Compassion

A third reading of *Pesaḥ* is offered in the commentary of Abraham Ibn Ezra (1080–1164, Spain) and also mentioned by Rashi on Exodus 12:13: *v'ḥamalti*, or "I will have mercy." Ibn Ezra (Exodus 12:27) adds, "because God had compassion on the first-born Israelite males as a result of the blood of the lamb, the lamb is rightfully called '*pesaḥ*' (Paschal) [as it symbolizes God's mercy]." Such an interpretation is reinforced when one turns to the Akkadian cognate *pasaḥu* which means "to soothe, placate, or be soothed."

According to this understanding, *mercy* and *compassion* are the most compelling and elemental messages emanating from the Israelite experience in Egypt. While one would have expected the suffering and oppression of the Israelites to harden their hearts, Torah repeatedly cautions us that we should not oppress the stranger, orphan, or widow in our midst (see Exodus 22:20, Leviticus 19:33–34, Deuteronomy 10:19, and Deuteronomy 24:17–18); we are obligated to remember that we too were strangers in a foreign land. God's acts of mercy and compassion on the eve of departure model the only appropriate response to oppression.

As evidence of this core message, one need look no further than the text at the heart of the haggadah. The rabbis deliberately selected the opening chapter of *Parashat Ki Tavo*. There, we read of the ritual of *hava'at bikkurim*, "the bringing of the first fruits" to the Sanctuary or Temple. As these fruits were presented, the Israelite farmer declared to the priest:

> My ancestor was a fugitive Aramean. He went down to Egypt with meager numbers and sojourned there; but there he became a very populous nation. The Egyptians dealt harshly with us and oppressed us; they imposed heavy labors on us. We cried to the Lord, the God of our fathers, and the Lord heard our plea and saw our plight, our misery, and our oppression. The Lord freed us from Egypt by a mighty hand, by an outstretched arm and awesome power, and by signs and portents. God brought us to this place and gave us this land, a land flowing with milk and honey. Wherefore I now bring the first fruits of the soil which You, O Lord, have given me (Deuteronomy 26:5–10).

With its midrashic accretions, this excerpt forms the heart of the haggadah. The passage chronicles God's compassion: protecting Jacob, helping us prosper in Egypt, hearing the cry of the people, delivering the Israelites from bondage, giving the gift of the Land of Israel, and providing its fruits. The text is noticeably silent on "The Ten Plagues"; nor is there any mention of calling forth God's vengeance on the Egyptians. The desire "to rejoice at the downfall of one's enemies" is wholly and rightfully absent from the core text of the haggadah.

Passover Preparations

Toward Redemption

This month will be to you the beginning of all months;
it will be the first month of the year to you.
Exodus 12:2

Nisan, the Hebrew month in which *Pesaḥ* occurs, is the beginning of the year for the Jewish people. While most of us are more familiar with another new year's celebration, namely *Rosh Hashanah* (which commemorates the birth of the world and occurs on the first of *Tishrei*, the seventh month of the calendar), *Pesaḥ* (which marks the birth of the Israelite people and begins on the eve of the fourteenth of *Nisan*) is the more significant new year for us as a nation (see *Mishnah Rosh Hashanah 1:1*). Since each festival is a liminal moment, it is not surprising that they share similar qualities. First, both involve a period of preparation and heightened consciousness. *Elul*, the month leading up to *Tishrei*, is a time of reflection and return; the weeks leading up to *Pesah* offer a parallel opportunity.

Second, both are times of renewal and rebirth. On the High Holidays, we are given the chance to begin again. Seasonally, *Pesah* reflects a similar experience. As Song of Songs teaches, "the winter has passed and the rains have ended; the blossoms have appeared in the land" (Song of Songs 2:11-12). Marked by nature's rebirth, the cycle of the year begins anew.

Third, it is said on *Rosh Hashanah* that "repentance, prayer, and righteousness avert the severity of the decree." In *Pesah* too, these three acts are abundantly evident. Removing the *hametz* (leavened bread) from our dwelling places represents a removal of the negative (puffed up) qualities in ourselves, a spiritual cleansing (as will be discussed in greater detail below under *Bedikat Hametz*). The seder includes various forms of prayer, and there are synagogue services throughout the holiday. We are expected to give *tzedakah* before the holiday so that all Jews have enough food to celebrate with dignity, as we are enjoined to open our doors to guests on seder night.

Turning Outward
Me'ot Hittin: Coins for Wheat (Giving)

Given the emphasis on *hesed* (compassion) this evening, it is imperative that all members of the community be allowed to savor the taste of freedom. The festival celebrates redemption from slavery; the rabbis recognized the hollowness of such a commemoration if people ignored suffering in their own midst. To rejoice while turning a blind eye to starvation and need is a perversion of the essential message of *Pesah*.

The first mishnah of Tractate *Pesahim* teaches, "Even a poor person in Israel does not eat without reclining. And those who distribute *tzedakah* must ensure that every poor person should not have fewer than four cups of wine, even if they are being provided from the community soup kitchen" (*Mishnah Pesahim 10:1*). We are not free until each person can live and celebrate with dignity, symbolized on seder night by reclining and drinking the four cups.

The obligation of providing for the needy became known as *Me'ot Hittin*, "coins for wheat" (*Shulhan Arukh, Orah Hayyim 429:1*) and has alternatively been referred to as *kimha d'Pishah* or "*Pesah* flour." Perhaps even more important is inviting the poor to one's seder table—a tradition at the heart of the *Ha Lahma Anya* section of *Maggid*.

Tzedakah provides the opportunity for all to celebrate meaningfully. This tradition trains one's self (and children) in the importance of giving. Furthermore, since family, community, and nation represent three foci of identity, this is a chance to foster generosity within the family, to donate to local community pantries (Jewish and non-Jewish alike), and to allocate *tzedakah* to Jews in other parts of the world, especially in Israel. Giving *tzedakah* transforms one from being a slave of Pharaoh to becoming a servant of God. Slavery compels a focus on one's own needs; freedom gives one the God-like ability to care for others. As *Pesaḥ* approaches, consider making a *Me'ot Ḥittin Tzedakah* Box. In the days leading up to Passover, be sure that every family member contributes to this *tzedakah* box strategically placed by the *mezuzah* (doorpost). Just as the blood of the Paschal Lamb led to the continuity of life, so too do the funds collected in this box mark the nourishing of life. A few days before *Pesaḥ*, make a list of *tzedakah* funds—locally, nationally, and in Israel—to which you might contribute. Decide democratically how to allocate your *Me'ot Ḥittin*.

Turning Inward

Bedikat Ḥametz: Searching the Home for Leavened Bread

Seven days you will eat unleavened bread; the first day, you will discard leaven from your homes.
Exodus 12:15

One of the most cherished traditions among both children and adults is *bedikat ḥametz* (the search for leavened bread). This tradition concludes weeks of conscientious efforts to clean the home and rid one's self of all leaven products. Typically, ten pieces of leaven are hidden in various parts of the home. By the light of a candle or flashlight, family members search for the bread, then set it aside to be burned the following morning (*biur ḥametz*). A declaration is recited expressing that all *ḥametz* which may have been overlooked and accidentally remains in one's possession is to be considered null and void, as the dust of the earth. This act, along with the selling of *ḥametz* through a local rabbi, releases us from owning any leaven in our dwelling throughout the holiday of *Pesaḥ* (an explicit Biblical prohibition). Though the ritual is often understood on a physical level (getting rid of the last *ḥametz*), other commentators endow this act with greater significance. Rabbi Moses Alsheikh understood *bedikat hametz* as not only the cleaning of one's physical surroundings but also as a time of introspection. *Ḥametz* represents that which has become leaven in us—arrogance, hubris, pride. Alsheikh encourages us all to "examine our ways" in a second annual opportunity for introspection, cleansing, and renewal.

Note the setting in which this ritual occurs: within one's own dwelling, enveloped by darkness, and slightly illuminated by the glow of a candle or flashlight. In so many ways, this act reflects the individual days of our lives. We exist within our own worlds. And too often we are enveloped by the darkness of this world. Yet, the opportunity is given to us at every single moment of our lives to kindle a light which, although modest in its illumination, can guide us through the darkness and extend our scope of vision.

Only by journeying in multiple vectors—outward by giving *tzedakah*, and then inward by improving the self —can we realize the potential transformation and rebirth that can be actualized on *Pesaḥ*.

Before *bedikat ḥametz*, think about the ways in which your home is a like a "sanctuary in miniature." What qualities do you love about your home? Name some other qualities that you would like to make a part of your home. Then turn to yourself. Reflect on the year that has passed and how you have aspired to living in the image of God. How have you fallen short? How have you succeeded?

One of the members of the household hides pieces of ḥametz (usually ten) around the house. Before searching for the ḥametz with a candle or flashlight, the participants say:

בָּרוּךְ אַתָּה יְיָ אֱלֹהֵינוּ מֶלֶךְ הָעוֹלָם, אֲשֶׁר קִדְּשָׁנוּ בְּמִצְוֹתָיו, וְצִוָּנוּ עַל בְּעוּר חָמֵץ.

Blessed are You, Adonai, our God, Sovereign of the Universe, who has sanctified us with the commandments and commanded us to remove leaven from our dwelling places.

The search ensues as all the revealed pieces of hametz are gathered together. Once the final remnant is found, participants say:

כָּל חֲמִירָא דְּאִכָּא בִרְשׁוּתִי, דְּלָא חֲמִתֵּיה וּדְלָא בְעַרְתֵּיה, לִבָּטֵל וְלֶהֱוֵי הֶפְקֵר כְּעַפְרָא דְאַרְעָא.

Let every remnant of leaven which is in my possession that I have not seen nor removed be null and void as the dust of the earth.

יְהִי רָצוֹן מִלְּפָנֶיךָ יי אֱלֹהֵינוּ וֵאלֹהֵי אֲבוֹתֵינוּ (וְאִמּוֹתֵינוּ), שֶׁכְּשֵׁם שֶׁאֲנִי מְבַעֵר (מְבַעֶרֶת) חָמֵץ מִבֵּיתִי וּמֵרְשׁוּתִי כָּךְ תְּבַעֵר אֶת יִצְרֵנוּ הָרָע מֵאִתָּנוּ וְתִתֶּן לָנוּ לֵב בָּשָׂר. וְכָל הָרִשְׁעָה כְּעָשָׁן תִּכְלֶה וְתַעֲבִיר מֶמְשֶׁלֶת זָדוֹן מִן הָאָרֶץ. וְטַהֵר לִבֵּנוּ לְעָבְדְּךָ בֶּאֱמֶת וְיַחֵד לְבָבֵנוּ לְאַהֲבָה וּלְיִרְאָה אֶת שְׁמֶךָ.

May it be Your will, Adonai, our God and God of our ancestors, that as I have removed leaven from my dwelling and from my possessions, so may You help me to eliminate the evil inclination from my life. Instill within me and within all of your creations a heart of compassion. May all oppression and cruelty vanish from the world like smoke. Purify my heart to serve You in truth and may the inclination of all our hearts aspire to love and honor Your Name.

In the morning, as the ḥametz is burned, say:

כָּל חֲמִירָא וַחֲמִיעָא דְּאִכָּא בִרְשׁוּתִי, דַּחֲזִתֵּה וּדְלָא חֲזִתֵּה, דַּחֲמִתֵּה וּדְלָא חֲמִתֵּה, דְּבִעַרְתֵּה וּדְלָא בְעַרְתֵּה, לִבָּטֵל וְלֶהֱוֵי הֶפְקֵר כְּעַפְרָא דְאַרְעָא.

Let every remnant of leaven which is in my possession that I have not seen nor removed be null and void as the dust of the earth.

Ta'anit Bekhorot: Fast of the First Born

The teaching that "one should not rejoice at the downfall of one's enemy" (Proverbs 24:17) is taken to heart before and during Passover festivities. While the first-born male Egyptians were killed during the tenth and final plague, the first born male Israelites were protected. Rather than celebrating this decree, we respond with somber reflection. It is a custom[1] for first-born males to fast on the day prior to the seder, from sunrise to sunset. Nevertheless, a tradition developed called a *siyyum bekhorot*, in which a tractate of the Mishnah or Talmud (or a book of the Bible or Midrash) is completed the morning of the fourteenth of Nisan. A celebration ensues, and by virtue of participating in the learning and *seudat mitzvah* (festive meal), those who attend are exempt from fasting.

[1] The Babylonian Talmud does not mention this fast and the Jerusalem Talmud rules explicitly that it is not obligatory. It is first mentioned as a custom in Tractate *Soferim* (21:3).

Setting the Table

When the Temple stood, one effected atonement through the bringing of sacrifices to the altar.
Now that there is no longer a Temple, the table of one's home effects atonement for the individual.
BT Menaḥot 97a

The rabbis effectively transferred ritual from the Temple to the home; domestic space became an inner-sanctum. Part of that transition involved a symbolic reinterpretation. A table is no longer simply a table; it is an altar with the capacity to bring the human and the Divine closer together. The ritual that occurs around the Shabbat and Festival table underscores this notion. Candles recall the menorah that stood in the precincts of the sanctum. Salt used with *ha-motzi* (the blessing over the bread) recalls its use with animal sacrifices. Wine, the vehicle by which the day is sanctified, echoes libations common in Temple practice. And just as the priests were attentive to the details of the sacrificial rites, we too attend to the details of the altar in our midst.

Particular to *Pesaḥ* is the *ke'arah* or seder plate. There are various ways of arranging the symbolic foods on the plate. Two methods are described here. Figure 1 places the items chronologically according to their use over the evening. Figure 2 reflects the more widespread, kabbalistic arrangement. The most logical is to place the foods in the order in which they will be used over the course of the evening. Accordingly, the Rema (Rabbi Moses Isserles, 1525-1572, Poland) says to place the *mei melaḥ* (salt water) and *karpas* (vegetable) at the bottom of the plate, then the three *matzot, maror* (bitter herb) and *ḥaroset* (fruit and nut chutney) in the middle, and finally at the farthest part of the plate (from the leader if one plate is being used or from each individual if each has a separate seder plate), the *beitzah* (a hard boiled egg) and the *zeroa'* (shankbone). Thus one is not compelled to "pass over" or "insult" any of the symbols; they appear in the proper order in which they will be employed over the evening. The second, more widespread (and kabbalistic) arrangement is consonant with Rabbi Yitzḥak Luria, the Ari. Diagrams appear below:

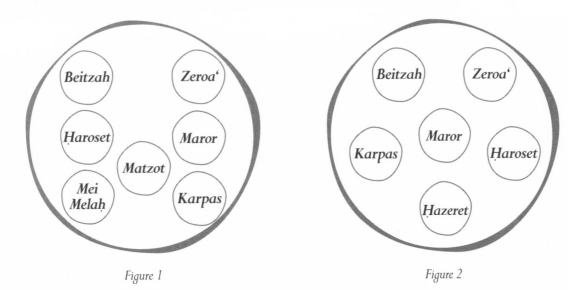

Figure 1   Figure 2

Each item on the table is significant:

1. *Karpas*—any vegetable other than lettuce, endive, or horseradish (as these may be used for the bitter herb); parsley is recommended. This food symbolizes spring and rebirth. After the winds and cold of a long winter, vegetation is a welcome sign of life reborn. Nurtured from a plant of water-seeking roots, the green vegetable symbolizes not only *Pesaḥ* as *Ḥag-HaAviv*, "the festival of spring," but also the birth and continued renaissance of the Jewish people.

2. *Mei Melaḥ*—salt water representative of the tears cried in the midst of oppression. Though we rejoice in the coming of spring and its redemptive powers, that joy is diminished as we remind ourselves of past pain. Redemption is not without a price; many souls, children and adults, suffered in order for a nation to be born. We are reminded how easy it is for a plant or green vegetable to wither away. Freedom is indeed fragile.

3. *Matzot*—unleavened bread. Matzah must be made within eighteen minutes of mixing the flour with water. On the evening of the seder, it is a *mitzvah* to eat *matzah shmurah*, guarded matzah. Such matzah is quite literally watched from the time the wheat is harvested in the field, through to its storage and actual baking. The meticulous supervision of the process gives special merit to this Passover "delicacy." Just as the matzah is guarded so diligently from its harvest, so were the Israelites protected by God. *Pesaḥ* evening is called *leyl shimurim*, "the night of protection." There is a special sense of vigilance on this night. God is closer to us and we are closer to God as we recall God's attentiveness and protection.

4. *Maror*—the bitter herb reminds us of the bitter slavery which our ancestors endured in the land of Egypt; though grated horseradish is most commonly used, the ideal is to employ *ḥazeret,* which is romaine lettuce. Chicory or endive may also be used. At first, romaine lettuce is sweet to the palate. However, the longer it stays in the ground, the more bitter it tastes. Such was our experience in Egypt: at first Joseph and his brothers are welcomed and prosper. Yet their affluence calls attention to them; soon after, the subtle enslavement begins as Pharaoh declares, "Let us deal wisely with them lest they increase" (Exodus 1:10). First-born Israelite males are cast into the Nile, and complete slavery ensues.

5. *Ḥaroset*—fruit and nut chutney, represents the mortar and bricks with which the Israelites built store cities and pyramids for Pharaoh. Though the sweet taste of the *ḥaroset* belies its message, perhaps the irony is intentional. In the midst of their slavery, the Israelites managed to be both productive and creative. Not only did they build cities for Pharaoh, but they also continued to propagate. One beautiful midrash claims that once Pharaoh decreed against the first–born males, the Israelite women gave birth under apple trees (*BT Sotah 11b*). In this way, the Egyptians could not find their babies. Given their protective role during persecution, apples now have a place of honor at the seder table.

6. *Beitzah*—hard boiled egg reminiscent of spring and rebirth; symbolizes the *ḥagigah*, the festival offering. It is also explained that the egg was chosen because of its Aramaic equivalent, *bei'a*. An expression in Aramaic teaches, "*be'a raḥmana u' farkinan*," "God desired and redeemed us." Additionally, the *Ḥatam Sofer* adds that while most foods soften when boiled, the egg becomes harder. Similarly, slavery strengthened the Israelites and forged their sense of identity.

7. *Zeroa'*—shankbone, a reminder of the Paschal Lamb which served as the core ritual in the Biblical observance of Passover. The Israelites were pressed on the eve of their exodus and so, as a sign of their great anticipation and eagerness, they rushed through their meal. From this first observance of *Pesaḥ* (circa 1240 BCE) through the Second Temple Period (until 70 CE), the Israelites observed Passover via the slaughter and roasting of the Paschal Lamb.[2] Torah ordains that the lamb be eaten "in haste" and with "loins girded, shoes on one's feet, and staff in hand" (Exodus 12:11). The Israelites were commanded to take a lamb on the tenth day of Nisan, slaughter the animal at dusk on the fourteenth, roast it, and eat it by the break of dawn. Families too small to consume an entire animal were to invite neighbors to join them. Today, in the absence of a Temple (and with the prohibition on offering sacrifices outside its precincts) we are left only with the ability to recount, relive, and renew our ancestral covenant through words and symbols.

Cup of Elijah

Elijah was an Israelite prophet active in the ninth century BCE. He is best known for decrying the idolatrous practices of the Israelites, such as worshipping the Canaanite god Ba'al. Elijah is a passionate loyalist of the Israelite God (I Kings 19:10) and seeks to kill the prophets of Ba'al. According to II Kings 2:1–11, Elijah did not die but was carried away to Heaven in a fiery chariot (II Kings 2:11). Malachi's final prophecy, "Behold, I will send the prophet Elijah to you before the coming of the awesome, fearful day of the Lord" (Malachi 3:23), leads to the association of Elijah with the Messianic Period. *BT Rosh Hashanah 11a* teaches, "It is in the month of Nisan that the Israelites will be redeemed." Since the Messiah is anticipated in this month and Elijah will herald this new era, Elijah's Cup eventually found a place at the seder. A goblet is filled with wine; the door is opened, the passage *shfokh ḥamatkhah*, "pour out Your wrath on the nations who know you not…" is read, and a song is chanted to Elijah. This ritual affords us a moment to reflect on hope, zealotry, and promised redemption.

Miriam's Cup

As the older sister of Moses, Miriam plays a key role in the redemption of the Israelites. Midrash teaches that it was because of Miriam that Amram and Yocheved conceived Moses, despite the fear of Pharaoh's decree against male Israelites. She watched over Moses as he floated down the Nile (Exodus 2:4) and secured her own mother to nurse him until Pharaoh's daughter (Batya) could raise him. Miriam dances with other Israelite women once they cross the Reed Sea (Exodus 15:20–21). Tradition teaches that the Israelites were blessed with water during their trek in the desert through Miriam's merit (Numbers 20:1 and *BT Ta'anit 9a*). Water is life-affirming and nurturing, much as Miriam was in her familial and national roles. Miriam provides a welcome balance to Elijah: while the latter represents zeal and even destruction of those who disagree, the former symbolizes cooperation and compassion. In this modern ritual, a decorative cup is placed on the table. Guests all add some water from their own cups to Miriam's Cup (see below, pp. 130–133), indicating that we each contribute to community and to *tikkun olam* (repairing a broken world).

[2] Continuity of the Paschal sacrifice was interrupted by the years between the destruction of the First Temple and the building of the Second Temple; during these years (586–516 BCE), the *Pesaḥ* was not offered.

Other Interesting Customs to Adopt for Your Seder

- Decorate the seder table with jewelry! The Jews of Nadishurani and Rakoshpaluta in Hungary decorated the seder table with all of their gold and silver jewelery. This tradition recalls all the gold and silver which the Israelites "borrowed" from the Egyptians (see Exodus 3:22; 11:2; 12:35).

The seder leader or others may wear a *kittel*, a white robe. Regarding this powerful symbol, Edward Greenstein teaches:

> The *kittel* is worn to symbolize a new beginning, as on the High Holy Days, when we repent and acquire a new chance in life. The father of a newborn boy wears a *kittel* at the *brit milah* [circumcision ceremony], acting as proxy for the boy who is entering the Covenant. A bridegroom wears a *kittel*, opening a new life for himself and his prospective family. When we die, we pass into Life Eternal buried in a *kittel*. At *Pesaḥ*, we each free ourselves from Egypt, and, as befits this renewal, we wear a *kittel*.

- Leave the door open at the beginning of the seder. This recalls the tradition of Rav Huna who, whenever he would sit down to a meal, would open the door to his home and declare, "let all who are hungry come and eat" (*BT Ta'anit 20b*). Indeed, Rav Mattityahu Gaon (Babylon, ninth century) says that the custom of our ancestors was to leave the door open during the seder so that poor Jews would join the celebration. Let the open door be an opportunity to speak of those in need.

- Give candy to children at the beginning of the seder. This is based on a teaching of Rabbi Tarfon (*BT Pesaḥim 109a*) that one distributes parched grain and nuts to children on *Erev Pesaḥ* (seder night) so that they should ask questions and not fall asleep. By beginning with candy, you will prompt the children to ask questions, setting the tone for the evening.

- Conduct the *Maggid* section (Telling of the Story) in a family or living room. As the seder is based on Greek symposia meals, where guests would lounge on cushions around a low table, it is appropriate to create a similar scene for your own family and friends. Participants will not only be impressed by your creativity but will also be more engaged in the telling of the story.

Lighting the Candles

Candles should be lit before nightfall on the first night; they must be lit after nightfall on the second night.
Kindle the lights, cover your eyes, and say:

בָּרוּךְ אַתָּה יְיָ אֱלֹהֵינוּ מֶלֶךְ הָעוֹלָם, אֲשֶׁר קִדְּשָׁנוּ בְּמִצְוֹתָיו, וְצִוָּנוּ לְהַדְלִיק נֵר שֶׁל (שַׁבָּת וְשֶׁל) יוֹם טוֹב.

Barukh atah Adonai Eloheinu Melekh ha'olam, asher kid'shanu b'mitzvotav, vetzivanu l'hadlik ner shel (Shabbat v'shel) Yom Tov.

Blessed are You, Adonai, our God, Sovereign of the Universe, who has sanctified us with the commandments and commanded us to kindle the light of (Shabbat and of) the Festival.

Then recite the following blessing:

בָּרוּךְ אַתָּה יְיָ אֱלֹהֵינוּ מֶלֶךְ הָעוֹלָם, שֶׁהֶחֱיָנוּ וְקִיְּמָנוּ וְהִגִּיעָנוּ לַזְּמַן הַזֶּה.

Barukh atah Adonai Eloheinu Melekh ha'olam, sheheḥeyanu, v'kiyemanu, v'higiyanu laz'man hazeh.

Blessed are You, Adonai, our God, Sovereign of the Universe, who has kept us alive, sustained us, and enabled us to reach this sacred time.

Journeys

For forty years the Holy Blessed One made Israel wander through the wilderness, saying,
"If I lead them on a straight route, everyone will take possession of a field or a vineyard and regard themselves as not obligated to
study Torah. I will therefore lead them by way of the wilderness, where they will eat manna, drink the waters of the well, and so give
themselves to the study of Torah, which will then become a part of them."
Midrash Tanḥuma, B'shalaḥ 1

Leader:
Passover celebrates two milestones. It marks the birth of the Israelite nation in their departure from Egypt and their entry into the land of Israel forty years later. These events frame the Israelite wanderings in the desert. This evening we set out on another journey, toward personal and communal redemption.

Participant:
Once the people were settled in Israel, they presented their first fruits to the priest and offered appreciation for their blessings; the Israelites placed the fruits near the altar and recounted the story of their journey from slavery to freedom.

Reflections
- Think of personal "first fruits." What blessings have you received this year?
- How much do you attribute to the efforts of your own labor, and to what extent do you perceive God's role in these gifts?
- What opportunities do you take to express gratitude?

Activity
- Identify the fruits and plants in the papercut. Why do these particular fruits represent Israel?

Sing Hinei Ma Tov:

Hinei ma tov uma na-im shevet aḥim gam yaḥad.　　　　　הִנֵּה מַה טּוֹב, וּמַה נָּעִים שֶׁבֶת אַחִים גַּם יָחַד.

Behold, how good and how pleasant it is for brothers and sisters to dwell together in unity (Psalms 133:1).

❦

When You Enter the Land
Plate 1

I acknowledge this day before the Lord your God that I have entered the land that the Lord swore to our ancestors to assign to us.
Deuteronomy 26:3

The papercut depicts the ritual of hava'at bikkurim, "bringing of the first fruits," along with the quote, "And you will take from the first fruits of the ground that you harvest from your land" (Deuteronomy 26:2). The woven basket overflows with the seven species. Gazelles above the basket symbolize the grace and beauty of Israel, which is referred to as eretz ha-tzvi, "the land of the gazelle" (Daniel 11:16, 41).

TRANSITION

The Holy Blessed One said to Moses, "The Land is precious to Me and Israel are precious to Me.
I will bring Israel who are precious to Me into the Land that is precious to Me."
Bemidbar Rabbah 23:7

Leader:

The transition from Egypt to Israel is dramatic:

> For the land that you are about to enter and possess is not like the land of Egypt from which you have come. There, the grain you sowed had to be watered by your own labors, like a vegetable garden; but the land you are about to cross into and possess soaks up water from the rains of the heavens (Deuteronomy 11:10–11).

The change in physical landscape is a model for our spiritual growth.

Participant:

Israel is a land dependent on God and the heavens for rain and protection. We too can be nourished and inspired from above even as we engage and improve the world below.

Reflections

- What are some of the ways we are "nourished from above"?
- How have you changed internally since last year's seder, and how do you hope to transform yourself before next year's seder?
- Recall times this year when you depended on other people or on God. Did you resent needing others, or was it reassuring to know they were there to support you?

●●●

Saturating its Furrows

Plate 2

It is a land which the Lord your God tends,
over which the Lord your God always keeps watch, from year's beginning to year's end.
Deuteronomy 11:12

A picture of Beit Netofah in the Northern Galilee taken by Nogah Hareuveni, founder of Neot Kedumim Biblical Landscape Reserve,
inspired this page. The panoramic view conveys the blessing and variety of the Israeli landscape: desert, mountains, fertile plains, and rolling hills.
We begin the seder where we will end—with thoughts of Israel.

DISCIPLINE

Seek freedom and become captive of your desires.
Seek discipline and find your liberty.
Frank Herbert

Participant:
The evening unfolds according to a prescribed order. The precision of the seder reflects the thoughtful creation of the world.

Reflections
- The haggadah encourages us to think about the role *order* plays in our life. How disciplined are we? What boundaries do we define for ourselves? To what extent do routines and rituals—religious, familial, or personal—play a role in creating each day?
- How do you understand the connection between the order of creation and the order of the seder?

Activity
- What was created on each of the seven days? (See Plate 3 for clues).

●●●

The Order of the Seder
Plate 3

The order of Jewish living is meant to be not a set of rituals,
but an order of all of man's existence, shaping all of his traits, interests, and dispositions.
[For it is] not so much the performance of single acts . . . as the pursuit of a way. . .
not so much the act of fulfilling as the state of being committed to the task . . .
moral episodes become part of a complete pattern.
Abraham Joshua Heschel

*This page adopts the theme of creation, with the seven days of the week in the center column and
the order of the seder on either side. The Hebrew letter for each day and each seder step is integrated
into the drawing. The letter zayin for the seventh day forms part of the Hebrew word, Shabbat.
The ritual order of the evening reflects a larger order.*

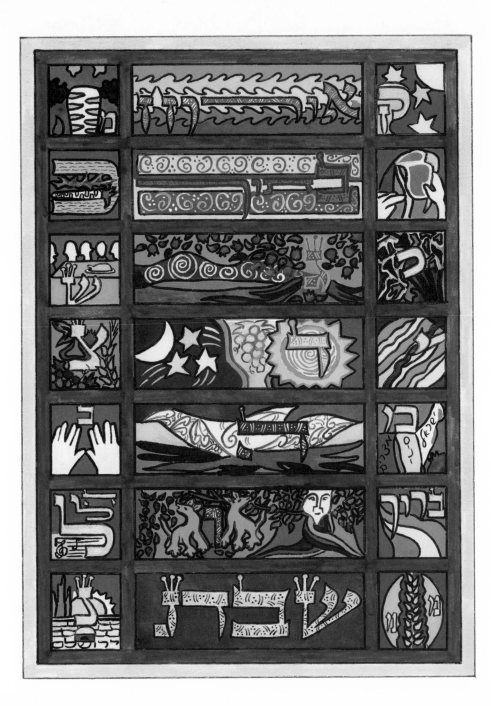

All join together in singing the steps of the seder:

קַדֵּשׁ וּרְחַץ כַּרְפַּס יַחַץ

מַגִּיד רָחְצָה מוֹצִיא מַצָּה

מָרוֹר כּוֹרֵךְ שֻׁלְחָן עוֹרֵךְ

צָפוּן בָּרֵךְ הַלֵּל נִרְצָה

Kadesh
Blessing over Wine

Urḥatz
Washing Hands

Karpas
Eating Vegetables

Yaḥatz
Breaking Middle Matzah

Maggid
Telling Story

Raḥtzah
Washing Hands with Blessing

Motzi Matzah
Blessings over Matzah

Maror
Eating Bitter Herb

Korekh
Assembling Pesaḥ Sandwich

Shulḥan Orekh
Festive Meal

Tzafun
Eating Afikoman

Barekh
Blessing After Meal

Hallel
Songs of Praise

Nirtzah
Concluding Prayers

· KADESH · קַדֵּשׁ ·

SANCTIFICATION

Human beings are the source of holiness and human will is the anvil upon which holiness is formed.

Abraham Joshua Heschel

Pour the first glass of wine. We recommend that each person be served by another, reflecting the idea that all are aristocracy this evening.

Activity
● Before blessing the wine, turn to a friend or family member and offer your own blessing.

Reflections
● *YaKNeHaZ:* **What's in an acronym?**   יקנה"ז

Below, you will see an image of a rabbit hunt, a print that was commonly joined with *kiddush* in medieval *haggadot* between the fifteenth and seventeenth centuries. What is the connection between a rabbit hunt and *kiddush*? Two explanations are given. First, this picture is a visual pun reminding the reader of a standard mnemonic device. When seder evening occurs on *Motza'ei Shabbat*, Saturday night, the seder must dovetail with the *havdalah* ceremony. The rabbis of the Talmud created an acronym to remember the order of ritual, *YaKNeHaZ*, which stands for the blessing over wine, *yayin*; the sanctification of the day, *kiddush*; the blessing over the candle of *havdalah*, *ner*; the blessing of separation, *havdalah*; and finally the blessing of time, *z'man* (otherwise known as *sheheheyanu*). As it turns out, the German expression for rabbit hunt, *Jag den Has*, sounds like the rabbinic mnemonic *YaKNeHaZ*. However, as Rabbi David Golinkin points out, pictures of rabbit hunts also appear in the *Sarajevo* and *John Rylands Haggadot* which were illuminated in Spain in the fourteenth century. Therefore, it seems that this picture is a symbol of spring which later was reinterpreted as a hint at *YaKNeHaZ*.

The Prague Haggadah, 1526. Image provided by The Library of The Jewish Theological Seminary

- **The Magical ATBASH** אתב״ש

The rabbis of the Talmud discovered a fascinating pattern in the Jewish calendar. The first seven letters of the *aleph-bet* stand for the days of *Pesah*. Each of the last letters stands for a holiday whose name starts with that letter. If you line up the first seven letters against the last seven letters, such that *aleph* corresponds to *tav* and *bet* corresponds to *shin*, etc., a remarkable discovery emerges. Each holiday begins on the corresponding day of the week in that calendar year. All you have to do to use this chart each year is recalibrate the "Day of the Week" column. Even more remarkable is that nothing corresponded to *zayin* until the twentieth century gave us "*Atzma'ut*," *Yom Ha'atzma'ut*, the birthday of the State of Israel!

Day of *Pesah*		Day of Week	Corresponding Observance	
First	(א)	Sunday	(ת)	*Tisha b'Av*, 9th of Av
Second	(ב)	Monday	(ש)	*Shavuot*
Third	(ג)	Tuesday	(ר)	*Rosh HaShanah*
Fourth	(ד)	Wednesday	(ק)	"*Kriat HaTorah*," Simhat Torah
Fifth	(ה)	Thursday	(צ)	"*Tzom Kippur*," Yom Kippur
Sixth	(ו)	Friday	(פ)	*Purim*
Seventh	(ז)	Saturday	(ע)	"*Atzma'ut*," Israeli Independence Day

מוזגים כוס ראשונה לכל המסובין ומקדשים.

בשבת מתחילים:

וַיְהִי עֶרֶב וַיְהִי בֹקֶר יוֹם הַשִּׁשִּׁי, וַיְכֻלּוּ הַשָּׁמַיִם וְהָאָרֶץ וְכָל צְבָאָם. וַיְכַל אֱלֹהִים בַּיּוֹם הַשְּׁבִיעִי מְלַאכְתּוֹ אֲשֶׁר עָשָׂה. וַיִּשְׁבֹּת בַּיּוֹם הַשְּׁבִיעִי מִכָּל מְלַאכְתּוֹ אֲשֶׁר עָשָׂה. וַיְבָרֶךְ אֱלֹהִים אֶת יוֹם הַשְּׁבִיעִי וַיְקַדֵּשׁ אוֹתוֹ כִּי בוֹ שָׁבַת מִכָּל מְלַאכְתּוֹ אֲשֶׁר בָּרָא אֱלֹהִים לַעֲשׂוֹת.

בחול מתחילים כאן:

סַבְרִי חֲבֵרִי

בָּרוּךְ אַתָּה יי אֱלֹהֵינוּ מֶלֶךְ הָעוֹלָם בּוֹרֵא פְּרִי הַגָּפֶן.

בָּרוּךְ אַתָּה יי אֱלֹהֵינוּ מֶלֶךְ הָעוֹלָם אֲשֶׁר בָּחַר בָּנוּ מִכָּל עָם וְרוֹמְמָנוּ מִכָּל לָשׁוֹן וְקִדְּשָׁנוּ בְּמִצְוֹתָיו, וַתִּתֶּן לָנוּ יי אֱלֹהֵינוּ בְּאַהֲבָה (שַׁבָּתוֹת לִמְנוּחָה וּ) מוֹעֲדִים לְשִׂמְחָה חַגִּים וּזְמַנִּים לְשָׂשׂוֹן, אֶת יוֹם (הַשַּׁבָּת הַזֶּה וְאֶת יוֹם) חַג הַמַּצּוֹת הַזֶּה זְמַן חֵרוּתֵנוּ (בְּאַהֲבָה) מִקְרָא קֹדֶשׁ זֵכֶר לִיצִיאַת מִצְרָיִם, כִּי בָנוּ בָחַרְתָּ וְאוֹתָנוּ קִדַּשְׁתָּ מִכָּל הָעַמִּים (וְשַׁבָּת) וּמוֹעֲדֵי קָדְשֶׁךָ (בְּאַהֲבָה וּבְרָצוֹן) בְּשִׂמְחָה וּבְשָׂשׂוֹן הִנְחַלְתָּנוּ, בָּרוּךְ אַתָּה יי מְקַדֵּשׁ (הַשַּׁבָּת וְ) יִשְׂרָאֵל וְהַזְּמַנִּים.

במוצאי שבת מוסיפים:

בָּרוּךְ אַתָּה יי אֱלֹהֵינוּ מֶלֶךְ הָעוֹלָם בּוֹרֵא מְאוֹרֵי הָאֵשׁ.

בָּרוּךְ אַתָּה יי אֱלֹהֵינוּ מֶלֶךְ הָעוֹלָם הַמַּבְדִּיל בֵּין קֹדֶשׁ לְחֹל, בֵּין אוֹר לְחֹשֶׁךְ בֵּין יִשְׂרָאֵל לָעַמִּים, בֵּין יוֹם הַשְּׁבִיעִי לְשֵׁשֶׁת יְמֵי הַמַּעֲשֶׂה, בֵּין קְדֻשַּׁת שַׁבָּת לִקְדֻשַּׁת יוֹם טוֹב הִבְדַּלְתָּ, וְאֶת יוֹם הַשְּׁבִיעִי מִשֵּׁשֶׁת יְמֵי הַמַּעֲשֶׂה קִדַּשְׁתָּ, הִבְדַּלְתָּ וְקִדַּשְׁתָּ אֶת עַמְּךָ יִשְׂרָאֵל בִּקְדֻשָּׁתֶךָ. בָּרוּךְ אַתָּה יי הַמַּבְדִּיל בֵּין קֹדֶשׁ לְקֹדֶשׁ:

בָּרוּךְ אַתָּה יי אֱלֹהֵינוּ מֶלֶךְ הָעוֹלָם שֶׁהֶחֱיָנוּ וְקִיְּמָנוּ וְהִגִּיעָנוּ לַזְּמַן הַזֶּה.

ושותים בהסיבת שמאל.

Leader chants kiddush to sanctify the day as all rise and raise their cups:

On Friday night, begin:
It was evening and it was morning, the sixth day. Heaven, earth, and all their creations were completed. God finished creating on the seventh day. On that day, God refrained from all the work that God had done. God blessed the seventh day and sanctified it—for on that day God rested from all the work that God had created and made.

On any other night, begin:

Friends, let us bless!

Blessed are You, Adonai, our God, Sovereign of the Universe, who creates the fruit of the vine.

Blessed are You, Adonai, our God, Sovereign of the Universe, who chose us from among all peoples and raised us above all languages and separated us through God's commandments. You have lovingly given us (Shabbat for rest and) seasons for happiness, festivals and times for rejoicing, this day of (Shabbat and) the Festival of Unleavened Bread, the time of our freedom (in love), a holy gathering in remembrance of the Exodus from Egypt. For You have chosen us and separated us from all nations, and (Shabbat and) Your holy festivals (lovingly and favorably) in happiness and rejoicing You have made our inheritance. Blessed are You, Adonai, Sanctifier of (the Shabbat and) Israel and the seasons.

On Saturday night add:
Blessed are You, Adonai, our God, Sovereign of the Universe, who creates the lights of fire.
Blessed are You, Adonai, our God, Sovereign of the Universe, who separates between holy and common, between light and darkness, between Israel and the nations, between the seventh day and the six days of work. Indeed, You distinguished between the holiness of Shabbat and the sanctity of a festival; and You made holy the distinction between the seventh day and the six days of creative acts. You have separated and sanctified Your people Israel with Your Holiness. Blessed are You, Adonai, the One who separates between sacred times.

Continue:

Blessed are You, Adonai, our God, Sovereign of the Universe, who has given us life, sustained us and brought us to this day.

Drink the first cup while reclining to the left.

· URḤATZ · וּרְחַץ ·

SILENCE

Rabbi Akiva said, "Silence is a fence which protects wisdom."
Avot 3:17

Leader:

This evening is a departure from routine. All is open to question. Washing the hands (*netilat yadayim*) is usually accompanied by a blessing. Now, each participant washes silently. This act is meant to spark questions. It is in silence that questions are born. It is in silence that God's Presence is felt.

All wash their hands without saying the usual blessing.

Reflections

- Use this pause to think of times in which you have experienced God's Presence.
- When do you carve out times for silence and reflection, and what happens when you do?

In These Hands
by Sheila Peltz Weinberg

A silent washing another door to freedom
Hands open to receive the cool water
Our bodies awaken.

Listen as you begin to relax, let go of slaveries, habits,
hurts let go,
even of expectations for tonight.
Take a quiet moment.
What does the water of life feel like on your fingers, palm,
on the back of your hand?

A silent washing
The blessing is in this silence.
In these hands.
In this moment.
Now we draw closer
To dip
To taste
To tell
To remember
To rejoice!

• KARPAS • כַּרְפַּס •

HEALING

There is more madness than sanity in this world.
Israel is one of the few healing herbs that have not withered away
in the dust-laden winds of history. It is a unique source in the spiritual life of mankind . . .
Abraham Joshua Heschel

Leader:

A green vegetable—symbol of life, sustenance, and renewal—is diminished by the tears of our ancestors.

Dip a vegetable in salt water and recite the following blessing before eating the vegetable:

בָּרוּךְ אַתָּה יי אֱלֹהֵינוּ מֶלֶךְ הָעוֹלָם בּוֹרֵא פְּרִי הָאֲדָמָה.

Blessed are You, Adonai, our God, Sovereign of the Universe, who creates the fruit of the ground.

Participant:

Karpas recalls the birth of the nation. Jacob and his descendants came down to Egypt for a new beginning. Escaping famine, seeking sustenance and life, they were given land in Goshen and thrived. Yet, their happiness was bounded by tears. Comfort gave way to deception and enslavement. Harsh labor weakened them and their hope for redemption.

Reflections

⚜ How can we be more attuned to life's blessings while recognizing that pain and loss is part of that experience?

· YAḤATZ · יַחַץ ·

INCOMPLETENESS

Nothing is more whole than a broken heart.
The Kotzker Rebbe

Leader:
Like the washing of the hands, this ritual is not accompanied by words. The only sound we hear is the crumbling of matzah. Our lives seek to recapture a sense of wholeness.

All:
We focus now on what is broken—in ourselves, among our people, and in our world.

Break the middle matzah into two unequal pieces; the smaller remnant is returned to its place between the two whole matzot. The larger piece is wrapped and hidden (by the seder leader or the children, according to custom); it will be used later for the afikoman.

Participant:
How fitting it is that the hidden piece is the larger portion of matzah. All too often we fail to see the larger picture. Much of the world is hidden—sometimes by God, sometimes by ourselves—and we must search for the missing piece like the *afikoman*.

Reflections
- Only when we give something up can we make room for the new; only when we admit we are broken can we begin the journey toward healing. Where are we lacking as individuals? Within the community? Where will we begin our search?
- Why do we use three *matzot*, symbolically and halakhically? It is a tradition on Shabbat and Festivals to place two complete loaves of bread on the table (commemorating two portions of manna in the desert). Since we break the middle matzah at this point of the seder, we need a full two "loaves" for later.

Activity
- Try to have three *matzot* at everyone's plate. Every participant will then break and hide an *afikoman*.

"Replete is the world with spiritual radiance, replete with sublime and marvelous secrets. But a small hand held against the eye hides it all," said the Ba'al Shem. "Just as a small coin held over the face can block out the sight of a mountain, so can the vanities of living block out the sight of the infinite light."
Abraham Joshua Heschel

Bread of Affliction

Plate 4

The Israelites are commanded to act justly not as the Egyptians acted; and the motive of
their action is to be the memory of the injustice their ancestors suffered in Egypt.
Michael Walzer

*This illustration underscores several messages. First, the festive meal is bracketed top and bottom by
history—slavery and redemption. We move stylistically from the slavery of Egypt to the redemption
of Jerusalem. We transition to redemption by taking care of the needs of the poor and by inviting
guests, by broadening our definition of family to include community.*

· MAGGID · מַגִּיד ·

GENEROSITY

You only have what you give.
It's by spending yourself that you become rich.
Isabel Allende

Leader:
Before sitting down to a meal, Rav Huna would open his door and declare: "Let all who are in need come and eat"
(*BT Ta'anit 20b*).

Participant:
Maimonides teaches, "Whoever locks the doors of the courtyard, and eats and drinks with his family and does not provide food and drink for the poor or suffering people, this is not a *mitzvah* celebration, but a celebration of the stomach, and this kind of celebration is a disgrace" (*Mishneh Torah, Yom Tov 6:18*).

All:
We sanctify freedom only when we are mindful of the needs of others.

Uncover the matzot, lift the seder plate, and say:

מגלים את המצות, מגביהים את הקערה ואומרים:

This is the bread of affliction
which our ancestors ate
in the Land of Egypt.

All who are hungry, come and eat.
All who are in need, come and join this Passover gathering.
Now we are here; next year may we be in the Land of Israel!
Now we are slaves; next year may we be free!

הָא לַחְמָא עַנְיָא
דִי אֲכַלוּ אַבְהָתַנָא
בְּאַרְעָא דְמִצְרָיִם.

כָּל דִּכְפִין יֵיתֵי וְיֵכֹל, כָּל דִּצְרִיךְ יֵיתֵי וְיִפְסַח.
הָשַׁתָּא הָכָא, לְשָׁנָה הַבָּאָה בְּאַרְעָא דְיִשְׂרָאֵל.
הָשַׁתָּא עַבְדֵי, לְשָׁנָה הַבָּאָה בְּנֵי חוֹרִין.

Reflections

- What does the presence of guests add to the seder?
- How can our community be more responsive to those who need hospitality and support?

Activity

- Reenact the Exodus in keeping with a widespread custom described by Yisrael ben Yosef Benjamin in 1853. Dress up one of the children as an Israelite, with staff in hand and satchel on shoulder. The following dialogue ensues between the leader of the seder and the child:

Leader: From where do you come O pilgrim?
Child: From the land of Egypt.
Leader: Did you go out to freedom from the bondage of Egypt?
Child: Yes indeed and now I am a free person.
Leader: Where are you going?
Child: I am going to Jerusalem.

With great joy, the participants begin to tell the story of the Exodus.

- According to another custom, everyone parades around the table with *matzot* slung over their shoulders.

Samuel explained that we call matzah *lehem oni* because we answer (*onim*) many words over it. . .
Another explanation: . . . it is like the [bread] of a poor person (*ani*).
BT Pesaḥim 115b

How Different is This Night!

Plate 5

They mix the second cup of wine, and here the child asks the parent. And if the
child does not have the knowledge to ask, his father teaches him:
"How different is this night from all other nights!
On all other nights we eat leavened or unleavened bread,
but on this night we eat only matzah.
On all other nights we eat many different vegetables,
but on this night we must eat bitter herbs.
On all other nights we eat roasted, cooked, or boiled meat,
but on this night we eat only roasted meat.
On all other nights we dip our foods once, but on this night we dip twice."
Mishnah Pesaḥim, 10:4

*The design reflects the original version of "The Four Questions." A lamb gazes at the center, since this
animal reflects the Biblical observance of Pesaḥ. The Mishnah's original third "question," regarding
the Paschal Lamb, is inscribed in the background. Each column is devoted to one of "The Four
Questions" of today, moving from, "On all other nights" at the top of the page to "On this night" at
the bottom. The fourth panel juxtaposes sitting upright to reclining, a symbol of freedom. Shackles
transform into crowns. We are all aristocracy this evening, reclining like royalty and learning Torah.
True aristocracy in Judaism is not the human ruler but the Divine word.*

CURIOSITY

On seder night, even two Sages well-versed in the laws of Pesaḥ
should still ask each other questions.
BT Pesaḥim 116a

How different is this night from all other nights!

מַה נִּשְׁתַּנָּה הַלַּיְלָה הַזֶּה מִכָּל הַלֵּילוֹת!

On all other nights we eat leavened or unleavened bread,
but on this night we eat only matzah.

שֶׁבְּכָל הַלֵּילוֹת אָנוּ אוֹכְלִין חָמֵץ וּמַצָּה,
הַלַּיְלָה הַזֶּה – כֻּלּוֹ מַצָּה.

On all other nights we eat many different vegetables,
but on this night we must eat bitter herbs.

שֶׁבְּכָל הַלֵּילוֹת אָנוּ אוֹכְלִין שְׁאָר יְרָקוֹת,
הַלַּיְלָה הַזֶּה – מָרוֹר.

On all other nights we never dip our foods,
but on this night we dip twice.

שֶׁבְּכָל הַלֵּילוֹת אֵין אָנוּ מַטְבִּילִין אֲפִילוּ פַּעַם אֶחָת,
הַלַּיְלָה הַזֶּה – שְׁתֵּי פְעָמִים.

On all other nights we eat either sitting or reclining,
but on this night we all recline.

שֶׁבְּכָל הַלֵּילוֹת אָנוּ אוֹכְלִין בֵּין יוֹשְׁבִין וּבֵין מְסֻבִּין,
הַלַּיְלָה הַזֶּה – כֻּלָּנוּ מְסֻבִּין.

All:
We are now ready to fulfill the commandment of seder evening, "You will recount it to your child on that day" (Exodus 13:8).

Leader:
Every journey begins with questions. According to the mishnah quoted on page 46, the seder atmosphere inspired children to ask their own questions. Only if a child did not have the knowledge to ask, did the parent introduce "The Four Questions."

Reflections
- What questions are on our minds tonight?
- How can we engage children and adults throughout the year to explore the depth and beauty of Judaism in all its aspects?

Activity
- Ask your own four questions about the seder.
- Discuss why there is a lamb at the center of the illumination.

We Were Slaves to Pharaoh in Egypt

Plate 6

Rav Ḥanin[a] expounded: The Holy Blessed One, said to the tribes,
"You have sold Joseph into slavery. By your lives, every year will you recite,
'We were slaves to Pharaoh,' and thereby atone for the sin of selling Joseph."
And just as Joseph went forth from imprisonment to royalty,
so we too have gone forth from slavery to freedom . . .
Midrash Tehillim, Mizmor 10.

Mount Sinai and a pyramid mirror each other, two halves of a whole. The pyramid is upside down, demonstrating that slavery is unnatural. The midrash about Joseph and his brothers is inscribed in the background. The pyramid is draped with Joseph's multi-colored coat; the colors carry over into the border, a mosaic of multi-colored glass, reflecting the shattered love of a family torn apart by favoritism and hatred. Mount Sinai is upright, indicating that learning Torah is a natural state, the very purpose for which we were created. Further, the rabbis argue that true freedom comes from the observance of Torah, which "inverts the pyramid of Egypt." Freedom manifests itself in becoming a servant of God instead of a slave to Pharaoh.

RESPONSIBILITY

Slavery is begun and sustained by coercion,
while service is begun and sustained by covenant.
Michael Walzer

עֲבָדִים הָיִינוּ

לְפַרְעֹה בְּמִצְרַיִם

וַיּוֹצִיאֵנוּ יי אֱלֹהֵינוּ מִשָּׁם בְּיָד חֲזָקָה וּבִזְרוֹעַ נְטוּיָה.

וְאִלּוּ לֹא הוֹצִיא הַקָּדוֹשׁ בָּרוּךְ הוּא אֶת אֲבוֹתֵינוּ מִמִּצְרַיִם הֲרֵי אָנוּ וּבָנֵינוּ וּבְנֵי בָנֵינוּ מְשֻׁעְבָּדִים הָיִינוּ לְפַרְעֹה בְּמִצְרַיִם,

וַאֲפִילוּ כֻּלָּנוּ חֲכָמִים, כֻּלָּנוּ נְבוֹנִים, כֻּלָּנוּ זְקֵנִים, כֻּלָּנוּ יוֹדְעִים אֶת הַתּוֹרָה, מִצְוָה עָלֵינוּ לְסַפֵּר בִּיצִיאַת מִצְרַיִם.

וְכָל הַמַּרְבֶּה לְסַפֵּר בִּיצִיאַת מִצְרַיִם, הֲרֵי זֶה מְשֻׁבָּח.

We were slaves

to Pharaoh in Egypt, and God took us out of there with a strong hand and an outstretched arm.
But if the Holy Blessed One had not taken our ancestors out of Egypt, then we and our children and our grandchildren would still be enslaved to Pharaoh in Egypt.

Therefore, even if all of us were sages, scholars, or elders; even if all of us knew the entirety of the Torah, it would still be our sacred obligation to tell the story of the Exodus from Egypt. Indeed, it is praiseworthy to delve into and expand upon the narrative as much as possible.

Leader:
Why do we recite the passage *Avadim hayinu*, "We were slaves…"? According to Rav Ḥanina, it is to atone collectively for having sold our brother Joseph into slavery. Yet the enmity that plagued Joseph and his brothers still echoes in our world today.

Participant:
There is always the hope for repair. We become redeemed by repenting for our misdeeds. *Ahavat Yisrael*, unconditional love for fellow Jews, is desperately needed today. We are siblings, engaged in building a Jewish nation.

All:
By learning from the past, we move toward a more hopeful future.

Reflections
- What do Joseph and his brothers teach us about actions and consequences?
- Discuss the rabbinic statement "Only a person who studies Torah is [truly] free" (Avot 6:2).
- How do you deal with conflict among siblings or friends?

The Morning *Shema*

Plate 7

From when may one read the *Shema* in the morning? From [the moment that] one may distinguish between blue and white. Rabbi Eliezer says, "[From the moment we can distinguish] between blue and green, and one may finish reading the *Shema* until the sun peers over the ridge of the mountains." Rabbi Yehoshua teaches, "until the third hour of the morning."

Mishnah Berakhot 1:2

Five images related to the Shema adorn this illumination. The top left image shows two individuals facing each other with "four amot" inscribed in Hebrew letters. According to a Talmudic teaching, one may begin reading the Shema only when one can recognize an acquaintance at a distance of four amot (arm lengths) (BT Berakhot 9b). Before we declare our belief in God, we must be able to see the Image of God in our fellow humans The second image is a ḥilazon or field snail, the source of the dye for the thread of blue in the tzitzit (Numbers 15:38). The third image illustrates Rabbi Eliezer's opinion which calls for a later recitation time, when one can distinguish between blue and green. The lower left cartouche alludes to the teaching of the Sages, "Tekhelet resembles the sea, and the sea resembles the firmament, and the firmament resembles the sapir stone, and the sapir stone resembles the throne of glory" (BT Menaḥot 43b). This midrash links heaven and earth, as the recitation of the Shema bridges the earthly and heavenly realms. Finally, four tzitziot dance down the right panel, tied at the top but free-flowing at the base, suggesting that commitment to the mitzvot is compatible with freedom.

COMMITMENT

Rabbi Tarfon used to say, "You are not required to complete the task, but you are not free to desist from it."
Avot 2:21

מַעֲשֶׂה

בְּרַבִּי אֱלִיעֶזֶר, וְרַבִּי יְהוֹשֻׁעַ, וְרַבִּי אֶלְעָזָר בֶּן עֲזַרְיָה, וְרַבִּי עֲקִיבָא, וְרַבִּי טַרְפוֹן שֶׁהָיוּ מְסֻבִּין בִּבְנֵי בְרַק, וְהָיוּ מְסַפְּרִים בִּיצִיאַת מִצְרַיִם כָּל אוֹתוֹ הַלַּיְלָה, עַד שֶׁבָּאוּ תַלְמִידֵיהֶם וְאָמְרוּ לָהֶם: רַבּוֹתֵינוּ, הִגִּיעַ זְמַן קְרִיאַת שְׁמַע שֶׁל שַׁחֲרִית!

A story

of Rabbi Eliezer, Rabbi Yehoshua, Rabbi Elazar ben Azariah, Rabbi Akiva, and Rabbi Tarfon who were reclining around the Passover table in *B'nei Berak*. There they were telling the story of the Exodus from Egypt the entire night, until their students came and said to them, "Our teachers! The time for the recitation of the morning *Shema* has arrived!"

Leader:
These rabbis model devotion and commitment. So engaged were they in the Exodus narrative that they discussed the story all night until it was time to recite the morning *Shema*.

All:
Every word of the *Shema* must be carefully recited in its proper order. We savor the haggadah too, embellishing our telling of the Exodus far into the night.

Reflections
- Why is there a snail in the picture?
- Why did the rabbis need to be reminded that it was time to recite the *Shema*?
- The *Shema* is recited twice daily. How does repetition and regularity dovetail with spirituality? Discuss the balance between *keva* (routine) and *kavannah* (spontaneity) in Judaism.

אָמַר רַבִּי אֶלְעָזָר בֶּן עֲזַרְיָה: הֲרֵי אֲנִי כְּבֶן שִׁבְעִים שָׁנָה וְלֹא זָכִיתִי שֶׁתֵּאָמֵר יְצִיאַת מִצְרַיִם בַּלֵּילוֹת עַד שֶׁדְּרָשָׁהּ בֶּן זוֹמָא, שֶׁנֶּאֱמַר: לְמַעַן תִּזְכֹּר אֶת יוֹם צֵאתְךָ מֵאֶרֶץ מִצְרַיִם כָּל יְמֵי חַיֶּיךָ. יְמֵי חַיֶּיךָ - הַיָּמִים, כָּל יְמֵי חַיֶּיךָ - הַלֵּילוֹת. וַחֲכָמִים אוֹמְרִים, יְמֵי חַיֶּיךָ - הָעוֹלָם הַזֶּה, כָּל יְמֵי חַיֶּיךָ - לְהָבִיא לִימוֹת הַמָּשִׁיחַ.

Rabbi Elazar ben Azariah said, "Behold, I am like a man of seventy years of age and I never understood why the Exodus from Egypt should be mentioned at night until Ben Zoma explained it: as it is written, 'so that you will remember the day of your leaving the Land of Egypt all the days of your life' (Deuteronomy 16:3). 'Days of your life'—this refers literally to the daytime. 'All the days of your life'—this refers to the nights." The Sages offer an alternate explanation: "Days of your life"—this refers to this world. "All the days of your life"—this refers to the Days of the Messiah.

The Four Children

Plate 8

And if the child does not have the knowledge to ask, his father teaches him . . .
Mishnah Pesaḥim 10:4

A Biblical character represents each of the Four Children:

*1. **Devorah the Wise.** Devorah was a judge and a prophetess—courageous, discerning, and insightful. Blessed with these qualities, the Israelites sought Devorah for judgment and advice (Judges 4:5).*

*2. **King Aḥav the Wicked.** King Aḥav seeks to acquire his neighbor Navot's vineyard. Navot refuses, enraging the king. His wife Jezebel enlists two townspeople to testify falsely against Navot, reporting that he had cursed both God and the king. Navot is stoned to death, and Aḥav takes possession of the vineyard (I Kings 21).*

*3. **Lot the Simple.** When Abraham and his nephew Lot prosper and their possessions multiply, the men can no longer dwell in close proximity (Genesis 13). Abraham suggests, "Let us separate: if you go north, I will go south; and if you go south, I will go north." Lot chooses the plain of the Jordan (Sodom and Gemorrah). While a more mature individual would weigh other factors, Lot makes his decision based on visual appeal.*

*4. **Adam and Eve, Who Know Not How to Ask.** Childlike in their innocence, "The two of them were naked, the man and his wife, yet they felt no shame" (Genesis 2:25). Questioning and self-reflection were absent from their experience. Questions nurture identity and open the door for answers. Inquiry brings the power to understand and to challenge. Adam and Eve are depicted without mouths to show their inability, at this early stage of human development, to formulate questions.*

DIVERSITY

*Ben Azzai said, "Scorn no one and do not disdain anything,
for there is no human who does not have his hour and there is no thing that does not have its place."*
Avot 4:3

Leader:

Four times, the Torah anticipates children asking their parents about the Passover story (Exodus 12:26, Exodus 13:8, Exodus 13:14, and Deuteronomy 6:20). Later rabbis see these as models of four distinct types of children: the wise, the wicked, the simple, and the one who does not know how to question.

Participant:

Perhaps these "children" are four qualities within each of us. They may also represent four stages of our lives or even successive generations of a single family.

All:

Each child learns in a unique way; it is our responsibility to open the door.

Reflections

● Explain the ways in which each of us contains these four types.

● How can our schools, synagogues, camps, and other institutions be more responsive to many different types of children?

Activity

● Choose modern characters (political, artistic, etc.) or other Biblical personalities to represent The Four Children.

Blessed is The Place. Blessed is God.	בָּרוּךְ הַמָּקוֹם, בָּרוּךְ הוּא,
Blessed is the One Who Gave Torah to God's People Israel. Blessed is God.	בָּרוּךְ שֶׁנָּתַן תּוֹרָה לְעַמּוֹ יִשְׂרָאֵל, בָּרוּךְ הוּא.
The Torah Speaks Concerning Four Children: One Wise, and One Wicked, One Simple, and One Who Does Not Know How to Question.	כְּנֶגֶד אַרְבָּעָה בָנִים דִּבְּרָה תוֹרָה, אֶחָד חָכָם, וְאֶחָד רָשָׁע, וְאֶחָד תָּם, וְאֶחָד שֶׁאֵינוֹ יוֹדֵעַ לִשְׁאֹל.

Wise

חָכָם

מַה הוּא אוֹמֵר? מָה הָעֵדֹת וְהַחֻקִּים וְהַמִּשְׁפָּטִים אֲשֶׁר צִוָּה יי אֱלֹהֵינוּ אֶתְכֶם? וְאַף אַתָּה אֱמָר לוֹ כְּהִלְכוֹת הַפֶּסַח: אֵין מַפְטִירִין אַחַר הַפֶּסַח אֲפִיקוֹמָן.

The wise one, what does she ask? "What are these testimonies, ordinances, and laws that Adonai our God commanded you?" (Deuteronomy 6:20). And so you should explain to her according to the laws of Passover: "We do not eat anything else after the *afikoman*."

Wicked

רָשָׁע

מַה הוּא אוֹמֵר? מָה הָעֲבֹדָה הַזֹּאת לָכֶם? לָכֶם—וְלֹא לוֹ. וּלְפִי שֶׁהוֹצִיא אֶת עַצְמוֹ מִן הַכְּלָל כָּפַר בָּעִקָּר. וְאַף אַתָּה הַקְהֵה אֶת שִׁנָּיו וֶאֱמָר לוֹ: בַּעֲבוּר זֶה עָשָׂה יי לִי בְּצֵאתִי מִמִּצְרָיִם. לִי—וְלֹא לוֹ. וְאִלּוּ הָיָה שָׁם לֹא הָיָה נִגְאָל.

What does the wicked one ask? "What is this ritual to you?" (Exodus 12:26)—"to you" and not "to him". Since he has excluded himself from the community, he has denied the essence of this Passover celebration. Rebuke him and say, "It is because of what God did for me in my leaving Egypt" (Exodus 13:8). "For me" and not "for him". If he had been there, he would not have been redeemed.

Simple

תָּם

מַה הוּא אוֹמֵר? מַה זֹּאת? וְאָמַרְתָּ אֵלָיו בְּחֹזֶק יָד הוֹצִיאָנוּ יי מִמִּצְרַיִם מִבֵּית עֲבָדִים.

What does the simple one ask? "What is this?" (Exodus 13:14). You should say to her, "With a strong hand God took us out of Egypt, from the House of Slaves."

Does Not Know How to Question

וְשֶׁאֵינוֹ יוֹדֵעַ לִשְׁאֹל

אַתְּ פְּתַח לוֹ. שֶׁנֶּאֱמַר: וְהִגַּדְתָּ לְבִנְךָ בַּיּוֹם הַהוּא לֵאמֹר בַּעֲבוּר זֶה עָשָׂה יי לִי בְּצֵאתִי מִמִּצְרָיִם.

And with the one who does not know how to question, you must take the initiative, as it is written, "You will tell your child on that day, saying 'because of what the Lord did for me in my leaving Egypt . . .'" (Exodus 13:8).

61

"You will tell your child..."

Passover reminds us, through its domestic theater of the seder, that the ultimate incubator of Jewish values and behavior is the environment we create for our children at home. If we can saturate our homes with echoes of eternity, our children will naturally absorb Judaism as their center of gravity—a moral compass, a medium of expression, a source of pride.

Ismar Schorsch

יָכוֹל מֵרֹאשׁ חֹדֶשׁ? תַּלְמוּד לוֹמַר: בַּיּוֹם הַהוּא. אִי בַּיּוֹם הַהוּא, יָכוֹל מִבְּעוֹד יוֹם? תַּלְמוּד לוֹמַר: בַּעֲבוּר זֶה. בַּעֲבוּר זֶה לֹא אָמַרְתִּי אֶלָּא בְּשָׁעָה שֶׁיֵּשׁ מַצָּה וּמָרוֹר מוּנָּחִים לְפָנֶיךָ.

We might assume that the telling of the story should begin on the first of the new month of Nisan. For this reason, the Torah teaches, "on that day." And yet, since the text says, "on that day," we might think that we can begin telling the story while it is still daytime. Therefore the Torah says, "because of this," meaning at the time that matzah and *maror* are set before us (i.e., in the evening, at the seder table).

The Roots of the Nation

Plate 9

Your ancestors were settled on the other side (*b'ever*) of the river from long ago—
Teraḥ, the father of Abraham and of Naḥor—and they served other gods.
And I took your ancestor Abraham from the other side of the river and guided
him through the Land of Canaan . . .
Joshua 24:2-3

The linguistic progression begins with God's declaration at Mount Sinai, "Behold I come to you in the thickness (or darkness—av) of the cloud" (Exodus 19:9). It is out of darkness that the Divine Presence is revealed to the Israelites. The transition at Sinai reminds us of Abraham's journey from the darkness of idolatrous belief in his homeland to the light of the knowledge of one God. From the embryonic roots of the Jewish people, we segue to the Hebrew midwives (ha-meyaldot ha-ivriot, Exodus 1:15). In their courage, lovingkindness, and wisdom, they defy Pharaoh's orders and become a vehicle for national survival. Moses witnesses an Egyptian taskmaster brutally beating a slave whom he recognizes as a Hebrew and considers a brother (ish ivri me'eḥav, Exodus 2:11). This incident awakens Moses' identification as a Hebrew and marks the beginning of his leadership. The design culminates in the expression v'ha'avarta shofar teruah, "You will sound the shofar blast" (Leviticus 25:9), heralding the Jubilee Year in which all property and slaves are returned to God. Creating a transition from darkness to light, from slavery to freedom, the entire composition reflects the Biblical verses it portrays, as well as the hopeful direction of the seder narrative.

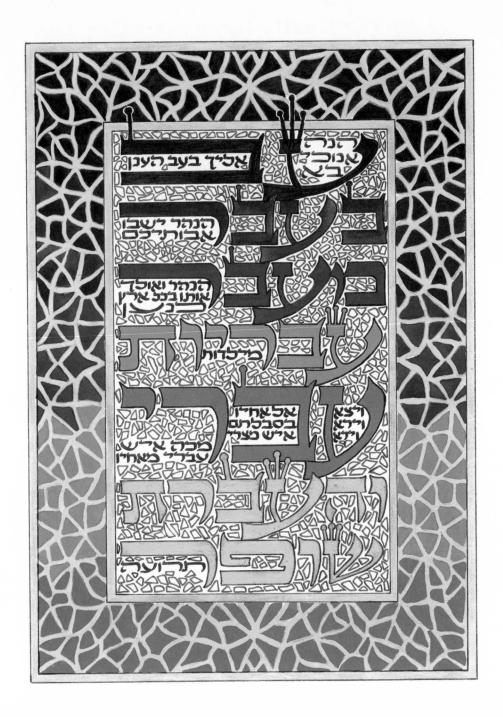

IDENTITY

One's name reflects one's essence.
I Samuel 25:25

מַתְחָלָה

עוֹבְדֵי עֲבוֹדָה זָרָה הָיוּ אֲבוֹתֵינוּ, וְעַכְשָׁו קֵרְבָנוּ הַמָּקוֹם לַעֲבוֹדָתוֹ שֶׁנֶּאֱמַר:

וַיֹּאמֶר יְהוֹשֻׁעַ אֶל כָּל הָעָם, כֹּה אָמַר יי אֱלֹהֵי יִשְׂרָאֵל, בְּעֵבֶר הַנָּהָר יָשְׁבוּ אֲבוֹתֵיכֶם מֵעוֹלָם, תֶּרַח אֲבִי אַבְרָהָם וַאֲבִי נָחוֹר, וַיַּעַבְדוּ אֱלֹהִים אֲחֵרִים, וָאֶקַּח אֶת אֲבִיכֶם אֶת אַבְרָהָם מֵעֵבֶר הַנָּהָר וָאוֹלֵךְ אוֹתוֹ בְּכָל אֶרֶץ כְּנָעַן, וָאַרְבֶּה אֶת זַרְעוֹ וָאֶתֶּן לוֹ אֶת יִצְחָק, וָאֶתֵּן לְיִצְחָק אֶת יַעֲקֹב וְאֶת עֵשָׂו, וָאֶתֵּן לְעֵשָׂו אֶת הַר שֵׂעִיר לָרֶשֶׁת אוֹתוֹ וְיַעֲקֹב וּבָנָיו יָרְדוּ מִצְרָיִם.

In the beginning

our ancestors were idol worshippers, but now, The Place (i.e. God) has brought us close to Divine service, as it is said, "Joshua declared to the people, 'Thus says Adonai, God of Israel: your ancestors were settled on the other side of the river from long ago—Teraḥ, the father of Abraham and Naḥor—and they served other gods. And I took your ancestor Abraham from the other side of the river and guided him through the Land of Canaan and increased his descendants and gave him Isaac; and to Isaac I gave Jacob and Esau; and to Esau I gave Mt. Seir, but Jacob and his sons went down to Egypt' " (Joshua 24:2-4).

Leader:
Based on the root *'ayin-vet-resh* (עבר), *Ivri* refers to "the one who crosses over." It alludes to the first *Ivri*, Abraham, who crossed over the Euphrates River as he journeyed to the Land of Canaan.

Participant:
We remember Abraham's humble roots on the other side of the river, acknowledging what he gave up in order to embrace the new.

Participant:
Each of us must sound the shofar of freedom and illuminate the darkness. Every day, as Jews and human beings, we must think how we can truly become *Ivrim*—ones who cross over from being self-centered to being God-directed.

Reflections
- When Jonah is asked to identify himself, he responds, "I am a Hebrew—*Ivri anokhi*" (Jonah 1:9). How would you answer this question? Has your answer changed over time, and how can you envisage it changing in the future?
- Abraham has to give up his family, faith, and familiar surroundings in order to acknowledge One God. Have you ever had to give up something in order to affirm your identity?

The Covenant Between the Parts
Plate 10

Look heavenward and count the stars—
if you are able to count them, so will your seed be.
Genesis 15:5

The left panel depicts God's promise to make Abraham's descendants as numerous as the stars. The second panel is split between two images. On the top, Abraham smashes the idols belonging to his father Teraḥ as we learn in a midrash (Genesis Rabbah 38:13), marking the first stage in his journey toward monotheism. The lower part showcases the produce of the Land of Canaan in full bloom, promising abundance and fertility. The third panel depicts the brit bein ha-betarim, "Covenant Between the Parts": God instructs Abraham, "Take a heifer, goat, ram, turtle dove, and pigeon and divide them." Darkness descends and God declares, "Know well that your descendants will be strangers in a land not theirs; they will serve them, and [this nation] will afflict them for four hundred years. But I will judge that nation, and afterward they [the Israelites] will go forth with great wealth" (Genesis 15:13-14). The fourth panel depicts the slavery predicted in the "Covenant Between the Parts." At the top, the Israelites cry out to God, eliciting God's empathy, precipitating their deliverance (Exodus 2:23-25).

VISION

Pay no attention to his appearance or his stature... for the Lord does not see as a person sees;
a person sees only what is visible, but the Lord sees into the heart.

I Samuel 16:7

Leader:

Ever hopeful, resourceful, and optimistic, the Jewish people has transformed periods of oppression into opportunities for growth. In this illumination (Plate 10), the taskmaster's whip turns into the roots of a tree. We imagine a better future for ourselves and for the world.

בָּרוּךְ שׁוֹמֵר הַבְטָחָתוֹ לְיִשְׂרָאֵל, בָּרוּךְ הוּא.

שֶׁהַקָּדוֹשׁ בָּרוּךְ הוּא חִשַׁב אֶת הַקֵּץ לַעֲשׂוֹת כְּמָה שֶׁאָמַר לְאַבְרָהָם אָבִינוּ בִּבְרִית בֵּין הַבְּתָרִים שֶׁנֶּאֱמַר:
וַיֹּאמֶר לְאַבְרָם יָדֹעַ תֵּדַע כִּי גֵר יִהְיֶה זַרְעֲךָ בְּאֶרֶץ לֹא לָהֶם וַעֲבָדוּם וְעִנּוּ אֹתָם אַרְבַּע מֵאוֹת שָׁנָה,
וְגַם אֶת הַגּוֹי אֲשֶׁר יַעֲבֹדוּ דָּן אָנֹכִי, וְאַחֲרֵי כֵן יֵצְאוּ בִּרְכֻשׁ גָּדוֹל.

Blessed is the One who upholds the promise to Israel, Blessed is God.

The Holy Blessed One determined when enslavement would end for the Israelites as promised to our ancestor Abraham, in the "Covenant Between the Parts." For God said, "Know well that your descendants will be strangers in a land not theirs; they will serve them and [this nation] will afflict them for four hundred years. But I will judge that nation, and afterward they [the Israelites] will go forth with great wealth" (Genesis 15:13–14).

Participant:

God offers Abraham a vision of a bright future, but one that will be punctuated by obstacles. How are we to understand a God who deliberately enslaves a Chosen People? Is there anything redeeming about the experience of slavery? What role does it play in the formation of Israelite identity?

Reflection

- Do you believe that God plans the course of history and knows all from the beginning? Why would God enslave the Israelites?

- How do we balance our need for memory of the troubles of our past with the need to build the future?

- Once Abraham realizes how alienated he is from his cultural milieu, he is ready to hear the call of *lekh lekha* ("go forth"), to cross over into Canaan, to become an *Ivri* (a Hebrew, literally "one who crosses over"). Have you ever thought about moving to Israel? Can you imagine yourself living there?

And "She" Stood by Us

Plate 11

I believe in the sun, even when it is not shining;
I believe in love, even when feeling it not;
I believe in God, even when He is silent.

Inscription found in a cellar in Cologne, Germany, where Jews hid from the Nazis

1. Lavan. The top left corner portrays Jacob, Rachel, and Leah standing before Jacob's deceptive uncle Lavan. What gave Jacob hope through these years of loneliness and estrangement from family? A promise: "Your descendants will be as the dust of the earth; you will spread out to the west and east . . ." (Genesis 28:14–15).

2. Amalek. The top right corner depicts Amalek's slaughter of the Israelites as they depart from Egypt (Deuteronomy 25:17–18). Here again, God's promise to Abraham gives the people strength to continue on their journey.

3. Haman. We move from Amalek to his descendant, Haman, the villain of the Purim narrative. In the lower left corner, King Ahasuerus and Queen Esther ponder the noose of Haman who sought to annihilate the Jewish people in the Persian empire. The covenantal promise gives Esther and the people the courage to confront Haman.

4. Shoah. This image in the lower right-hand corner recalls the Shoah (Holocaust), which strained the Jewish people's trust in the Divine Promise as never before. The image juxtaposes barbed wire, yellow badges, and flames of Kristallnacht. The word "Hatikvah" (The Hope) is inscribed in small golden letters, alluding to the hope that enabled people to survive, and foreshadowing the birth of the modern State of Israel.

FAITH

*It's really a wonder that I haven't dropped all my ideals,
because they seem so absurd and impossible to carry out. Yet I keep them, because,
in spite of everything, I still believe that people are really good at heart.*

Anne Frank

Raise the cup and say:

וְהִיא שֶׁעָמְדָה

It was She who stood by our ancestors and by us, in times of trouble and in joy.

לַאֲבוֹתֵינוּ וְלָנוּ,

For it is not just one tyrant who rose up to annihilate us,

שֶׁלֹּא אֶחָד בִּלְבַד עָמַד עָלֵינוּ לְכַלּוֹתֵנוּ,

but in every generation, they seek to destroy us.

אֶלָּא שֶׁבְּכָל דּוֹר וָדוֹר עוֹמְדִים עָלֵינוּ לְכַלּוֹתֵנוּ,

And the Holy Blessed One redeems us from their hands.

וְהַקָּדוֹשׁ בָּרוּךְ הוּא מַצִּילֵנוּ מִיָּדָם.

Replace the cup.

Leader:
Who or what stood by us throughout Jewish history? Some maintain that "She" must be God; others insist that "She" must refer to Torah or God's promise (*havtaḥato*).

Participant:
The image portrays three Biblical episodes and one later one suggesting an answer: God's promise to uphold the covenant allowed us to survive difficult times.

Reflection
- What is the significance of the stories depicted in the corners of the illumination?
- If "She" refers to God, do you constantly feel God's active presence? How can one live with perceived "absence" and still continue to have faith in God's goodness, power, and empathy?

Activity
- Sing *Ani Ma-amin*, "I Believe".

Ani Ma-amin

אֲנִי מַאֲמִין

Ani ma-amin be-emunah shelemah b'viat ha-mashiaḥ.

אֲנִי מַאֲמִין בֶּאֱמוּנָה שְׁלֵמָה בְּבִיאַת הַמָּשִׁיחַ

V'af al pi she-yitmahmei-a

וְאַף עַל פִּי שֶׁיִּתְמַהְמֵהַּ

im kol ze aḥakeh lo b'khol yom sheyavo.

עִם כָּל זֶה אֲחַכֶּה לוֹ בְּכָל יוֹם שֶׁיָּבוֹא.

I believe with perfect faith in the coming of the Messiah, and although he may tarry, I will wait daily for his coming.

Abundant as the Plants of the Field

Plate 12

Rabbi Yudan said, "At first a fig tree's fruit is picked one by one, then two by two, then three by three until the figs ripen so abundantly that baskets must be used to gather them. So too, at the beginning, 'Abraham was one and he inherited the Land' (Ezekiel 33:24). Then two: Abraham and Isaac. And after that, three: Abraham, Isaac, and Jacob. Until finally, 'The children of the Israel were fruitful and increased abundantly and multiplied and waxed exceedingly mighty' " (Exodus 1:7).

Genesis Rabbah 46:1

Rich colors illuminate this page, alluding to God enrobing the Israelites in embroidered garments (Ezekiel 16:10). The floral design at each corner represents arba kanfot ha'aretz, "the four corners of the world," to which the Israelites were dispersed. The design is inspired by the Nuremberg Maḥzor, an illuminated manuscript from 1330–1331. Just as Jacob's descendants integrated quickly into Egypt and lived for some time in relative calm and prosperity, so did Jews settle and prosper in Germany for centuries. But just as the sweet blessings of Egypt gradually turned sour, so did the promise of acceptance and prosperity in Germany prove illusory.

ABUNDANCE

Be fruitful and multiply, fill the earth and master it . . .
Genesis 1:28

Here begins the essence of the Maggid section, Deuteronomy 26:5–8 (the entire text is quoted below though the whole excerpt does not appear in the traditional haggadah). You are invited to read and discuss the following passage on your own, using some of the suggested questions to spark conversation, or you may continue with the traditional dialogue between the Biblical verses and rabbinic midrash. The next thirteen pages present a traditional Maggid reading and commentary of Deuteronomy 26:5–8. Slow reading is one of the hallmarks of rabbinic exegesis. The rabbis turn to the core passage around which the haggadah is structured. They savor the process of interpretation as they revel in embellishing the story of the Exodus. Their commentary goes deeper than the literal sense of the text. In fact, the rabbis created an acronym to describe the various levels of Torah interpretation: pardes, meaning "orchard." While the word is vivid in alluding to the fruit of one's labors, its constituent letters correspond to each of the four levels: (p) for pshat, the literal interpretation; (r) for remez, the hint that propels one in a particular direction; (d) for drash, the homiletical interpretation; and (s) for sod, the mystical reading of Torah. The citing and parsing of verses here tends to focus on the third level of meaning—drash or homiletical musings.

Leader:

The haggadah transports us back to the beginning of our Egyptian experience—to our ancestor Jacob and his travails. To move forward we return to our roots.

אֲרַמִּי אֹבֵד אָבִי וַיֵּרֶד מִצְרַיְמָה וַיָּגָר שָׁם בִּמְתֵי מְעָט; וַיְהִי שָׁם לְגוֹי גָּדוֹל עָצוּם וָרָב. וַיָּרֵעוּ אֹתָנוּ הַמִּצְרִים וַיְעַנּוּנוּ; וַיִּתְּנוּ עָלֵינוּ עֲבֹדָה קָשָׁה. וַנִּצְעַק אֶל יְהוָה אֱלֹהֵי אֲבֹתֵינוּ; וַיִּשְׁמַע יְהוָה אֶת קֹלֵנוּ וַיַּרְא אֶת עָנְיֵנוּ וְאֶת עֲמָלֵנוּ וְאֶת לַחֲצֵנוּ. וַיּוֹצִאֵנוּ יְהוָה מִמִּצְרַיִם בְּיָד חֲזָקָה וּבִזְרֹעַ נְטוּיָה וּבְמֹרָא גָּדֹל וּבְאֹתוֹת וּבְמֹפְתִים. וַיְבִאֵנוּ אֶל הַמָּקוֹם הַזֶּה; וַיִּתֶּן לָנוּ אֶת הָאָרֶץ הַזֹּאת, אֶרֶץ זָבַת חָלָב וּדְבָשׁ.

My ancestor was a wandering Aramean. He went down to Egypt and sojourned there few in number, and there too he became a nation—great, mighty, and numerous. And the Egyptians did evil to us, afflicted us and compelled us to do heavy labor. We cried out to Adonai, the God of our ancestors. God heard our voice, and God saw our suffering, our toil, and our oppression. Adonai brought us out of Egypt with a strong hand, an outstretched arm, great awe, signs, and wonders. God brought us to this place and gave us this land, a land flowing with milk and honey.
(Deuteronomy 26: 5–9)

Reflection

- Who was the wandering Aramean?
- Recount the steps that brought this ancestor "down to Egypt."
- What does it mean to become "a nation within a nation"? How does this situation parallel the state of Jewish communities today? Discuss tensions that arise from minority-majority interactions.

- How did we "cry out" to God? To what extent were the Israelites responsible for their redemption from Egypt?
- The final verse (Deuteronomy 26:9, in blue) describes arrival in the Promised Land. This verse, however, is not traditionally included in classical *haggadot*. As Prof. Moshe Benovitz explains, "Some say that this part was intentionally omitted from the haggadah either by Babylonian Jews who were comfortable where they were, or by people who did not want to antagonize the Romans and assert Jewish sovereignty." Given the modern return to Israel, should this verse now be included? What resonance does it have for us today? Discuss.

Go and learn　　　　　　　　　　　　　　צֵא וּלְמַד

מַה בִּקֵּשׁ לָבָן הָאֲרַמִּי לַעֲשׂוֹת לְיַעֲקֹב אָבִינוּ, שֶׁפַּרְעֹה לֹא גָזַר אֶלָּא עַל הַזְּכָרִים, וְלָבָן בִּקֵּשׁ לַעֲקֹר אֶת הַכֹּל, שֶׁנֶּאֱמַר:

אֲרַמִּי אֹבֵד אָבִי וַיֵּרֶד מִצְרַיְמָה. וַיָּגָר שָׁם בִּמְתֵי מְעָט, וַיְהִי שָׁם לְגוֹי גָּדוֹל עָצוּם וָרָב.

Go and learn what Lavan the Aramean sought to do to Jacob our father. Pharaoh decreed solely against the males, whereas Lavan sought to uproot everything, as it is said,
"An Aramean was destroying my father (alternately: My father was a wandering Aramean). He went down to Egypt and sojourned there few in number, and there too he became a nation—great, mighty, and numerous" (Deuteronomy 26:5).

- Why is Lavan's plan deemed more evil than Pharaoh's?

וַיֵּרֶד מִצְרַיְמָה – אָנוּס עַל פִּי הַדִּבּוּר.

וַיָּגָר שָׁם – מְלַמֵּד שֶׁלֹּא יָרַד לְהִשְׁתַּקֵּעַ בְּמִצְרַיִם אֶלָּא לָגוּר שָׁם, שֶׁנֶּאֱמַר: וַיֹּאמְרוּ אֶל פַּרְעֹה לָגוּר בָּאָרֶץ בָּאנוּ כִּי אֵין מִרְעֶה לַצֹּאן אֲשֶׁר לַעֲבָדֶיךָ כִּי כָבֵד הָרָעָב בְּאֶרֶץ כְּנָעַן וְעַתָּה יֵשְׁבוּ נָא עֲבָדֶיךָ בְּאֶרֶץ גֹּשֶׁן.

"He went down to Egypt"—compelled by God's Word.
"And he sojourned there"—This teaches that Jacob did not go down to Egypt to plant roots, but merely to sojourn there, as it is said, "They (Joseph's brothers) said to Pharaoh, 'We came to sojourn in the land, for there is no pasture for your servants' flock since the famine is severe in the Land of Canaan, and now, please let your subjects dwell in the land of Goshen.'" (Genesis 47:4).

- Why is the midrash so reluctant to say that Jacob planted roots in Egypt? What does this say about the centrality of the Land of Israel?

בִּמְתֵי מְעָט – כְּמָה שֶׁנֶּאֱמַר: בְּשִׁבְעִים נֶפֶשׁ יָרְדוּ אֲבֹתֶיךָ מִצְרַיְמָה וְעַתָּה שָׂמְךָ יי אֱלֹהֶיךָ כְּכוֹכְבֵי הַשָּׁמַיִם לָרֹב.

"Few in number"—as it is written, "With seventy souls your ancestors descended to Egypt and now, God has made you as numerous as the stars of the heavens" (Deuteronomy 10:22).

- Given God's promise of abundance, why did nearly every ancestral couple wrestle with infertility?

וַיְהִי שָׁם לְגוֹי – מְלַמֵּד שֶׁהָיוּ יִשְׂרָאֵל מְצֻיָּנִים שָׁם.

"And there they became a nation"—this teaches that the Israelites were a distinct community in Egypt.

● How do we balance our need to remain a distinct community with pressures for integration into the surrounding culture?

גָּדוֹל עָצוּם – כְּמָה שֶׁנֶּאֱמַר: וּבְנֵי יִשְׂרָאֵל פָּרוּ וַיִּשְׁרְצוּ וַיִּרְבּוּ וַיַּעַצְמוּ בִּמְאֹד מְאֹד, וַתִּמָּלֵא הָאָרֶץ אֹתָם.

"A nation great and mighty"—as it is said, "The Children of Israel were fruitful, swarmed, multiplied, and became very, very great, until the earth became full with them" (Exodus 1:7).

וָרָב – כְּמָה שֶׁנֶּאֱמַר: רְבָבָה כְּצֶמַח הַשָּׂדֶה נְתַתִּיךְ, וַתִּרְבִּי וַתִּגְדְּלִי וַתָּבֹאִי בַּעֲדִי עֲדָיִים שָׁדַיִם נָכֹנוּ וּשְׂעָרֵךְ צִמֵּחַ צִמֵּחַ וְאַתְּ עֵרֹם וְעֶרְיָה.

"Numerous"—as it is said, "I made you as abundant as the plants of the field and you multiplied and grew into exceptional beauty. Your breasts developed and your hair sprouted, but you were unclothed and vulnerable" (Ezekiel 16:7).

Leader:
Abundance and fertility form the heart of God's assurance to Abraham, "I will bestow my blessing on you and make your descendants as numerous as the stars of heaven and the sands on the seashore…" (Genesis 22:17).

Participant:
Ironically it is this blessing that leads the Egyptians to jealousy and suspicion: " . . . the more they were oppressed, the more they increased and spread out, so that the [Egyptians] came to dread the Israelites" (Exodus 1:12).

All:
A midrash quoted by the *Rishonim* (the medieval rabbis) teaches: "Israel is likened to the plants of the field. Why? The more you prune them back, the more vigorously they grow." The trials of Israel have made us a stronger, more resilient people.

Reflection
● What is the traditional Jewish attitude toward having large families? How does this dovetail with expectations of modernity?
● Discuss the challenges facing families with many children.
● How can our communities encourage and support larger families?

Activity
● Discuss your family's roots. Does your own family's journey share any aspects of the Israelite experience in Egypt?

SUFFERING

And the Egyptians did evil to us, afflicted us and compelled us to do heavy labor.

Deuteronomy 26:6

וַיָּרֵעוּ אֹתָנוּ הַמִּצְרִים
וַיְעַנּוּנוּ וַיִּתְּנוּ עָלֵינוּ
עֲבֹדָה קָשָׁה.

"And the Egyptians did evil to us"—as it is said,
"Come, let us deal wisely with them, lest they increase; otherwise,
in the event of war, they will join with our enemies and fight us
and rise up from the land" (Exodus 1:10).

וַיָּרֵעוּ אֹתָנוּ הַמִּצְרִים – כְּמָה שֶׁנֶּאֱמַר:
הָבָה נִתְחַכְּמָה לוֹ פֶּן יִרְבֶּה, וְהָיָה כִּי תִקְרֶאנָה מִלְחָמָה
וְנוֹסַף גַּם הוּא עַל שֹׂנְאֵינוּ וְנִלְחַם בָּנוּ וְעָלָה מִן הָאָרֶץ.

"They afflicted us"—as it is said,
"They appointed taskmasters over them to oppress them with burdens,
and they built storage cities for Pharaoh—Pithom and Raamses" (Exodus 1:11).

וַיְעַנּוּנוּ – כְּמָה שֶׁנֶּאֱמַר:
וַיָּשִׂימוּ עָלָיו שָׂרֵי מִסִּים לְמַעַן עַנֹּתוֹ בְּסִבְלֹתָם
וַיִּבֶן עָרֵי מִסְכְּנוֹת לְפַרְעֹה אֶת פִּתֹם וְאֶת רַעַמְסֵס.

"They compelled us to do heavy labor"—as it is said,
"The Egyptians ruthlessly imposed upon the Israelites harsh labor" (Exodus 1:13).

וַיִּתְּנוּ עָלֵינוּ עֲבֹדָה קָשָׁה – כְּמָה שֶׁנֶּאֱמַר:
וַיַּעֲבִדוּ מִצְרַיִם אֶת בְּנֵי יִשְׂרָאֵל בְּפָרֶךְ.

Maror: The Subtle Descent

Plate 13

Rabbi Shmuel bar Naḥmani taught, "Why were the Egyptians compared to *maror?* To teach that, just as *maror* is soft as it begins to grow and hard at the end, so were the Egyptians soft and mild at the beginning, but tough and hard in the end."

BT Pesaḥim 39a

The painting conveys the subtle descent into bondage, beginning with Joseph and his brothers. Sold into slavery, Joseph is brought to Egypt where he rises to become second in power to Pharaoh. His brothers go down to Egypt to secure provisions for the family. Ultimately, the entire family is welcomed by Pharaoh and given land in Goshen. Then, "a new king arose over Egypt who did not know Joseph" (Exodus 1:8). Joseph, who saved Egypt from famine, is forgotten; his descendants become marginalized. Pharaoh decrees that first-born males must be cast into the Nile. Next, Yokheved gently places her son, Moses, into a basket, hoping to save him from Egyptian persecution. Further downstream, Pharaoh's daughter removes Moses from the water and raises him, foreshadowing how she will raise him to adulthood. At the base of the picture, faceless Israelites slide into an abyss. Now fully enslaved, they have lost their individuality. Naked, powerless, bowed by burdens and abused by taskmasters, they risk losing their humanity as well.

VIGILANCE

Eternal vigilance is the price of liberty.

Wendell Phillips

Leader:

Romaine lettuce may be used for the bitter herb; it begins with a refreshing taste but gradually becomes more bitter, like our ancestors' experience in Egypt.

Participant:

Initially, Joseph's descendants prosper in Egypt. Then Pharaoh fears Israelite success. He declares to his people, "Come, let us deal wisely with them, lest they increase; otherwise, in the event of war, they will join with our enemies and fight us and rise up from the land" (Exodus 1:10).

All:

Chillingly familiar, Pharaoh's twin strategies of propaganda and dehumanization have characterized persecution and enslavement throughout history.

Reflections

* At what times in history has Rabbi Shmuel bar Nahmani's adage (see page 82) proven true?

* Where is vigilance required around the world today? What situations are deteriorating? And how can we prevent another "subtle descent"?

And We Cried Out

Plate 14

But if you search there [i.e. in exile] for the Lord your God, you will find God,
if only you seek God with all your heart and soul. . .

Deuteronomy 4:29

This design is inspired by the message underlying the Exodus narrative. "And we cried out" appears in various Hebrew styles. Elsewhere in the Tanakh, "crying out" is interpreted by commentators to mean prayer. The variety of lettering styles mirrors the many different ways in which individual Israelites "cried out" or prayed—personally and collectively—to elicit a response from above. Interspersed among the cries, appear the responses: vayishma', "And God heard"; vayizkor, "and God remembered"; vayar, "and God saw"; and vayeda', "and God knew."

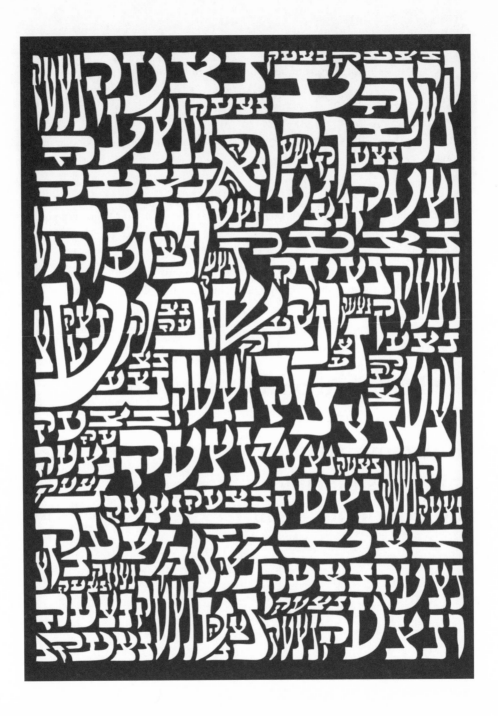

INITIATIVE

When I pray, I speak to God; but when I study, God speaks to me.
a medieval siddur

Leader:
A human act, the supplication of the Israelites, triggers a rapid succession of actions from God: God hears, God remembers, God looks, and God takes notice.

All:
God acts in partnership with us, but sometimes human action is a necessary precursor to a Divine response.

Participant:
Sometimes it takes much crying out to God before we hear a response. At times we cannot discern an answer, and sometimes God seems not to interfere. But in the Passover story, human prayer and communication ultimately cause God to intervene.

And we cried out to Adonai, the God of our ancestors. And God heard our voice, and God saw our suffering, our toil, and our oppression.

Deuteronomy 26:7

וַנִּצְעַק אֶל יי
אֱלֹהֵי אֲבֹתֵינוּ,
וַיִּשְׁמַע יי אֶת קֹלֵנוּ
וַיַּרְא אֶת עָנְיֵנוּ
וְאֶת עֲמָלֵנוּ וְאֶת לַחֲצֵנוּ.

וַנִּצְעַק אֶל יי אֱלֹהֵי אֲבֹתֵינוּ – כְּמָה שֶׁנֶּאֱמַר: וַיְהִי בַיָּמִים הָרַבִּים הָהֵם, וַיָּמָת מֶלֶךְ מִצְרַיִם, וַיֵּאָנְחוּ בְנֵי יִשְׂרָאֵל מִן הָעֲבֹדָה וַיִּזְעָקוּ, וַתַּעַל שַׁוְעָתָם אֶל הָאֱלֹהִים מִן הָעֲבֹדָה.

וַיִּשְׁמַע יי אֶת קֹלֵנוּ – כְּמָה שֶׁנֶּאֱמַר: וַיִּשְׁמַע אֱלֹהִים אֶת נַאֲקָתָם וַיִּזְכֹּר אֱלֹהִים אֶת בְּרִיתוֹ, אֶת אַבְרָהָם אֶת יִצְחָק וְאֶת יַעֲקֹב.

"And we cried out to Adonai, the God of our ancestors"—as it is said, "And it came to pass after many days, . . . the Children of Israel despaired because of their enslavement, and . . . their cry soared heavenward to God because of their slavery" (Exodus 2:23).
"God heard our voice"—as it is said, "And God heard their groaning, and God remembered the covenant with Abraham, with Isaac, and with Jacob" (Exodus 2:24).

וַיַּרְא אֶת עָנְיֵנוּ – זוֹ פְּרִישׁוּת דֶּרֶךְ אֶרֶץ, כְּמָה שֶׁנֶּאֱמַר: וַיַּרְא אֱלֹהִים אֶת בְּנֵי יִשְׂרָאֵל וַיֵּדַע אֱלֹהִים.

וְאֶת עֲמָלֵנוּ – אֵלוּ הַבָּנִים, כְּמָה שֶׁנֶּאֱמַר: כָּל הַבֵּן הַיִּלּוֹד הַיְאֹרָה תַּשְׁלִיכֻהוּ וְכָל הַבַּת תְּחַיּוּן.

וְאֶת לַחֲצֵנוּ – זֶה הַדְּחַק, כְּמָה שֶׁנֶּאֱמַר: וְגַם רָאִיתִי אֶת הַלַּחַץ אֲשֶׁר מִצְרַיִם לֹחֲצִים אוֹתָם.

"God saw our suffering"—this refers to the enforced separation between husbands and wives, as it is said (Exodus 2:25), "And God saw the plight of the Israelites, and God knew."

"Our toil"—this alludes to the annihilation of the male children, as it is said (Exodus 1:22), " 'Every boy that is born you will throw into the Nile, but let every girl live.' "

"Our oppression"—this means crushing oppression, as it is said (Exodus 3:9), "I have seen how the Egyptians oppress them relentlessly."

Reflections
- Why did the Israelites have to "cry out" before God responded?
- How do we sense God's responsiveness today?
- Do you turn to God more in times of need or in times of joy?

Adonai brought us out of Egypt with a strong hand, an outstretched arm, great awe, signs, and wonders.

Deuteronomy 26:8

וַיּוֹצִאֵנוּ יי מִמִּצְרַיִם

בְּיָד חֲזָקָה וּבִזְרֹעַ נְטוּיָה

וּבְמֹרָא גָּדֹל, וּבְאֹתֹת, וּבְמֹפְתִים.

וַיּוֹצִאֵנוּ יי מִמִּצְרַיִם–לֹא עַל יְדֵי מַלְאָךְ, וְלֹא עַל יְדֵי שָׂרָף, וְלֹא עַל יְדֵי שָׁלִיחַ, אֶלָּא הַקָּדוֹשׁ בָּרוּךְ הוּא בִּכְבוֹדוֹ וּבְעַצְמוֹ, שֶׁנֶּאֱמַר, וְעָבַרְתִּי בְאֶרֶץ מִצְרַיִם בַּלַּיְלָה הַזֶּה וְהִכֵּיתִי כָל בְּכוֹר בְּאֶרֶץ מִצְרַיִם מֵאָדָם וְעַד בְּהֵמָה, וּבְכָל אֱלֹהֵי מִצְרַיִם אֶעֱשֶׂה שְׁפָטִים אֲנִי יי.

וְעָבַרְתִּי בְאֶרֶץ מִצְרַיִם - אֲנִי וְלֹא מַלְאָךְ.
וְהִכֵּיתִי כָל בְּכוֹר בְּאֶרֶץ מִצְרַיִם - אֲנִי וְלֹא שָׂרָף.
וּבְכָל אֱלֹהֵי מִצְרַיִם אֶעֱשֶׂה שְׁפָטִים - אֲנִי וְלֹא הַשָּׁלִיחַ.
אֲנִי יי - אֲנִי הוּא וְלֹא אַחֵר.

"I will take you out of Egypt"—not by a messenger, nor by an angel, nor by a surrogate, but the Holy Blessed One through God's own Glorious Self, as it is said, "I will pass through the Land of Egypt on this night and I will strike every first born male in Egypt from human to beast; and I will exact judgment on the gods of Egypt—I Myself, Adonai, will do it" (Exodus 12:12).

"I will pass through the Land of Egypt"—I, and not a messenger.
"I will strike every first born male in Egypt"—I, and not an angel.
"I will exact judgment on the gods of Egypt"—I, and not a surrogate.
"I, Adonai"—I, and not another.

בְּיָד חֲזָקָה – זוֹ הַדֶּבֶר, כְּמָה שֶׁנֶּאֱמַר: הִנֵּה יַד יי הוֹיָה בְּמִקְנְךָ אֲשֶׁר בַּשָּׂדֶה, בַּסּוּסִים, בַּחֲמֹרִים, בַּגְּמַלִּים, בַּבָּקָר וּבַצֹּאן דֶּבֶר כָּבֵד מְאֹד.

וּבִזְרֹעַ נְטוּיָה – זוֹ הַחֶרֶב, כְּמָה שֶׁנֶּאֱמַר: וְחַרְבּוֹ שְׁלוּפָה בְּיָדוֹ נְטוּיָה עַל יְרוּשָׁלָיִם.

"With a strong hand"—this is the plague of pestilence, as it is said, "Behold, the hand of Adonai is upon your cattle in the field, your horses, your donkeys, your camels, your oxen, and your sheep—a very severe disease" (Exodus 9:3).

"And with an outstretched arm"—this refers to the sword, as it is said, "An unsheathed sword in God's hand stretched out over Jerusalem" (I Chronicles 21:16).

וּבְמֹרָא גָּדֹל—זֶה גִּלּוּי שְׁכִינָה, כְּמָה שֶׁנֶּאֱמַר: אוֹ הֲנִסָּה אֱלֹהִים לָבוֹא לָקַחַת לוֹ גוֹי מִקֶּרֶב גּוֹי בְּמַסֹּת בְּאֹתֹת וּבְמוֹפְתִים וּבְמִלְחָמָה וּבְיָד חֲזָקָה וּבִזְרוֹעַ נְטוּיָה וּבְמוֹרָאִים גְּדֹלִים, כְּכֹל אֲשֶׁר עָשָׂה לָכֶם יי אֱלֹהֵיכֶם בְּמִצְרַיִם לְעֵינֶיךָ.

וּבְאֹתוֹת—זֶה הַמַּטֶּה, כְּמָה שֶׁנֶּאֱמַר: וְאֶת הַמַּטֶּה הַזֶּה תִּקַּח בְּיָדֶךָ אֲשֶׁר תַּעֲשֶׂה בּוֹ אֶת הָאֹתֹת.

וּבְמוֹפְתִים—זֶה הַדָּם, כְּמָה שֶׁנֶּאֱמַר: וְנָתַתִּי מוֹפְתִים בַּשָּׁמַיִם וּבָאָרֶץ.

"And with great awe"—this is the revelation of the Divine Presence, as it is said, "Has God ever tried to take a nation from the midst of another nation with trials, signs, wonders, battle, a strong hand, an outstretched arm, awesome events—as all that Adonai, your God, did for you in Egypt before your very eyes?" (Deuteronomy 4:34).

"And with signs"—this is the rod, as it is said, "Take in your hand this rod with which you will make the signs" (Exodus 4:17).

"And with wonders"—this is the plague of blood, as it said, "I will place wonders in the heavens and on the earth . . ." (Joel 3:3).

It is customary to remove or spill a drop of wine from the cup with the declaration of each of the words in blue (a total of sixteen drops):

דָּם, וָאֵשׁ וְתִימְרוֹת עָשָׁן.

Blood, Fire, and Pillars of Smoke.

Joel 3:3

Another interpretation:
"With a strong hand"—two plagues.
"With an outstretched arm"—two plagues.
"With great awe"—two plagues.
"With signs"—two plagues.
"And with wonders"—two plagues.

דָּבָר אַחֵר:
בְּיָד חֲזָקָה - שְׁתַּיִם,
וּבִזְרוֹעַ נְטוּיָה - שְׁתַּיִם,
וּבְמֹרָא גָּדֹל - שְׁתַּיִם,
וּבְאֹתוֹת - שְׁתַּיִם,
וּבְמוֹפְתִים - שְׁתַּיִם.

אֵלּוּ עֶשֶׂר מַכּוֹת שֶׁהֵבִיא הַקָּדוֹשׁ בָּרוּךְ הוּא עַל הַמִּצְרִים בְּמִצְרַיִם, וְאֵלּוּ הֵן:

These are the Ten Plagues that the Holy Blessed One brought upon the Egyptians in Egypt:

דָּם, צְפַרְדֵּעַ, כִּנִּים, עָרוֹב, דֶּבֶר, שְׁחִין, בָּרָד, אַרְבֶּה, חֹשֶׁךְ, מַכַּת בְּכוֹרוֹת.

Blood, Frogs, Lice, Mixed Beasts, Pestilence, Boils, Hail, Locusts, Darkness, and Slaying of the First Born.

רַבִּי יְהוּדָה הָיָה נוֹתֵן בָּהֶם סִימָנִים: דְּצַ"ךְ, עֲדַ"שׁ, בְּאַחַ"ב.

Rabbi Yehudah would use these acronyms: *D'tzakh, Adash, Be'aḥav.*

Plagues

Plates 15 and 16

Do not rejoice at the downfall of your enemy . . .
Proverbs 24:17

The design reflects Rabbi Akiva's teaching (see below) that each plague in Egypt was actually five separate plagues. The colors mirror the nature of each plague: a band of reds for blood, greens for the frogs, pale colors for the lice, a mixed spectrum for the mixed horde of beasts, shades of brown for the cattle pestilence, yellows for the boils, blues for hail, progressively darker grays for locusts gradually covering the skies, blackened tones for darkness, and reds again for the death of the first born. Burgundy and blue stippling around the plagues recalls the drops of wine removed from the cup. Eschewing realistic depictions of the plagues, this design parallels Rabbi Yehudah's acronym: d'tzach, adash, be'ahav—that is to say, avoiding the triumphant pronouncement of the plagues and sensitively minimizing their role in the Passover story.

ויש אומרים שהמנהג לשפוך טיפות יין מהכוס

באצבע אחת וכנגד עשר מכות וכנגד חרב אלהים

אלו עשר מכות שהביא הקדוש ברוך הוא

מִנַּיִן אַתָּה אוֹמֵר שֶׁלָּקוּ הַמִּצְרִים בְּמִצְרַיִם עֶשֶׂר מַכּוֹת, וְעַל הַיָּם לָקוּ חֲמִשִּׁים מַכּוֹת?
בְּמִצְרַיִם מָה הוּא אוֹמֵר? וַיֹּאמְרוּ הַחַרְטֻמִּים אֶל פַּרְעֹה אֶצְבַּע אֱלֹהִים הִיא, וְעַל הַיָּם מָה הוּא אוֹמֵר? וַיַּרְא יִשְׂרָאֵל אֶת הַיָּד הַגְּדֹלָה
אֲשֶׁר עָשָׂה יי בְּמִצְרַיִם וַיִּירְאוּ הָעָם אֶת יי וַיַּאֲמִינוּ בַּיי וּבְמֹשֶׁה עַבְדּוֹ.
כַּמָּה לָקוּ בְּאֶצְבַּע? עֶשֶׂר מַכּוֹת.
אֱמֹר מֵעַתָּה, בְּמִצְרַיִם לָקוּ עֶשֶׂר מַכּוֹת, וְעַל הַיָּם לָקוּ חֲמִשִּׁים מַכּוֹת.

Rabbi Yosse the Galilean says:

How do we know that the Egyptians were stricken by ten plagues in Egypt and fifty by the Reed Sea?
Concerning Egypt, the text states, "The magicians said to Pharaoh, 'This is the finger of God.' " (Exodus 8:15).
And concerning the Reed Sea, Torah teaches, "Israel saw the great hand with which Adonai had stricken Egypt and the people feared Adonai; they believed in Adonai and in Moses, God's servant" (Exodus 14:31).
How many plagues from a finger of God? Ten plagues.
So from this, you may deduce that since the Israelites saw "the great hand" of God at the Reed Sea, the Egyptians were stricken there by fifty plagues.

רַבִּי אֱלִיעֶזֶר אוֹמֵר:

מִנַּיִן שֶׁכָּל מַכָּה וּמַכָּה שֶׁהֵבִיא הַקָּדוֹשׁ בָּרוּךְ הוּא עַל הַמִּצְרִים בְּמִצְרַיִם הָיְתָה שֶׁל אַרְבַּע מַכּוֹת? שֶׁנֶּאֱמַר: יְשַׁלַּח בָּם חֲרוֹן אַפּוֹ
עֶבְרָה וָזַעַם וְצָרָה, מִשְׁלַחַת מַלְאֲכֵי רָעִים. עֶבְרָה - אַחַת, וָזַעַם - שְׁתַּיִם, וְצָרָה - שָׁלֹשׁ, מִשְׁלַחַת מַלְאֲכֵי רָעִים - אַרְבַּע.
אֱמֹר מֵעַתָּה, בְּמִצְרַיִם לָקוּ אַרְבָּעִים מַכּוֹת, וְעַל הַיָּם לָקוּ מָאתַיִם מַכּוֹת.

Rabbi Eliezer says:

How do we know that each plague which God brought upon the Egyptians was actually four plagues?
Scripture states, "God sent anger: wrath, retribution, sorrow, and a cabal of evil messengers" (Psalms 78:49).
Wrath—one. Retribution—two. Sorrow—three. A cabal of evil messengers—four.
So one may conclude that in Egypt they were stricken by forty plagues and at the Reed Sea, two hundred plagues.

רַבִּי עֲקִיבָא אוֹמֵר:

מִנַּיִן שֶׁכָּל מַכָּה וּמַכָּה שֶׁהֵבִיא הַקָּדוֹשׁ בָּרוּךְ הוּא עַל הַמִּצְרִים בְּמִצְרַיִם הָיְתָה שֶׁל חָמֵשׁ מַכּוֹת? שֶׁנֶּאֱמַר: יְשַׁלַּח בָּם חֲרוֹן אַפּוֹ,
עֶבְרָה וָזַעַם, וְצָרָה מִשְׁלַחַת מַלְאֲכֵי רָעִים. חֲרוֹן אַפּוֹ - אַחַת, עֶבְרָה - שְׁתַּיִם, וָזַעַם - שָׁלֹשׁ, וְצָרָה - אַרְבַּע, מִשְׁלַחַת מַלְאֲכֵי רָעִים - חָמֵשׁ.
אֱמֹר מֵעַתָּה, בְּמִצְרַיִם לָקוּ חֲמִשִּׁים מַכּוֹת וְעַל הַיָּם לָקוּ חֲמִשִּׁים וּמָאתַיִם מַכּוֹת.

Rabbi Akiva says:

How do we know that each plague was actually five plagues?
Scripture teaches, "God sent anger, wrath, retribution, sorrow, and a cabal of evil messengers" (Psalms 78:49).
Anger—one. Wrath—two. Retribution—three. Sorrow—four. A cabal of evil messengers—five.
So one may conclude that in Egypt they were stricken by fifty plagues and at the Reed Sea, two hundred fifty plagues.

Leader:

Why are the rabbis so intent on multiplying the plagues? Their interpretations magnify God's grandeur and power.
Yet our joy is restrained—for freedom was attained through the suffering of others. Wine is a symbol of joy. A full cup of wine represents joy overflowing. By diminishing the wine, we temper our joy.

All:

It is written, "Do not rejoice at the downfall of your enemy, nor let your heart be glad when he stumbles" (Proverbs 24:17).

Participant:

All people are God's creatures, even when they are not on "our side." The suffering of others, even of our enemies, is no cause for celebration. As a freed people, we aspire to a higher morality. We are commanded not to oppress others. Here, we go further, symbolically recognizing the other's pain.

Reflections

- Why are the plagues in Plates 15 and 16 represented abstractly rather than figuratively?
- What is the significance of the dotted borders?
- What educational messages does the haggadah seek to convey? Does the message of the plagues support or contradict these values?

כַּמָּה מַעֲלוֹת טוֹבוֹת
לַמָּקוֹם עָלֵינוּ!

אִלּוּ הוֹצִיאָנוּ מִמִּצְרַיִם וְלֹא עָשָׂה בָהֶם שְׁפָטִים   דַּיֵּנוּ!

אִלּוּ עָשָׂה בָהֶם שְׁפָטִים וְלֹא עָשָׂה בֵאלֹהֵיהֶם   דַּיֵּנוּ!

אִלּוּ עָשָׂה בֵאלֹהֵיהֶם וְלֹא הָרַג אֶת בְּכוֹרֵיהֶם   דַּיֵּנוּ!

אִלּוּ הָרַג אֶת בְּכוֹרֵיהֶם וְלֹא נָתַן לָנוּ אֶת מָמוֹנָם   דַּיֵּנוּ!

אִלּוּ נָתַן לָנוּ אֶת מָמוֹנָם וְלֹא קָרַע לָנוּ אֶת הַיָּם   דַּיֵּנוּ!

אִלּוּ קָרַע לָנוּ אֶת הַיָּם וְלֹא הֶעֱבִירָנוּ בְתוֹכוֹ בֶּחָרָבָה   דַּיֵּנוּ!

אִלּוּ הֶעֱבִירָנוּ בְתוֹכוֹ בֶּחָרָבָה, וְלֹא שִׁקַּע צָרֵינוּ בְּתוֹכוֹ   דַּיֵּנוּ!

אִלּוּ שִׁקַּע צָרֵינוּ בְּתוֹכוֹ, וְלֹא סִפֵּק צָרְכֵּנוּ בַּמִּדְבָּר אַרְבָּעִים שָׁנָה   דַּיֵּנוּ!

אִלּוּ סִפֵּק צָרְכֵּנוּ בַּמִּדְבָּר אַרְבָּעִים שָׁנָה וְלֹא הֶאֱכִילָנוּ אֶת הַמָּן   דַּיֵּנוּ!

אִלּוּ הֶאֱכִילָנוּ אֶת הַמָּן וְלֹא נָתַן לָנוּ אֶת הַשַּׁבָּת   דַּיֵּנוּ!

אִלּוּ נָתַן לָנוּ אֶת הַשַּׁבָּת וְלֹא קֵרְבָנוּ לִפְנֵי הַר סִינַי   דַּיֵּנוּ!

אִלּוּ קֵרְבָנוּ לִפְנֵי הַר סִינַי וְלֹא נָתַן לָנוּ אֶת הַתּוֹרָה   דַּיֵּנוּ!

אִלּוּ נָתַן לָנוּ אֶת הַתּוֹרָה וְלֹא הִכְנִיסָנוּ לְאֶרֶץ יִשְׂרָאֵל   דַּיֵּנוּ!

אִלּוּ הִכְנִיסָנוּ לְאֶרֶץ יִשְׂרָאֵל וְלֹא בָּנָה לָנוּ אֶת בֵּית הַבְּחִירָה   דַּיֵּנוּ!

How exceedingly great is all that God has done for us!

If God had taken us out of Egypt and not exacted judgment, **it would have been enough.**

If God had exacted judgment on the Egyptians and not on their gods, **it would have been enough.**

If God had punished their gods and not killed their first born, **it would have been enough.**

If God had killed their first born and not given us reparations, **it would have been enough.**

If God had given us reparations and not split the Reed Sea, **it would have been enough.**

If God had split the Reed Sea and not carried us onto dry land, **it would have been enough.**

If God had carried us onto dry land and not drowned our enemies, **it would have been enough.**

If God had drowned our enemies and not provided for our needs in the desert for forty years, **it would have been enough.**

If God had provided for our needs in the desert for forty years and not fed us manna, **it would have been enough.**

If God had fed us manna and not given us the Shabbat, **it would have been enough.**

If God had given us the Shabbat and not led us to Mount Sinai, **it would have been enough.**

If God had led us to Mount Sinai and not given us the Torah, **it would have been enough.**

If God had given us the Torah and not brought us into the Land of Israel, **it would have been enough.**

If God had brought us into the Land of Israel and not built the Temple, **it would have been enough.**

עַל אַחַת כַּמָּה וְכַמָּה

טוֹבָה כְפוּלָה וּמְכֻפֶּלֶת

לַמָּקוֹם עָלֵינוּ:

שֶׁהוֹצִיאָנוּ מִמִּצְרַיִם,

וְעָשָׂה בָהֶם שְׁפָטִים,

וְעָשָׂה בֵאלֹהֵיהֶם,

וְהָרַג אֶת בְּכוֹרֵיהֶם,

וְנָתַן לָנוּ אֶת מָמוֹנָם,

וְקָרַע לָנוּ אֶת הַיָּם,

וְהֶעֱבִירָנוּ בְתוֹכוֹ בֶּחָרָבָה,

וְשִׁקַּע צָרֵינוּ בְּתוֹכוֹ,

וְסִפֵּק צָרְכֵּנוּ בַּמִּדְבָּר אַרְבָּעִים שָׁנָה,

וְהֶאֱכִילָנוּ אֶת הַמָּן,

וְנָתַן לָנוּ אֶת הַשַּׁבָּת,

וְקֵרְבָנוּ לִפְנֵי הַר סִינַי,

וְנָתַן לָנוּ אֶת הַתּוֹרָה,

וְהִכְנִיסָנוּ לְאֶרֶץ יִשְׂרָאֵל,

וּבָנָה לָנוּ אֶת בֵּית הַבְּחִירָה, לְכַפֵּר עַל כָּל עֲוֹנוֹתֵינוּ.

**How numerous then,
doubled and redoubled,
are the great blessings which
God has bestowed upon us:**

bringing us forth from Egypt,

exacting judgment on the Egyptians

and their gods,

killing their first born,

giving us reparations,

splitting the sea,

carrying us onto dry land,

drowning our enemies,

providing for our needs in the desert for forty years,

feeding us manna,

giving us the Shabbat,

leading us to Mount Sinai,

giving us the Torah,

bringing us into the Land of Israel,

and building a Temple to provide atonement for our sins.

The Teaching of Rabban Gamliel
Plate 17

The Israelites will not be a holy nation until they are, all of them, participants in a world
of ritual remembering; until they celebrate the Passover, rest on *Shabbat*, study the law;
until they actively "break every yoke" . . . This is God's kingdom, and in some ultimate sense,
every place else is Egypt.

Michael Walzer

The illumination is divided into three horizontal bands, echoing the structure of the mishnah:
Pesaḥ, Matzah, and Maror. Rabban Gamliel's teaching forms the frame—built of square,
brick-colored letters, the foundation of the seder experience. The name of each segment appears,
divided between the right and left margins.

1. Pesaḥ. The Pesaḥ or Paschal Lamb and the pilgrimage which preceded its slaughter at twilight on the
fourteenth of Nisan comprise the essential Biblical observance of Passover (Exodus 12:3-8).

2. Matzah. Seder night is called leyl shimurim, "the night of protection," because God watched over the
houses of the Israelites. In our own act of watching, we recall God's watchful eye.
The painting outlines many of the steps involved in baking matzah.

3. Maror. This window begins in servitude, with an Israelite bent under his burden, and continues with
the varied menu of bitter herbs. The legal codes offer several choices for bitter vegetables.

LANGUAGE

*Language is the very means by which
the imprisoned heart gains freedom.*
Avivah Gottlieb Zornberg

רַבָּן גַּמְלִיאֵל הָיָה אוֹמֵר:

כָּל שֶׁלֹּא אָמַר שְׁלֹשָׁה דְבָרִים אֵלּוּ בַּפֶּסַח לֹא יָצָא יְדֵי חוֹבָתוֹ, וְאֵלּוּ הֵן:

פֶּסַח, מַצָּה, וּמָרוֹר.

Rabban Gamliel used to say: Whoever does not mention these three symbols on Passover, has not fulfilled the obligation for seder evening: the Paschal Lamb, the Unleavened Bread, and the Bitter Herb.

Participant:

The requirement for discussing these three foods derives from Exodus 12:27. In response to children asking, "What does this service mean to you?" the Torah commands, "You will say, it is the Passover sacrifice to the Lord, because God protected the homes of the Israelites in Egypt when God smote the Egyptians but saved our houses." Since the verse opens, "You will *say*," Rabban Gamliel understands an obligation *to speak* about the Passover sacrifice (see also Exodus 13:8).

All:

Since *matzah* and *maror* were eaten with the *Pesaḥ* in Temple times and earlier, rabbinic logic extends the obligation to "speaking about" these items as well.

Reflections

- What symbols or steps of the seder do you consider most important?
- Why do we recall Temple rituals when they are no longer observed?
- If there were a Temple today, what purposes would it serve?

Paschal Lamb   פֶּסַח

שֶׁהָיוּ אֲבוֹתֵינוּ אוֹכְלִים בִּזְמַן שֶׁבֵּית הַמִּקְדָּשׁ הָיָה קַיָם עַל שׁוּם מָה? עַל שׁוּם שֶׁפָּסַח הַקָּדוֹשׁ בָּרוּךְ הוּא עַל בָּתֵּי אֲבוֹתֵינוּ

בְּמִצְרַיִם שֶׁנֶּאֱמַר: וַאֲמַרְתֶּם זֶבַח פֶּסַח הוּא לַיי אֲשֶׁר פָּסַח עַל בָּתֵּי בְנֵי יִשְׂרָאֵל בְּמִצְרַיִם, בְּנָגְפּוֹ אֶת מִצְרַיִם וְאֶת בָּתֵּינוּ הִצִּיל

וַיִּקֹּד הָעָם וַיִּשְׁתַּחֲווּ.

The *Pesaḥ* which was consumed by our ancestors when the Temple stood (until 70 C.E.)—why was it eaten? Because the Holy Blessed One protected (*pasaḥ al*) the homes of our ancestors in Egypt, as it is written, "You will say, 'This is a Passover Sacrifice to Adonai who protected the homes of the Children of Israel in Egypt when God struck the Egyptians; indeed, God saved our homes.' And the people bowed their heads and prostrated themselves in prayer" (Exodus 12:27).

Raise the matzah and say:

Unleavened Bread   מַצָּה

זוֹ שֶׁאָנוּ אוֹכְלִים עַל שׁוּם מָה? עַל שׁוּם שֶׁלֹּא הִסְפִּיק בְּצֵקָם שֶׁל אֲבוֹתֵינוּ לְהַחֲמִיץ עַד שֶׁנִּגְלָה עֲלֵיהֶם מֶלֶךְ מַלְכֵי הַמְּלָכִים הַקָּדוֹשׁ בָּרוּךְ הוּא וּגְאָלָם, שֶׁנֶּאֱמַר: וַיֹּאפוּ אֶת הַבָּצֵק אֲשֶׁר הוֹצִיאוּ מִמִּצְרַיִם עֻגֹת מַצּוֹת כִּי לֹא חָמֵץ, כִּי גֹרְשׁוּ מִמִּצְרַיִם וְלֹא יָכְלוּ לְהִתְמַהְמֵהַּ וְגַם צֵדָה לֹא עָשׂוּ לָהֶם.

This matzah which we eat this evening—what is its significance? Because the dough of our ancestors did not have time to rise when the Holy Blessed One, King of all kings, appeared and redeemed them, as it is said, "They baked the dough that they took out of Egypt into cakes of unleavened bread because it did not have time to rise. For they were expelled from Egypt hurriedly and could not delay; they did not even organize provisions for themselves" (Exodus 12:39).

Replace the matzah.

Rabbi Naḥman of Bratslav comments on "they did not even organize provisions for themselves":
"When you are about to leave Egypt, any Egypt, do not stop to think, 'but how will I earn a living out there?'
One who stops to 'organize provisions' will never get out of Egypt."

Raise the bitter herb and say:

Bitter Herb   מָרוֹר

זֶה שֶׁאָנוּ אוֹכְלִים עַל שׁוּם מָה? עַל שׁוּם שֶׁמֵּרְרוּ הַמִּצְרִים אֶת חַיֵּי אֲבוֹתֵינוּ בְּמִצְרָיִם שֶׁנֶּאֱמַר: וַיְמָרְרוּ אֶת חַיֵּיהֶם בַּעֲבֹדָה קָשָׁה, בְּחֹמֶר וּבִלְבֵנִים וּבְכָל עֲבֹדָה בַּשָּׂדֶה אֵת כָּל עֲבֹדָתָם אֲשֶׁר עָבְדוּ בָהֶם בְּפָרֶךְ.

Maror—why do we eat it this evening? Because the Egyptians embittered the lives of our ancestors in Egypt, as it said, "The Egyptians embittered Hebrew lives with burdensome labor, with mortar, bricks and every task done in the field; all the work the Hebrews did, they were ruthlessly forced to do" (Exodus 1:14).

Replace the bitter herb.

In Every Generation

Plate 18

What is at stake in our lives is more than the fate of one generation. In this moment, we, the living, are Israel. The tasks begun by the patriarchs and prophets and carried out by countless Jews of the past are now entrusted to us… we are the only channel of Jewish tradition, those who must save Judaism from oblivion, those who must hand over the entire past to the generations to come.

Abraham Joshua Heschel

The text of the haggadah is hollowed over a map of the journey from Egypt to Israel. The visual effect (white letters) suggests the purity of God, who kept all promises to the Israelites. The large letters declare, "God redeemed us with them!" The square shapes framing the map each present a maze of personal and collective history.

EMPATHY

You will not wrong or oppress a stranger, for you were strangers in the land of Egypt.
Exodus 22:20

בְּכָל דּוֹר וָדוֹר

חַיָּב אָדָם לִרְאוֹת אֶת עַצְמוֹ כְּאִילוּ הוּא יָצָא מִמִּצְרַיִם שֶׁנֶּאֱמַר: וְהִגַּדְתָּ לְבִנְךָ בַּיּוֹם הַהוּא לֵאמֹר, בַּעֲבוּר זֶה עָשָׂה יי לִי בְּצֵאתִי מִמִּצְרַיִם, שֶׁלֹּא אֶת אֲבוֹתֵינוּ בִּלְבַד גָּאַל הַקָּדוֹשׁ בָּרוּךְ הוּא, אֶלָּא אַף אוֹתָנוּ גָּאַל עִמָּהֶם, שֶׁנֶּאֱמַר: וְאוֹתָנוּ הוֹצִיא מִשָּׁם לְמַעַן הָבִיא אֹתָנוּ לָתֶת לָנוּ אֶת הָאָרֶץ אֲשֶׁר נִשְׁבַּע לַאֲבוֹתֵינוּ.

In every generation

each person is obligated to relate to the Exodus as if it had been a personal journey, as it said, "You will tell your child on that day saying, 'It is because of what Adonai did for me when I went free from Egypt…'" (Exodus 13:8).
It was not our ancestors alone whom God redeemed, but we who are present here today also were redeemed with them, as it is written, "God brought us out of there for the sake of giving us the land which God had promised to our ancestors" (Deuteronomy 6:23).

Leader:
"In every generation" is a brilliant expression of our relationship to the past. Our history has shaped us, as individuals and as a people, and will continue to influence the direction and destination of our journeys. With each festival, national history becomes personal memory. The experience of one generation becomes the active memory of another.

Participant:
To be a Jew is to define ourselves through each of these memories, across the generations. Having been slaves, we are obligated to care for the weak and needy of society, seeing each person as a world worth cultivating. For "whoever rescues a single soul, Scripture credits with saving an entire world" (*Mishnah Sanhedrin 4:5*).

All:
While it is difficult for us to imagine living in slavery, the more we are able to empathize with our ancestors, the sweeter the celebration of freedom becomes on seder night.

Activity

- If you hid names of historical figures before the seder, lift your plates to reveal a character. Each person role plays and discusses what freedom means.

- Try re-enacting part of the Exodus narrative—Yokheved and Amram, Moses's parents, deciding what to do about Pharaoh's decree; Pharaoh's daughter Batya finding the baby and deciding to raise him; Moses growing up in the palace and coming to terms with his Jewish identity; Moses' call to leadership at the burning bush. Refer to the Biblical story and add rabbinic interpretation or your own ideas and words. Use costumes, song . . . use the whole room as your stage. . .

Raise the cup of wine and say:

לְפִיכָךְ אֲנַחְנוּ חַיָּבִים

לְהוֹדוֹת, לְהַלֵּל, לְשַׁבֵּחַ, לְפָאֵר, לְרוֹמֵם, לְהַדֵּר, לְבָרֵךְ, לְעַלֵּה וּלְקַלֵּס לְמִי שֶׁעָשָׂה לַאֲבוֹתֵינוּ וְלָנוּ אֶת כָּל הַנִּסִּים הָאֵלֶּה: הוֹצִיאָנוּ מֵעַבְדוּת לְחֵרוּת, מִיָּגוֹן לְשִׂמְחָה, מֵאֵבֶל לְיוֹם טוֹב, וּמֵאֲפֵלָה לְאוֹר גָּדוֹל, וּמִשִּׁעְבּוּד לִגְאֻלָּה, וְנֹאמַר לְפָנָיו שִׁירָה חֲדָשָׁה, הַלְלוּיָהּ.

We are obligated to thank, to praise, to extol, to glorify, to exalt, to honor, to bless, to raise, and to acclaim the One who brought miracles to our ancestors and to us. God brought us from slavery to freedom, from misery to joy, from mourning to celebration, from darkness to great light, from enslavement to redemption. And so we sing a new song before God: Halleluyah!

Replace the cup of wine. We now recite the first half of Hallel, which will be completed after the meal.

109

Halleluyah!

Praise all servants of God, praise the name of Adonai.
May the name of Adonai be blessed,
now and forevermore.
From the eastern rising of the sun to its setting in the west,
may the name of Adonai be praised.
Adonai is raised above all nations;
God's honor extends to the heavens.
Who is like Adonai, our God,
who resides in the uppermost heaven,
but descends to examine
the heavens and the earth!
God raises up the poor from the dust,
God raises the destitute from the chaff
to place them among nobility,
the noble ones of God's people.
God transforms the childless woman
into a joyful mother of many children.
Halleluyah!

Psalms 113

הַלְלוּיָהּ!

הַלְלוּ עַבְדֵי יי הַלְלוּ אֶת שֵׁם יי.

יְהִי שֵׁם יי מְבֹרָךְ מֵעַתָּה וְעַד עוֹלָם.

מִמִּזְרַח שֶׁמֶשׁ עַד מְבוֹאוֹ מְהֻלָּל שֵׁם יי.

רָם עַל כָּל גּוֹיִם יי עַל הַשָּׁמַיִם כְּבוֹדוֹ.

מִי כַּיי אֱלֹהֵינוּ הַמַּגְבִּיהִי לָשָׁבֶת.

הַמַּשְׁפִּילִי לִרְאוֹת בַּשָּׁמַיִם וּבָאָרֶץ.

מְקִימִי מֵעָפָר דָּל מֵאַשְׁפֹּת יָרִים אֶבְיוֹן

לְהוֹשִׁיבִי עִם נְדִיבִים עִם נְדִיבֵי עַמּוֹ,

מוֹשִׁיבִי עֲקֶרֶת הַבַּיִת אֵם הַבָּנִים שְׂמֵחָה,

הַלְלוּיָהּ.

110

When Israel left Egypt

the House of Jacob departed from a nation of foreign language.
Judah became God's sanctuary,
Israel became God's governance.
The sea witnessed and fled,
the Jordan River flowed backward,
the mountains danced like gazelles,
the hills like lambs.
Sea, why do you flee?
Jordan River, why do you flow backward?
Mountains, why do you prance like gazelles?
Hills, why do you dance like lambs?
The earth trembles before the Master,
before the God of Jacob,
who turned the rock into a lake,
the flint into a spring of water.

Psalms 114

בְּצֵאת יִשְׂרָאֵל מִמִּצְרַיִם

בֵּית יַעֲקֹב מֵעַם לֹעֵז.

הָיְתָה יְהוּדָה לְקָדְשׁוֹ, יִשְׂרָאֵל מַמְשְׁלוֹתָיו.

הַיָּם רָאָה וַיָּנֹס, הַיַּרְדֵּן יִסֹּב לְאָחוֹר.

הֶהָרִים רָקְדוּ כְאֵילִים, גְּבָעוֹת כִּבְנֵי צֹאן.

מַה לְּךָ הַיָּם כִּי תָנוּס, הַיַּרְדֵּן תִּסֹּב לְאָחוֹר.

הֶהָרִים תִּרְקְדוּ כְאֵילִים, גְּבָעוֹת כִּבְנֵי צֹאן.

מִלִּפְנֵי אָדוֹן חוּלִי אָרֶץ, מִלִּפְנֵי אֱלוֹהַּ יַעֲקֹב.

הַהֹפְכִי הַצּוּר אֲגַם מָיִם, חַלָּמִישׁ לְמַעְיְנוֹ מָיִם.

111

Israel's Departure

Plate 19

Rabbi Judah said to Rabbi Meir: One tribe said, "I will not be the first to go into the sea," and another tribe said, "I will not be the first to go into the sea." While they were standing there deliberating, Naḥshon the son of Aminadav of the tribe of Judah sprang forward and was the first to go down into the sea. Because it was Naḥshon who came forward, Judah obtained royal dominion in Israel: "The sea saw him and fled" (Psalms 114:3).

BT Sotah 36b-37a

Like the psalm, the illustration is filled with movement: hills dance like gazelles. Below, the sea parts as the Israelites pass through on the sandy sea bed. Midrashim offer various opinions about exactly how the water parted; this rendering follows the literal text from Exodus 14:29, "The waters were like a wall for them, to their right and to their left." The transition from sea to hills to sky also evokes the complementary themes of creation and separation.

BIRTH

We Jews stand between redemptions, as it were, looking back in order to look forward. We thus come to see that we also stand among redemptions—acts of freedom, births of possibility—that we might not have seen, or assisted in, without the paradigm of Pesaḥ.

Arnold Eisen

Leader:
Creation is accompanied by an act of separation, dividing light from darkness, heavens from earth, sea from dry land. Here, in birthing the nation, God separates the Israelites from their Egyptian surroundings before they become a free people.

Participant:
Psalm 114, the second Psalm in the *Hallel*, celebrates the redemption from Egypt. This transformative event marks the Israelites' coalescence even before the covenant at Sinai.

Reflections
- Pain and loss accompany every birth. What did the Israelites lose in leaving Egypt?
- The natural imagery of Psalm 114 encourages us to think about our impact on the environment. How does human behavior affect the natural world? What can we do to improve the situation?

Raise the cup of wine, and say:

בָּרוּךְ אַתָּה יי אֱלֹהֵינוּ מֶלֶךְ הָעוֹלָם אֲשֶׁר גְּאָלָנוּ וְגָאַל אֶת אֲבוֹתֵינוּ מִמִּצְרַיִם, וְהִגִּיעָנוּ לַלַּיְלָה הַזֶּה לֶאֱכָל בּוֹ מַצָּה וּמָרוֹר, כֵּן יי אֱלֹהֵינוּ וֵאלֹהֵי אֲבוֹתֵינוּ יַגִּיעֵנוּ לְמוֹעֲדִים וְלִרְגָלִים אֲחֵרִים הַבָּאִים לִקְרָאתֵנוּ לְשָׁלוֹם, שְׂמֵחִים בְּבִנְיַן עִירֶךָ וְשָׂשִׂים בַּעֲבוֹדָתֶךָ, וְנֹאכַל שָׁם מִן הַזְּבָחִים וּמִן הַפְּסָחִים אֲשֶׁר יַגִּיעַ דָּמָם עַל קִיר מִזְבַּחֲךָ לְרָצוֹן, וְנוֹדֶה לְךָ שִׁיר חָדָשׁ עַל גְּאֻלָּתֵנוּ וְעַל פְּדוּת נַפְשֵׁנוּ.

בָּרוּךְ אַתָּה יי גָּאַל יִשְׂרָאֵל.

בָּרוּךְ אַתָּה יי אֱלֹהֵינוּ מֶלֶךְ הָעוֹלָם
בּוֹרֵא פְּרִי הַגָּפֶן.

Blessed are You Adonai, Sovereign of the Universe, for redeeming us and our ancestors from Egypt, and for sustaining us to this evening in which we eat matzah and *maror*. So too, Adonai, our God and God of our ancestors, allow us to reach other special times and festivals in peace, happy in the building of Your city and joyous in Your service. We will eat there from the Passover offerings, and we will thank You with a new song for our redemption and the deliverance of our souls.

Blessed are You, Adonai, who redeemed Israel.

**Blessed are You, Adonai, our God,
Sovereign of the Universe,
who creates the fruit of the vine.**

Drink the second cup of wine while reclining to the left.

• RAHTZAH • רָחְצָה •

Wash the hands, this time reciting the blessing:

בָּרוּךְ אַתָּה יי אֱלֹהֵינוּ מֶלֶךְ הָעוֹלָם אֲשֶׁר קִדְּשָׁנוּ בְּמִצְוֹתָיו וְצִוָּנוּ עַל נְטִילַת יָדָיִם.

Blessed are You, Adonai, our God, Sovereign of the Universe, who sanctified us with the commandments and commanded us to wash the hands.

• MOTZI MATZAH • מוֹצִיא מַצָּה •

Hold the three matzot from the seder plate and say the first blessing:

בָּרוּךְ אַתָּה יי אֱלֹהֵינוּ מֶלֶךְ הָעוֹלָם הַמּוֹצִיא לֶחֶם מִן הָאָרֶץ.

Blessed are You, Adonai, our God, Sovereign of the Universe, who brings forth bread from the earth.

While holding the middle broken matzah, say the second blessing:

בָּרוּךְ אַתָּה יי אֱלֹהֵינוּ מֶלֶךְ הָעוֹלָם אֲשֶׁר קִדְּשָׁנוּ בְּמִצְוֹתָיו וְצִוָּנוּ עַל אֲכִילַת מַצָּה.

Blessed are You, Adonai, our God, Sovereign of the Universe, who sanctified us with the commandments and commanded us to eat matzah.

Eat a piece of the upper complete matzah and the middle broken matzah while recling to the left.

· MAROR · מָרוֹר

Take an "olive's volume" (generous portion) of the bitter herb, dip it in ḥaroset, and without reclining say:

בָּרוּךְ אַתָּה יי אֱלֹהֵינוּ מֶלֶךְ הָעוֹלָם אֲשֶׁר קִדְּשָׁנוּ בְּמִצְוֹתָיו וְצִוָּנוּ עַל אֲכִילַת מָרוֹר.

Blessed are You, Adonai, our God, Sovereign of the Universe, who sanctified us with the commandments and commanded us to eat the bitter herb.

Eat the bitter herb and ḥaroset.

· KOREKH · כּוֹרֵךְ

Take two pieces of the bottom matzah, place an olive's volume of bitter herb and some ḥaroset between the pieces of matzah, and eat while reclining to the left, after saying:

זֵכֶר לַמִּקְדָּשׁ כְּהִלֵּל, כֵּן עָשָׂה הִלֵּל בִּזְמַן שֶׁבֵּית הַמִּקְדָּשׁ הָיָה קַיָּם, הָיָה כּוֹרֵךְ פֶּסַח, מַצָּה וּמָרוֹר וְאוֹכֵל בְּיַחַד, לְקַיֵּם מַה שֶּׁנֶּאֱמַר: עַל מַצּוֹת וּמְרֹרִים יֹאכְלֻהוּ.

A remembrance of the Temple according to Hillel the Sage: this is what Hillel would do when the Temple stood. He would combine the Paschal sacrifice, matzah, and *maror* and eat them together, to fulfill what is written, "They will eat [the Paschal Lamb] with *matzot* and bitter herbs" (Numbers 9:11).

Reflections
- A haggadah printed in Spanish for use by Marranos after their return to the Jewish community (Leghorn, Italy, 1654), says in the recipe for *ḥaroset*: "Then mix in a bit of brick dust, in memory of the bricks which our fathers made in Egypt." The *Bet David* by Rabbi Yosef Philosof (Salonika, 1740) reports that "in Salonika the elders testified that they used to put chopped calermini stone in the *ḥaroset*."

· SHULḤAN OREKH · שֻׁלְחָן עוֹרֵךְ

Enjoy the festive meal, recognizing the blessing that God has bestowed on us. Remember to save some room for the afikoman!

·TZAFUN· צָפוּן ·

At the end of the meal, the leader of the seder takes an olive's volume of the matzah that was hidden earlier as the afikoman and distributes the rest of the afikoman to the seder participants. Reclining to the left, all declare:

זֵכֶר לְקָרְבַּן פֶּסַח הַנֶּאֱכָל עַל הַשֹּׂבַע.

A remembrance of the Paschal Lamb which was eaten on a full stomach.

Reflections

- The *afikoman* was believed to have protective powers. In Poland, they would "break a piece off of the *afikoman*, pierce it, and hang it on the wall." . . . In Libya and Tunisia, the *afikoman* was carried by sea travelers as an antidote to a raging sea. In Persia, it was kept in the pocket as a charm for plenty and blessing. It was also used as a charm for pregnant women to ensure male children, to help the mute speak, to ensure silos full of grain, to protect against bullets, and to prevent a river from overflowing its banks.

ᐧ BAREKH ᐧ בָּרֵךְ ᐧ

Pour the third cup of wine and recite Birkat Hamazon (the Blessing after the Meal):

שִׁיר הַמַּעֲלוֹת

בְּשׁוּב יי אֶת שִׁיבַת צִיּוֹן הָיִינוּ כְּחֹלְמִים. אָז יִמָּלֵא שְׂחוֹק פִּינוּ וּלְשׁוֹנֵנוּ רִנָּה.
אָז יֹאמְרוּ בַגּוֹיִם הִגְדִּיל יי לַעֲשׂוֹת עִם אֵלֶּה. הִגְדִּיל יי לַעֲשׂוֹת עִמָּנוּ הָיִינוּ שְׂמֵחִים.
שׁוּבָה יי אֶת שְׁבִיתֵנוּ כַּאֲפִיקִים בַּנֶּגֶב. הַזֹּרְעִים בְּדִמְעָה בְּרִנָּה יִקְצֹרוּ.
הָלוֹךְ יֵלֵךְ וּבָכֹה נֹשֵׂא מֶשֶׁךְ הַזָּרַע בֹּא יָבֹא בְרִנָּה נֹשֵׂא אֲלֻמֹּתָיו.

אם המסובים הם שלושה או יותר מזמנים. ואם יש עשרה מוסיפים "אלוהינו" שבסוגריים.

המזמן: חֲבֵרַי נְבָרֵךְ.
הכל עונים: יְהִי שֵׁם יי מְבֹרָךְ מֵעַתָּה וְעַד עוֹלָם.
המזמן: יְהִי שֵׁם יי מְבֹרָךְ מֵעַתָּה וְעַד עוֹלָם.
המזמן: בִּרְשׁוּת חֲבֵרַי נְבָרֵךְ (אֱלֹהֵינוּ) שֶׁאָכַלְנוּ מִשֶּׁלּוֹ.
הכל עונים: בָּרוּךְ (אֱלֹהֵינוּ) שֶׁאָכַלְנוּ מִשֶּׁלּוֹ וּבְטוּבוֹ חָיִינוּ.
המזמן: בָּרוּךְ (אֱלֹהֵינוּ) שֶׁאָכַלְנוּ מִשֶּׁלּוֹ וּבְטוּבוֹ חָיִינוּ.
כולם ביחד: בָּרוּךְ הוּא וּבָרוּךְ שְׁמוֹ.

אם אין שלושה מסובים, מתחילים כאן:

בָּרוּךְ אַתָּה יי אֱלֹהֵינוּ מֶלֶךְ הָעוֹלָם, הַזָּן אֶת הָעוֹלָם כֻּלּוֹ בְּטוּבוֹ בְּחֵן, בְּחֶסֶד וּבְרַחֲמִים, הוּא נוֹתֵן לֶחֶם לְכָל בָּשָׂר כִּי לְעוֹלָם חַסְדּוֹ
וּבְטוּבוֹ הַגָּדוֹל תָּמִיד לֹא חָסַר לָנוּ וְאַל יֶחְסַר לָנוּ מָזוֹן לְעוֹלָם וָעֶד בַּעֲבוּר שְׁמוֹ הַגָּדוֹל כִּי הוּא אֵל זָן וּמְפַרְנֵס לַכֹּל וּמֵטִיב לַכֹּל וּמֵכִין
מָזוֹן לְכָל בְּרִיּוֹתָיו אֲשֶׁר בָּרָא בָּרוּךְ אַתָּה יי הַזָּן אֶת הַכֹּל.

A Song of Ascents

When Adonai brought the exiles back to Zion, we were like dreamers. Then God filled our mouths with laughter and our tongues with shouts of joy. The nations said, "Adonai has done great things for them." Indeed, Adonai has done great things for us, so that we are jubilant. Return, Adonai, our exiles as the flood waters of the Negev. Those who sow in tears will reap in joy. Though one weeps on the way, carrying seed, one will return in joy carrying sheaves.

Psalms 126

If there are three or more people, one of them recites the following invitation to bless.
If there are ten, "our God" (in parentheses) is added:

Leader: Friends, let us bless.
The others respond: May the name of Adonai be blessed now and forever.
Leader repeats the above verse and continues: By permission of all those who have participated in this meal, let us bless (our God) from whose food we have eaten.
The others respond: Blessed is the One (our God) from whose food we have eaten and whose goodness sustains us.
Leader: Blessed is the One (our God) from whose food we have eaten and whose goodness sustains us.
All declare together: Blessed is God and blessed is God's Name.

If there are fewer than three, omit the above invitation to bless and continue here:
Blessed are You Adonai, our God, Sovereign of the Universe, who nourishes the whole world through goodness, grace, lovingkindness, and mercy. God gives sustenance to all creatures; God's lovingkindness endures forever. God's great goodness is never lacking. May we never lack sustenance. For the sake of God's great name, God sustains and supports all and is beneficent to all, and prepares food for all creatures that God created. Blessed are You, Adonai, who nourishes all.

נוֹדֶה לְךָ יי אֱלֹהֵינוּ. עַל שֶׁהִנְחַלְתָּ לַאֲבוֹתֵינוּ אֶרֶץ חֶמְדָּה טוֹבָה וּרְחָבָה, וְעַל שֶׁהוֹצֵאתָנוּ יי אֱלֹהֵינוּ מֵאֶרֶץ מִצְרַיִם, וּפְדִיתָנוּ מִבֵּית עֲבָדִים, וְעַל בְּרִיתְךָ שֶׁחָתַמְתָּ בִּבְשָׂרֵנוּ, וְעַל תּוֹרָתְךָ שֶׁלִּמַּדְתָּנוּ, וְעַל חֻקֶּיךָ שֶׁהוֹדַעְתָּנוּ, וְעַל חַיִּים, חֵן וָחֶסֶד שֶׁחוֹנַנְתָּנוּ, וְעַל אֲכִילַת מָזוֹן שָׁאַתָּה זָן וּמְפַרְנֵס אוֹתָנוּ תָּמִיד בְּכָל יוֹם וּבְכָל עֵת וּבְכָל שָׁעָה.

וְעַל הַכֹּל יי אֱלֹהֵינוּ אֲנַחְנוּ מוֹדִים לָךְ, וּמְבָרְכִים אוֹתָךְ יִתְבָּרַךְ שִׁמְךָ בְּפִי כָּל חַי תָּמִיד לְעוֹלָם וָעֶד. כַּכָּתוּב וְאָכַלְתָּ וְשָׂבָעְתָּ וּבֵרַכְתָּ אֶת יי אֱלֹהֶיךָ עַל הָאָרֶץ הַטֹּבָה אֲשֶׁר נָתַן לָךְ. בָּרוּךְ אַתָּה יי עַל הָאָרֶץ וְעַל הַמָּזוֹן.

רַחֵם נָא יי אֱלֹהֵינוּ עַל יִשְׂרָאֵל עַמֶּךָ, וְעַל יְרוּשָׁלַיִם עִירֶךָ וְעַל צִיּוֹן מִשְׁכַּן כְּבוֹדֶךָ וְעַל מַלְכוּת בֵּית דָּוִד מְשִׁיחֶךָ, וְעַל הַבַּיִת הַגָּדוֹל וְהַקָּדוֹשׁ שֶׁנִּקְרָא שִׁמְךָ עָלָיו. אֱלֹהֵינוּ, אָבִינוּ, רְעֵנוּ, זוּנֵנוּ, פַּרְנְסֵנוּ וְכַלְכְּלֵנוּ, וְהַרְוִיחֵנוּ, וְהַרְוַח לָנוּ יי אֱלֹהֵינוּ מְהֵרָה מִכָּל צָרוֹתֵינוּ. וְנָא אַל תַּצְרִיכֵנוּ יי אֱלֹהֵינוּ, לֹא לִידֵי מַתְּנַת בָּשָׂר וָדָם, וְלֹא לִידֵי הַלְוָאָתָם, כִּי אִם לְיָדְךָ הַמְּלֵאָה, הַפְּתוּחָה, הַקְּדוֹשָׁה וְהָרְחָבָה, שֶׁלֹּא נֵבוֹשׁ, וְלֹא נִכָּלֵם לְעוֹלָם וָעֶד.

בְּשַׁבָּת מוֹסִיפִים אֶת הַסָּעִיף הַבָּא:

רְצֵה וְהַחֲלִיצֵנוּ יי אֱלֹהֵינוּ בְּמִצְוֹתֶיךָ וּבְמִצְוַת יוֹם הַשְּׁבִיעִי הַשַּׁבָּת הַגָּדוֹל וְהַקָּדוֹשׁ הַזֶּה כִּי יוֹם זֶה גָּדוֹל וְקָדוֹשׁ הוּא לְפָנֶיךָ לִשְׁבָּת בּוֹ וְלָנוּחַ בּוֹ בְּאַהֲבָה כְּמִצְוַת רְצוֹנֶךָ וּבִרְצוֹנְךָ הָנִיחַ לָנוּ יי אֱלֹהֵינוּ שֶׁלֹּא תְהֵא צָרָה וְיָגוֹן וַאֲנָחָה בְּיוֹם מְנוּחָתֵנוּ וְהַרְאֵנוּ יי אֱלֹהֵינוּ בְּנֶחָמַת צִיּוֹן עִירֶךָ וּבְבִנְיַן יְרוּשָׁלַיִם עִיר קָדְשֶׁךָ כִּי אַתָּה הוּא בַּעַל הַיְשׁוּעוֹת וּבַעַל הַנֶּחָמוֹת.

אֱלֹהֵינוּ וֵאלֹהֵי אֲבוֹתֵינוּ יַעֲלֶה וְיָבֹא וְיַגִּיעַ וְיֵרָאֶה וְיֵרָצֶה וְיִשָּׁמַע וְיִפָּקֵד וְיִזָּכֵר זִכְרוֹנֵנוּ וּפִקְדוֹנֵנוּ וְזִכְרוֹן אֲבוֹתֵינוּ וְזִכְרוֹן מָשִׁיחַ בֶּן דָּוִד עַבְדֶּךָ וְזִכְרוֹן יְרוּשָׁלַיִם עִיר קָדְשֶׁךָ וְזִכְרוֹן כָּל עַמְּךָ בֵּית יִשְׂרָאֵל לְפָנֶיךָ לִפְלֵיטָה לְטוֹבָה לְחֵן וּלְחֶסֶד וּלְרַחֲמִים לְחַיִּים וּלְשָׁלוֹם בְּיוֹם חַג הַמַּצּוֹת הַזֶּה. זָכְרֵנוּ יי אֱלֹהֵינוּ בּוֹ לְטוֹבָה, וּפָקְדֵנוּ בוֹ לִבְרָכָה, וְהוֹשִׁיעֵנוּ בוֹ לְחַיִּים, וּבִדְבַר יְשׁוּעָה וְרַחֲמִים חוּס וְחָנֵּנוּ וְרַחֵם עָלֵינוּ וְהוֹשִׁיעֵנוּ כִּי אֵלֶיךָ עֵינֵינוּ כִּי אֵל מֶלֶךְ חַנּוּן וְרַחוּם אָתָּה.

וּבְנֵה יְרוּשָׁלַיִם עִיר הַקֹּדֶשׁ בִּמְהֵרָה בְיָמֵינוּ, בָּרוּךְ אַתָּה יי בּוֹנֵה בְרַחֲמָיו יְרוּשָׁלַיִם, אָמֵן!

בָּרוּךְ אַתָּה יי אֱלֹהֵינוּ מֶלֶךְ הָעוֹלָם הָאֵל אָבִינוּ, מַלְכֵּנוּ, אַדִּירֵנוּ, בּוֹרְאֵנוּ, גּוֹאֲלֵנוּ, יוֹצְרֵנוּ, קְדוֹשֵׁנוּ, קְדוֹשׁ יַעֲקֹב, רוֹעֵנוּ רוֹעֵה יִשְׂרָאֵל, הַמֶּלֶךְ הַטּוֹב וְהַמֵּטִיב לַכֹּל, שֶׁבְּכָל יוֹם וָיוֹם הוּא הֵטִיב, הוּא מֵטִיב, הוּא יֵיטִיב לָנוּ, הוּא גְמָלָנוּ, הוּא גוֹמְלֵנוּ, הוּא יִגְמְלֵנוּ לָעַד, לְחֵן וּלְחֶסֶד וּלְרַחֲמִים וּלְרֶוַח, הַצָּלָה וְהַצְלָחָה, בְּרָכָה וִישׁוּעָה, נֶחָמָה, פַּרְנָסָה וְכַלְכָּלָה וְרַחֲמִים וְחַיִּים וְשָׁלוֹם וְכָל טוֹב וּמִכָּל טוּב לְעוֹלָם אַל יְחַסְּרֵנוּ.

We thank You, Adonai, our God, for the gift of a desirable, good, and spacious land which You gave to our ancestors, for taking us out of the Land of Egypt and redeeming us from the House of Slavery, for the covenant that You have sealed in our flesh, for the Torah that You taught us, for the ordinances You have made known to us, for life, grace, and lovingkindness that You have bestowed on us, and for the food with which You feed and sustain us every day, every moment, every hour.

For everything, Adonai, our God, we thank You and we bless You. Let Your Name be blessed eternally in the mouth of every living creature, as it is written, "When you eat and are satisfied, you shall bless Adonai, your God, for the good land that God has given you" (Deuteronomy 8:10). Blessed are You, Adonai, for the land and for the food.

Please, Adonai, our God, have mercy on Your people Israel, on Your city Jerusalem, on Zion, the indwelling of Your glory, on the kingship of the House of David, Your anointed one, and on Your great and holy House over which we call Your Name. Our God, our Parent, guide us, sustain us, feed us, support us, make us prosper, deliver us, and speedily save us, Adonai, our God, from all of our sorrows. And please, Adonai our God, may we never be dependent on the charity of others or on their loans, but only upon Your full, open, overflowing, and beneficent hand. May we never be embarrassed or ashamed at any time.

On Shabbat, add the following paragraph:

May You desire, Adonai our God, to strengthen us in Your commandments, and especially in the observance of the seventh day, this great and holy Shabbat, for this day is wonderful and holy before You, that we may refrain from work and rest lovingly according to Your desire. And may it be Your will that you provide respite, Adonai our God, from all sorrow, pain, and trouble on the day of our rest. And show us, Adonai, our God, the comfort of Zion, Your City, and the rebuilding of Jerusalem, Your Holy City, for You are a God of redemption and of consolation.

Our God and God of our ancestors, may the remembrance of us, the recalling of us, the memory of our ancestors, the memory of the Messiah, son of David, Your servant, the memory of Jerusalem, Your sacred city, and the memory of Your people, the House of Israel, ascend, journey, arrive, appear, be accepted, be heard, be noted and be remembered for deliverance, for goodness, for grace, for kindness, for mercy, for life, and for peace on this day of the Festival of *Matzot*. Remember us, Adonai, our God, for goodness; recall us for blessing; redeem us for life. And for the sake of redemption and mercy, have pity on us, be kind to us, have mercy on us, and redeem us, for it is to You that our eyes are turned, because You are a gracious and merciful God.

Rebuild Jerusalem, the sacred city, speedily in our days. Blessed are You, Adonai, merciful Builder of Jerusalem. Amen!

Blessed are You, Adonai, our God, Sovereign of the world, our parent, our monarch, our precious one, our creator, our redeemer, our maker, our sacred one, the sanctifier of Jacob, our shepherd, the leader of Israel, the total sovereign, who is good to all; who every day did good, does good, and will do good for us. God gave us grace, God gives us grace, and God will give us grace forever—for favor, for kindness, for mercy, for salvation, for prosperity, for blessing, for comfort, for support, for mercy, for life, for peace, and for all good. May we never lack for anything.

הָרַחֲמָן הוּא יִמְלֹךְ עָלֵינוּ לְעוֹלָם וָעֶד: הָרַחֲמָן הוּא יִתְבָּרַךְ בַּשָּׁמַיִם וּבָאָרֶץ. הָרַחֲמָן הוּא יִשְׁתַּבַּח לְדוֹר דּוֹרִים, וְיִתְפָּאַר בָּנוּ לָעַד וּלְנֵצַח נְצָחִים, וְיִתְהַדַּר בָּנוּ לָעַד וּלְעוֹלְמֵי עוֹלָמִים. הָרַחֲמָן הוּא יְפַרְנְסֵנוּ בְּכָבוֹד. הָרַחֲמָן הוּא יִשְׁבֹּר עֻלֵּנוּ מֵעַל צַוָּארֵנוּ וְהוּא יוֹלִיכֵנוּ קוֹמְמִיּוּת לְאַרְצֵנוּ. הָרַחֲמָן הוּא יִשְׁלַח לָנוּ בְּרָכָה מְרֻבָּה בַּבַּיִת הַזֶּה וְעַל שֻׁלְחָן זֶה שֶׁאָכַלְנוּ עָלָיו. הָרַחֲמָן הוּא יִשְׁלַח לָנוּ אֶת אֵלִיָּהוּ הַנָּבִיא זָכוּר לַטּוֹב וִיבַשֶּׂר לָנוּ בְּשׂוֹרוֹת טוֹבוֹת יְשׁוּעוֹת וְנֶחָמוֹת.

ניתן לומר אחת מן הברכות הבאות:

הָרַחֲמָן הוּא יְבָרֵךְ אֶת בַּעַל הַבַּיִת הַזֶּה וְאֶת בַּעֲלַת הַבַּיִת הַזֶּה, אוֹתָם וְאֶת בֵּיתָם וְאֶת זַרְעָם וְאֶת כָּל אֲשֶׁר לָהֶם...

הָרַחֲמָן הוּא יְבָרֵךְ אֶת אָבִי מוֹרִי וְאֶת אִמִּי מוֹרָתִי, אוֹתָם וְאֶת בֵּיתָם וְאֶת זַרְעָם וְאֶת כָּל אֲשֶׁר לָהֶם...

הָרַחֲמָן הוּא יְבָרֵךְ אֶת כָּל הַמְּסֻבִּין כָּאן...

ולהמשיך:

...אוֹתָנוּ וְאֶת כָּל אֲשֶׁר לָנוּ, כְּמוֹ שֶׁנִּתְבָּרְכוּ אִמּוֹתֵינוּ שָׂרָה, רִבְקָה, רָחֵל וְלֵאָה וַאֲבוֹתֵינוּ אַבְרָהָם, יִצְחָק וְיַעֲקֹב, "בַּכֹּל", "מִכֹּל", "כֹּל", כֵּן יְבָרֵךְ אוֹתָנוּ כֻּלָּנוּ יַחַד בִּבְרָכָה שְׁלֵמָה וְנֹאמַר אָמֵן.

בַּמָּרוֹם יְלַמְּדוּ עֲלֵיהֶם וְעָלֵינוּ זְכוּת שֶׁתְּהֵא לְמִשְׁמֶרֶת שָׁלוֹם, וְנִשָּׂא בְרָכָה מֵאֵת יי וּצְדָקָה מֵאֱלֹהֵי יִשְׁעֵנוּ וְנִמְצָא חֵן וְשֵׂכֶל טוֹב בְּעֵינֵי אֱלֹהִים וְאָדָם.

בשבת מוסיפים:

הָרַחֲמָן הוּא יַנְחִילֵנוּ יוֹם שֶׁכֻּלוֹ שַׁבָּת וּמְנוּחָה לְחַיֵּי הָעוֹלָמִים.

הָרַחֲמָן הוּא יַנְחִילֵנוּ יוֹם שֶׁכֻּלוֹ טוֹב.

הָרַחֲמָן הוּא יְבָרֵךְ אֶת מְדִינַת יִשְׂרָאֵל, רֵאשִׁית צְמִיחַת גְּאֻלָּתֵנוּ.

הָרַחֲמָן הוּא יְבָרֵךְ אֶת חַיָּלֵי צְבָא הַהֲגַנָּה לְיִשְׂרָאֵל וְיָגֵן עֲלֵיהֶם.

הָרַחֲמָן הוּא יְבָרֵךְ אֶת אַחֵינוּ בְּנֵי יִשְׂרָאֵל הַנְּתוּנִים בַּצָּרָה, וְיוֹצִיאֵם מֵאֲפֵלָה לְאוֹרָה.

הָרַחֲמָן הוּא יְזַכֵּנוּ לִימוֹת הַמָּשִׁיחַ וּלְחַיֵּי הָעוֹלָם הַבָּא.

122

May the Merciful One rule over us forever. May the Merciful One always be blessed in the heavens and on earth. May the Merciful One be praised for all generations, glorified through our actions forever and ever, and sanctified through us forever. May the Merciful One sustain us in dignity. May the Merciful One break the yoke from our necks and guide us proudly toward the Land of Israel. May the Merciful One send us abundant blessings on this house and upon this table from which we have eaten. May the Merciful One send Elijah the prophet, remembered for good, and may he deliver good news of redemption and comfort.

Choose the appropriate blessing:

May the Merciful One bless our host and hostess together with their entire family and all that belongs to them...

May the Merciful One bless my father and my mother, my teachers, together with their entire family and all that belongs to them...

May the Merciful One bless all those who recline around our table, us and all that belongs to us...

Continue:

just as God blessed our ancestors Sarah, Rebecca, Rachel and Leah, Abraham, Isaac, and Jacob—"in everything," "from everything," " in every way," so too may God bless all of us together with a complete blessing and let us say, Amen!

May their merit and ours be remembered in the Heavens above as an assurance for protective peace. May the blessing from Adonai arise and righteousness from the God of our redemption; and may we find favor and good in the eyes of God and humanity.

On Shabbat:

May the Merciful One give us a day which is entirely Shabbat and eternal rest.

May the Merciful One give us a day which is entirely good.

May the Merciful One protect the State of Israel, the first flowering of our redemption.

May the Merciful One bless the soldiers of Israel and defend them.

May the Merciful One bless our fellow Jews who are in distress and deliver them from darkness to light.

May the Merciful One cause us to merit the days of the Messiah and the World to Come.

מִגְדּוֹל יְשׁוּעוֹת מַלְכּוֹ וְעֹשֶׂה חֶסֶד לִמְשִׁיחוֹ לְדָוִד וּלְזַרְעוֹ עַד עוֹלָם, עֹשֶׂה שָׁלוֹם בִּמְרוֹמָיו הוּא יַעֲשֶׂה שָׁלוֹם עָלֵינוּ וְעַל כָּל יִשְׂרָאֵל וְאִמְרוּ אָמֵן. יְראוּ אֶת יי קְדוֹשָׁיו כִּי אֵין מַחְסוֹר לִירֵאָיו, כְּפִירִים רָשׁוּ וְרָעֵבוּ וְדוֹרְשֵׁי יי לֹא יַחְסְרוּ כָל טוֹב. הוֹדוּ לַיי כִּי טוֹב כִּי לְעוֹלָם חַסְדּוֹ. פּוֹתֵחַ אֶת יָדֶךָ וּמַשְׂבִּיעַ לְכָל חַי רָצוֹן. בָּרוּךְ הַגֶּבֶר אֲשֶׁר יִבְטַח בַּיי וְהָיָה יי מִבְטַחוֹ. נַעַר הָיִיתִי גַּם זָקַנְתִּי וְלֹא רָאִיתִי צַדִּיק נֶעֱזָב וְזַרְעוֹ מְבַקֶּשׁ לָחֶם. יי עֹז לְעַמּוֹ יִתֵּן יי יְבָרֵךְ אֶת עַמּוֹ בַשָּׁלוֹם.

ומברכים:

בָּרוּךְ אַתָּה יי אֱלֹהֵינוּ מֶלֶךְ הָעוֹלָם בּוֹרֵא פְּרִי הַגָּפֶן.

שותים בהסיבת שמאל.

God is a tower of salvation to God's chosen king and acts compassionately to the anointed one, to David and his descendants forever. May the One who makes peace on high, bring peace to us and to all Israel and let us say: Amen. May God's sacred ones fear Adonai, for those who fear God lack nothing. Young lions want and are hungry, but those who seek Adonai lack nothing. Give thanks to Adonai, for God is good! God's mercy endures forever. You open your hand and satisfy every living being with favor. Blessed is the one who trusts in Adonai; Adonai becomes her security. I was a youth and now I am old; have I ever seen a righteous person abandoned or his children begging for food? May Adonai give strength to God's people, may Adonai bless God's people with peace.

Each participant takes a cup of wine in hand and says:

Blessed are You, Adonai, our God, Sovereign of the Universe, who creates the fruit of the vine.

Drink the third cup of wine while reclining to the left.

Pour Out Your Wrath

Plate 20

God of retribution, Lord, God of retribution appear! Rise up, Judge of the earth,
give the arrogant their desserts! How long will the wicked exult, will they utter insolent
speech, will all evildoers vaunt themselves? They crush Your people, Lord,
they afflict Your very own . . .
Psalms 94:1-5

*Since the declaration "pour out your wrath…" is juxtaposed in the seder with Elijah's Cup, this
design depicts an upside down wine goblet. The text, a mirror image of "pour out your wrath," is
inverted to show that our recitation is ambivalent. This upside down Kiddush cup also forms a
doorway. We are both inside the doorway shouting "shfokh hamatkha," and outside with God and
Elijah the Prophet, looking in. How will God respond to our plea for retribution? Perhaps instead
of vengeance, God will stand with us in our suffering.*

COMFORT

Rabbi Abbahu said,
"A man should always strive to be of the persecuted and not of the persecutors. For among the birds none are more persecuted than doves and pigeons, yet only these were declared by Torah to be fit for the altar."
BT Bava Kamma 93a

Fill Elijah's Cup and open the door.

Leader:
Context is essential in order to gain a deeper understanding of this passage. "Pour out your wrath" does not appear in any haggadah until around the year 1100 (notably emerging after the First Crusade in 1096). The experience of persecution, blood libels, and expulsions shaped this cry of anguish and vengeance. In our recitation tonight, we remember the pain of our ancestors.

Participant:
Still, while it may be natural to wish for revenge, a sensitive soul restrains this urge. Vengeance, even if justified, too often brings further destruction and chaos. Self-control becomes the flowering of our redemption.

Together we say:

Pour out Your wrath

on the nations which do not know You and

upon governments which have not called upon Your Name.

For the enemy has consumed Jacob and destroyed his refuge (Psalms 79:6–7).

Pour out Your wrath upon them and let Your rage overpower them (Psalms 69:25).

Angrily pursue them and erase them from under God's sky (Lamentations 3:66).

שְׁפֹךְ חֲמָתְךָ

אֶל הַגּוֹיִם אֲשֶׁר לֹא יְדָעוּךָ,

וְעַל מַמְלָכוֹת אֲשֶׁר בְּשִׁמְךָ לֹא קָרָאוּ.

כִּי אָכַל אֶת יַעֲקֹב, וְאֶת נָוֵהוּ הֵשַׁמּוּ.

שְׁפָךְ עֲלֵיהֶם זַעְמֶךָ וַחֲרוֹן אַפְּךָ יַשִּׂיגֵם.

תִּרְדֹּף בְּאַף וְתַשְׁמִידֵם מִתַּחַת שְׁמֵי יי.

Activity
- Sing *Eliyahu Ha-Navi.*

Eliyahu Ha-Navi

Eliyahu ha-Navi, Eliyahu ha-Navi,

Eliyahu, Eliyahu, Eliyahu ha-Giladi (x2)

Bimheyrah v'yameinu, yavo aleinu,

im Mashiah ben David. (x2)

Elijah the Prophet, come to us soon,
for you herald Messianic days.

All:

Let us also call out in the words of Isaiah, " 'Comfort, oh comfort My People,' says your God. Speak tenderly to Jerusalem, and declare to her that her term of service is over, that her iniquity is expiated; for she has received at the hand of the Lord double for all her sins" (Isaiah 40:1–2).

Reflections

- Why are the words in the illustration reversed?
- Is there a place for anger and wishes for vengeance within Judaism?
- What, besides wrath, would we like to "pour out" on those who do not wish us well?
- Elijah remarks, "I am moved by zeal for the Lord, the God of Hosts" (I Kings 19:10). While Elijah's zeal leads to loyalty, it also leads to fundamentalism. What can we do to confront fundamentalism in all religions? How can we find a balance between religious passion and respect for other paths and beliefs?
- If you were writing a haggadah, would you include this section or omit it, change it or leave it intact?
- A modern Israeli haggadah includes the following text. How do you respond to its sentiment?

Pour out Your love

on the nations who know You,

and on kingdoms who call Your name.

For the good which they do for the seed of Jacob,

and they shield Your people Israel from their enemies.

May they merit to see the good of Your chosen,

and to rejoice in the joy of Your nation.

אֵלִיָּהוּ הַנָּבִיא

אֵלִיָּהוּ הַנָּבִיא אֵלִיָּהוּ הַתִּשְׁבִּי

אֵלִיָּהוּ אֵלִיָּהוּ אֵלִיָּהוּ הַגִּלְעָדִי (2x)

בִּמְהֵרָה בְיָמֵינוּ יָבֹא אֵלֵינוּ

עִם מָשִׁיחַ בֶּן דָּוִד: (2x)

שְׁפֹךְ אַהֲבָתְךָ

שְׁפֹךְ אַהֲבָתְךָ עַל הַגּוֹיִם אֲשֶׁר יְדָעוּךָ

וְעַל מַמְלָכוֹת אֲשֶׁר בְּשִׁמְךָ קוֹרְאִים

בִּגְלַל חֲסָדִים שֶׁהֵם עוֹשִׂים עִם זֶרַע יַעֲקֹב

וּמְגִנִּים עַל עַמְּךָ יִשְׂרָאֵל מִפְּנֵי אוֹכְלֵיהֶם

יִזְכּוּ לִרְאוֹת בְּטוֹבַת בְּחִירֶיךָ

וְלִשְׂמוֹחַ בְּשִׂמְחַת גּוֹיֶיךָ.

Miriam

Plate 21

Then Miriam the Prophetess, Aaron's sister, took a timbrel in her hand, and all the women went out after her in dance with timbrels. And Miriam chanted for them, "Sing to the Lord, for God has triumphed gloriously; horse and driver, God has hurled into the sea."
Exodus 15:20-21

Vivid colors animate this illumination. "Halleluyah," the refrain of many Hallel psalms, floats boldly at the top of the design. A mosaic of blues evokes the movement of the sea. Miriam stands amidst a crowd of women, musical instruments in hand, dancing to celebrate their salvation. Scrolled around the frame is the Hebrew excerpt from Parashat Beshalaḥ (Exodus 15). Thirty-six women surround our Prophetess. Abbaye, a Babylonian scholar of the Talmudic period, teaches, "There are not fewer than thirty-six righteous individuals in the world who receive the Divine Presence" (BT Sanhedrin 97b and BT Sukkah 45b). These individuals are credited with God's daily decision to sustain the world. Later tradition teaches us that the identities of the thirty-six righteous individuals in every generation are not revealed to others or even themselves. Only the Heavens know their identity. Let each of us aspire to this ideal, acting as if the world's survival depended on our righteousness. And let us treat others with respect and deference, knowing that any one of them might be one of the thirty-six.

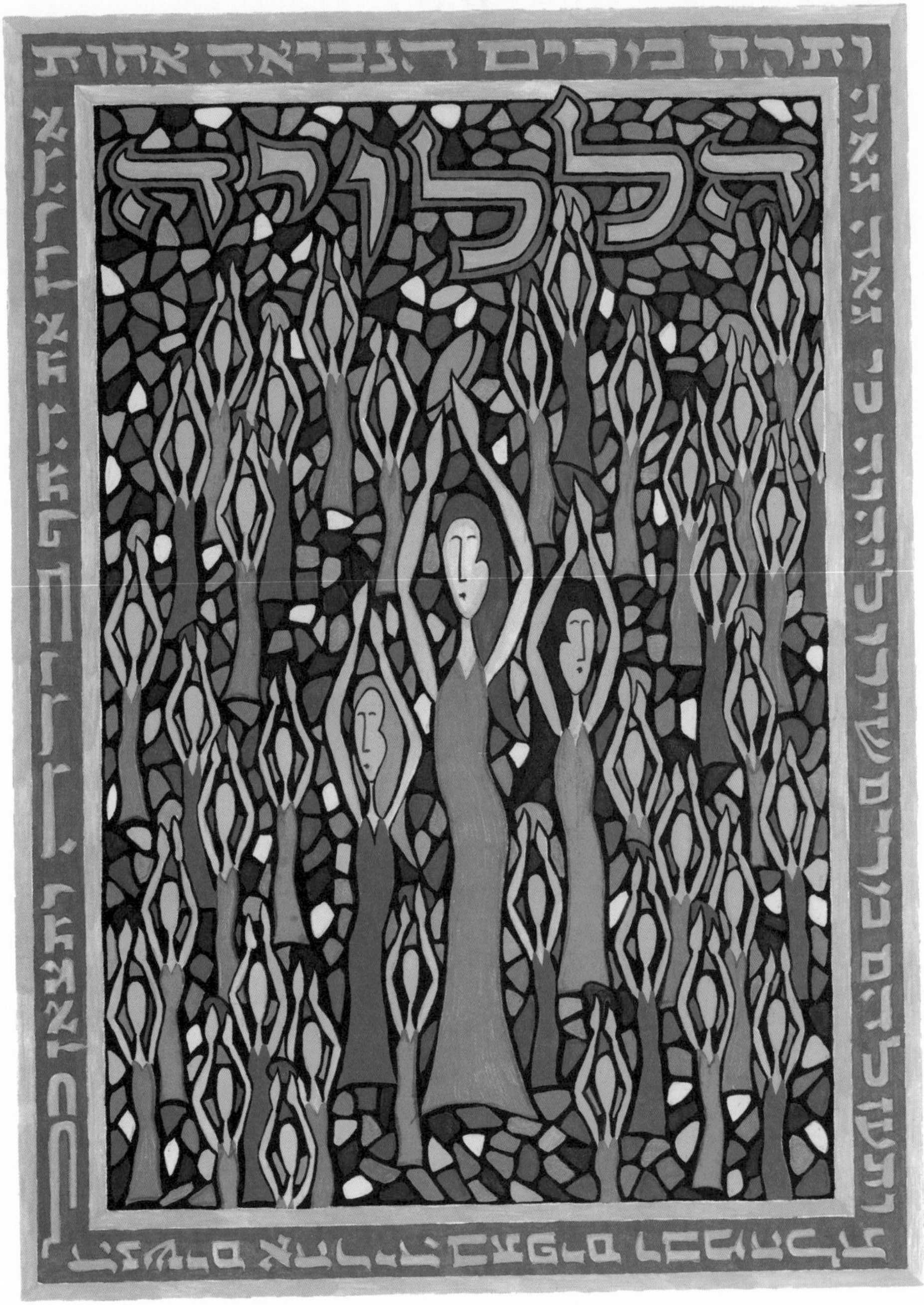
ותקח מרים הנביאה אחות
הללויה

JOY

Occasionally in life there are those moments of unutterable fulfillment
which cannot be completely explained by those symbols called words.
Their meanings can only be articulated by the inaudible language of the heart.

Martin Luther King, Jr.

Participant:

Miriam the Prophetess, joined by other Israelite women, celebrates freedom by the Reed Sea. We too sing God's praises during the completion of *Hallel*.

Participant:

Miriam has already played a pivotal role in her family. According to a midrash (*BT Sotah 12a*), after her parents divorced to avoid Pharaoh's decree, she convinced them to remarry and have more children. Miriam watched over Moses in the basket and arranged for Yokheved, Moses' own mother, to be his wet nurse until he was weaned.

All:

Now Miriam leads the women in song and dance as they express their gratitude and joy.

Activity

➤ In a modern custom developed at feminist *sedarim* (see page 23), each participant pours a bit of water into a special goblet designated as Miriam's Cup. As we add our individual waters, we are reminded that community is formed only when individuals join together in a common purpose. We also acknowledge that it was due to Miriam's merit that the Israelites received water (*be'er Miriam*, or Miriam's well) through their wanderings in the desert. Miriam nourished the Israelites as we now nourish each other and sing to the tune of *Eliyahu Ha-Navi*:

Miriam ha-Neviah

מִרְיָם הַנְּבִיאָה

מִרְיָם הַנְּבִיאָה עֹז וְזִמְרָה בְּיָדָהּ.

מִרְיָם תִּרְקוֹד אִתָּנוּ לְהַגְדִּיל זִמְרַת הָעוֹלָם.

מִרְיָם תִּרְקוֹד אִתָּנוּ לְתַקֵּן אֶת הָעוֹלָם.

בִּמְהֵרָה בְיָמֵינוּ הִיא תְּבִיאֵנוּ

אֶל מֵי הַיְשׁוּעָה אֶל מֵי הַיְשׁוּעָה:

Miriam ha-Neviah oz v'zimra b'yadah.
Miriam, tirkod itanu, l'hagdil zimrat ha'olam.
Miriam, tirkod itanu, l'takein et ha'olam.
Bimheyrah v'yameinu, hi tavi'einu.
El mei ha'yeshua. El mei ha'yeshua.

Miriam the Prophetess, strength and song are in her hand.
Miriam will dance with us to increase the world's song.
Miriam will dance with us to heal the world.
Soon, and in our time, she will lead us
to the water of salvation.

Ushavtem mayim b'sasson

Ushavtem mayim b'sasson
Mi-ma'ayanei ha-yeshua.

Joyfully shall you draw upon
The fountains of deliverance.
Isaiah 12:3

ּוּשְׁאַבְתֶּם מַיִם בְּשָׂשׂוֹן

ּוּשְׁאַבְתֶּם מַיִם בְּשָׂשׂוֹן,
מִמַּעַיְנֵי הַיְשׁוּעָה.

Reflections

- How many women are in the picture? Why?
- Rabbi Naḥman of Bratslav said *Mitzvah gedolah lihiyot besimḥa tamid*, "It is a great *mitzvah* to always be happy." How can we bring more joy into our daily lives?
- What should be the role of music in our worship?

· HALLEL · הַלֵּל

מוֹזְגִים כּוֹס רְבִיעִית וְגוֹמְרִים עָלֶיהָ אֶת הַהַלֵּל:

Pour the fourth cup of wine and complete the recitation of Hallel which was begun before the meal:

Not for us, Adonai, not for our sake,
but for the sake of Your Name, grant honor,
for the sake of Your Lovingkindness and Your Truth.
Why should the nations ask,
"Where is their God?"
when our God is indeed in the heavens.
Everything God desires is accomplished.
Their idols are silver and gold,
the work of human hands.
They have mouths but cannot speak,
eyes but cannot see, ears but cannot hear,
noses but cannot smell,
hands but cannot feel,
legs but cannot walk;
they cannot make sounds with their throats.
Those who fashion these idols will become like them,
everyone who places their faith in them.
Israel, trust in Adonai,
our Help and our Protector.
House of Aaron, trust in Adonai,
our Help and our Protector.
Those who revere Adonai, trust in Adonai,
our Help and our Protector.

Adonai has remembered us and will bless us.
God will bless the House of Israel,
God will bless the House of Aaron,
God will bless those who honor Adonai,
the small with the great.

לֹא לָנוּ יי לֹא לָנוּ כִּי לְשִׁמְךָ תֵּן כָּבוֹד
עַל חַסְדְּךָ עַל אֲמִתֶּךָ.
לָמָּה יֹאמְרוּ הַגּוֹיִם אַיֵּה נָא אֱלֹהֵיהֶם.
וֵאלֹהֵינוּ בַשָּׁמַיִם כֹּל אֲשֶׁר חָפֵץ עָשָׂה.
עֲצַבֵּיהֶם כֶּסֶף וְזָהָב מַעֲשֵׂה יְדֵי אָדָם.
פֶּה לָהֶם וְלֹא יְדַבֵּרוּ עֵינַיִם לָהֶם וְלֹא יִרְאוּ.
אָזְנַיִם לָהֶם וְלֹא יִשְׁמָעוּ אַף לָהֶם וְלֹא יְרִיחוּן.
יְדֵיהֶם וְלֹא יְמִישׁוּן רַגְלֵיהֶם וְלֹא יְהַלֵּכוּ
לֹא יֶהְגּוּ בִּגְרוֹנָם.
כְּמוֹהֶם יִהְיוּ עֹשֵׂיהֶם כֹּל אֲשֶׁר בֹּטֵחַ בָּהֶם.
יִשְׂרָאֵל בְּטַח בַּיי עֶזְרָם וּמָגִנָּם הוּא.
בֵּית אַהֲרֹן בִּטְחוּ בַיי עֶזְרָם וּמָגִנָּם הוּא.
יִרְאֵי יי בִּטְחוּ בַיי עֶזְרָם וּמָגִנָּם הוּא.

יי זְכָרָנוּ יְבָרֵךְ יְבָרֵךְ אֶת בֵּית יִשְׂרָאֵל
יְבָרֵךְ אֶת בֵּית אַהֲרֹן.
יְבָרֵךְ יִרְאֵי יי הַקְּטַנִּים עִם הַגְּדֹלִים.

134

Adonai will increase you,
you and your children.
Blessed are you to Adonai,
the Creator of the heavens and the earth.
The heavens belong to Adonai,
but the earth God gave to human beings.
The dead cannot sing praises to God,
nor anyone who descends into silence.
But we will bless God,
today and forever.
Halleluyah!

Psalms 115

יֹסֵף יי עֲלֵיכֶם עֲלֵיכֶם וְעַל בְּנֵיכֶם.

בְּרוּכִים אַתֶּם לַיי עֹשֵׂה שָׁמַיִם וָאָרֶץ.

הַשָּׁמַיִם שָׁמַיִם לַיי וְהָאָרֶץ נָתַן לִבְנֵי אָדָם.

לֹא הַמֵּתִים יְהַלְלוּ יָהּ וְלֹא כָּל יֹרְדֵי דוּמָה.

וַאֲנַחְנוּ נְבָרֵךְ יָהּ מֵעַתָּה וְעַד עוֹלָם

הַלְלוּיָהּ.

I love, for God hears my supplicating voice;

because God inclined the Divine ear toward me,
so I will call to God for all of my days.
The ropes of death surrounded me
and the straits of the netherworld found me;
I discovered sorrow and pain.
And so I called to Adonai,
"Please, Adonai, rescue me!"
Adonai is gracious and righteous;
our God is merciful.
Adonai protects the simple.
I was impoverished, but God redeemed me.
Return, my soul, to your rest,
for Adonai has been generous to you.
You saved my soul from death,
my eyes from tears, my feet from stumbling.
I will walk before Adonai
in the lands of the living.
I believe, that is why I speak.
I am sorely afflicted.
In my haste I said,
"Every person is a liar."

אָהַבְתִּי כִּי יִשְׁמַע יי אֶת קוֹלִי תַּחֲנוּנָי,

כִּי הִטָּה אָזְנוֹ לִי וּבְיָמַי אֶקְרָא.

אֲפָפוּנִי חֶבְלֵי מָוֶת וּמְצָרֵי שְׁאוֹל מְצָאוּנִי

צָרָה וְיָגוֹן אֶמְצָא.

וּבְשֵׁם יי אֶקְרָא אָנָּה יי מַלְּטָה נַפְשִׁי.

חַנּוּן יי וְצַדִּיק וֵאלֹהֵינוּ מְרַחֵם.

שֹׁמֵר פְּתָאִים יי דַּלּוֹתִי וְלִי יְהוֹשִׁיעַ.

שׁוּבִי נַפְשִׁי לִמְנוּחָיְכִי כִּי יי גָּמַל עָלָיְכִי.

כִּי חִלַּצְתָּ נַפְשִׁי מִמָּוֶת אֶת עֵינִי מִן דִּמְעָה

אֶת רַגְלִי מִדֶּחִי.

אֶתְהַלֵּךְ לִפְנֵי יי בְּאַרְצוֹת הַחַיִּים.

הֶאֱמַנְתִּי כִּי אֲדַבֵּר אֲנִי עָנִיתִי מְאֹד.

אֲנִי אָמַרְתִּי בְחָפְזִי כָּל הָאָדָם כֹּזֵב.

How can I repay Adonai

for all the goodness bestowed on me?
I will raise a cup of redemption
and will call out in Adonai's Name.
I will fulfill my vows to Adonai
in the presence of all of God's people.
Precious in the sight of Adonai
is the death of righteous ones.
Please Adonai, for I am truly Your servant,
I am Your servant,
the child of Your maidservant,
You have freed me from my bonds.
I will offer a thanksgiving sacrifice to You
and I will call upon the Name of Adonai.
I will fulfill my vows to Adonai,
in the presence of all God's people,
in the courts of the House of Adonai,
in the heart of Jerusalem.
Halleluyah!

Psalms 116

מָה אָשִׁיב לַיי כָּל תַּגְמוּלוֹהִי עָלָי.

כּוֹס יְשׁוּעוֹת אֶשָּׂא וּבְשֵׁם יי אֶקְרָא.

נְדָרַי לַיי אֲשַׁלֵּם נֶגְדָה נָּא לְכָל עַמּוֹ.

יָקָר בְּעֵינֵי יי הַמָּוְתָה לַחֲסִידָיו.

אָנָּה יי כִּי אֲנִי עַבְדֶּךָ אֲנִי עַבְדְּךָ בֶּן אֲמָתֶךָ

פִּתַּחְתָּ לְמוֹסֵרָי.

לְךָ אֶזְבַּח זֶבַח תּוֹדָה בְשֵׁם יי אֶקְרָא.

נְדָרַי לַיי אֲשַׁלֵּם נֶגְדָה נָּא לְכָל עַמּוֹ.

בְּחַצְרוֹת בֵּית יי בְּתוֹכֵכִי יְרוּשָׁלָיִם

הַלְלוּיָהּ.

All nations, sing to Adonai, praise God all peoples!

For God's lovingkindness has overwhelmed us, Adonai's truth endures forever.

Halleluyah! *Psalms 117*

הַלְלוּ אֶת יי כָּל גּוֹיִם שַׁבְּחוּהוּ כָּל הָאֻמִּים.

כִּי גָבַר עָלֵינוּ חַסְדּוֹ וֶאֱמֶת יי לְעוֹלָם הַלְלוּיָהּ.

Give thanks to Adonai, for God is good. God's mercy is everlasting.

Let Israel declare: God's mercy is everlasting.

Let the House of Aaron declare: God's mercy is everlasting.

Let those who fear Adonai declare: God's mercy is everlasting.

הוֹדוּ לַיי כִּי טוֹב כִּי לְעוֹלָם חַסְדּוֹ.

יֹאמַר נָא יִשְׂרָאֵל כִּי לְעוֹלָם חַסְדּוֹ.

יֹאמְרוּ נָא בֵית אַהֲרֹן כִּי לְעוֹלָם חַסְדּוֹ.

יֹאמְרוּ נָא יִרְאֵי יי כִּי לְעוֹלָם חַסְדּוֹ.

From the depths, I called out to God;

God graciously answered me.
Adonai is with me, I will not fear;
what can a human do to me?
God is a help to me;
I will see the end of those who hate me.
It is better to take refuge in God
than in human beings.
It is better to take refuge in God
than in princes.
All the nations surrounded me,
but in the Name of Adonai I defeated them.
They surrounded me like bees,
but they were extinguished as a brushfire—
in the Name of Adonai, I defeated them.
They sought to make me fall,
but Adonai came to my rescue.
God is my strength and my song;
God is my redemption.
The voice of joy and salvation
is in the tents of the righteous,
the right hand of Adonai acts bravely.
The right hand of Adonai is exalted,
the right hand of Adonai acts valiantly.
I will not die; I will live and I will tell of God's deeds.
God surely punished me,
but God has not allowed death to overtake me.
Open for me the gates of righteousness;
I will pass through them and thank God.
This is indeed God's gate,
through which the righteous will pass.

מִן הַמֵּצַר קָרָאתִי יָּהּ עָנָנִי בַמֶּרְחַב יָהּ.

יי לִי לֹא אִירָא מַה יַעֲשֶׂה לִי אָדָם.

יי לִי בְּעֹזְרָי וַאֲנִי אֶרְאֶה בְשֹׂנְאָי.

טוֹב לַחֲסוֹת בַּיי מִבְּטֹחַ בָּאָדָם.

טוֹב לַחֲסוֹת בַּיי מִבְּטֹחַ בִּנְדִיבִים.

כָּל גּוֹיִם סְבָבוּנִי בְּשֵׁם יי כִּי אֲמִילַם.

סַבּוּנִי גַם סְבָבוּנִי בְּשֵׁם יי כִּי אֲמִילַם.

סַבּוּנִי כִדְבוֹרִים דֹּעֲכוּ כְּאֵשׁ קוֹצִים
בְּשֵׁם יי כִּי אֲמִילַם.

דָּחֹה דְחִיתַנִי לִנְפֹּל וַיי עֲזָרָנִי.

עָזִּי וְזִמְרָת יָהּ וַיְהִי לִי לִישׁוּעָה.

קוֹל רִנָּה וִישׁוּעָה בְּאָהֳלֵי צַדִּיקִים
יְמִין יי עֹשָׂה חָיִל.

יְמִין יי רוֹמֵמָה יְמִין יי עֹשָׂה חָיִל.

לֹא אָמוּת כִּי אֶחְיֶה וַאֲסַפֵּר מַעֲשֵׂי יָהּ.

יַסֹּר יִסְּרַנִּי יָּהּ וְלַמָּוֶת לֹא נְתָנָנִי.

פִּתְחוּ לִי שַׁעֲרֵי צֶדֶק אָבֹא בָם אוֹדֶה יָהּ.

זֶה הַשַּׁעַר לַיי צַדִּיקִים יָבֹאוּ בוֹ.

I will give thanks because You answered me
and You became my salvation. (Repeat)

The stone which the builders rejected
became the cornerstone. (Repeat)

This came from Adonai;
it is wondrous in our eyes. (Repeat)

This is the day which Adonai made;
we will rejoice in it and celebrate. (Repeat)

Please, Adonai, rescue us!
Please, Adonai, rescue us!
Please, Adonai, grant us success!
Please, Adonai, grant us success!

Blessed is the one who comes in the name of Adonai,
We bless you from the House of Adonai. (Repeat)

Adonai is God who has given us light;
bind the festal offering to the horns of the altar with cords. (Repeat)

You are my Lord, and I will exalt You. (Repeat)

Give thanks to Adonai, for God is good. (Repeat)

Psalms 118

All your works will praise You, Adonai, our God.

And your pious ones, the righteous who do your will and
all your people, the House of Israel, will give thanks to you in joy;
they will bless, praise, glorify, exalt, fear, sanctify, and crown
your name, our Sovereign. For it is good to give thanks to you;
it is pleasant to sing to your name. Forever and ever, you are God.

אוֹדְךָ כִּי עֲנִיתָנִי וַתְּהִי לִי לִישׁוּעָה.
אוֹדְךָ כִּי עֲנִיתָנִי וַתְּהִי לִי לִישׁוּעָה.

אֶבֶן מָאֲסוּ הַבּוֹנִים הָיְתָה לְרֹאשׁ פִּנָּה.
אֶבֶן מָאֲסוּ הַבּוֹנִים הָיְתָה לְרֹאשׁ פִּנָּה.

מֵאֵת יי הָיְתָה זֹּאת הִיא נִפְלָאת בְּעֵינֵינוּ.
מֵאֵת יי הָיְתָה זֹּאת הִיא נִפְלָאת בְּעֵינֵינוּ.

זֶה הַיּוֹם עָשָׂה יי נָגִילָה וְנִשְׂמְחָה בוֹ.
זֶה הַיּוֹם עָשָׂה יי נָגִילָה וְנִשְׂמְחָה בוֹ.

אָנָּא יי הוֹשִׁיעָה נָּא!
אָנָּא יי הוֹשִׁיעָה נָּא!
אָנָּא יי הַצְלִיחָה נָּא!
אָנָּא יי הַצְלִיחָה נָּא!

בָּרוּךְ הַבָּא בְּשֵׁם יי בֵּרַכְנוּכֶם מִבֵּית יי.
בָּרוּךְ הַבָּא בְּשֵׁם יי בֵּרַכְנוּכֶם מִבֵּית יי.

אֵל יי וַיָּאֶר לָנוּ אִסְרוּ חַג בַּעֲבֹתִים עַד קַרְנוֹת הַמִּזְבֵּחַ.
אֵל יי וַיָּאֶר לָנוּ אִסְרוּ חַג בַּעֲבֹתִים עַד קַרְנוֹת הַמִּזְבֵּחַ.

אֵלִי אַתָּה וְאוֹדֶךָּ אֱלֹהַי אֲרוֹמְמֶךָּ.
אֵלִי אַתָּה וְאוֹדֶךָּ אֱלֹהַי אֲרוֹמְמֶךָּ.

הוֹדוּ לַיי כִּי טוֹב כִּי לְעוֹלָם חַסְדּוֹ.
הוֹדוּ לַיי כִּי טוֹב כִּי לְעוֹלָם חַסְדּוֹ.

יְהַלְלוּךָ יי אֱלֹהֵינוּ כָּל מַעֲשֶׂיךָ
וַחֲסִידֶיךָ צַדִּיקִים עוֹשֵׂי רְצוֹנֶךָ, וְכָל עַמְּךָ
בֵּית יִשְׂרָאֵל בְּרִנָּה יוֹדוּ וִיבָרְכוּ, וִישַׁבְּחוּ וִיפָאֲרוּ,
וִירוֹמְמוּ וְיַעֲרִיצוּ, וְיַקְדִּישׁוּ וְיַמְלִיכוּ אֶת שִׁמְךָ,
מַלְכֵּנוּ. כִּי לְךָ טוֹב לְהוֹדוֹת וּלְשִׁמְךָ נָאֶה לְזַמֵּר,
כִּי מֵעוֹלָם וְעַד עוֹלָם אַתָּה אֵל.

כִּי לְעוֹלָם חַסְדּוֹ	הוֹדוּ לַיי כִּי טוֹב
כִּי לְעוֹלָם חַסְדּוֹ	הוֹדוּ לֵאלֹהֵי הָאֱלֹהִים
כִּי לְעוֹלָם חַסְדּוֹ	הוֹדוּ לַאֲדֹנֵי הָאֲדֹנִים
כִּי לְעוֹלָם חַסְדּוֹ	לְעֹשֵׂה נִפְלָאוֹת גְּדֹלוֹת לְבַדּוֹ
כִּי לְעוֹלָם חַסְדּוֹ	לְעֹשֵׂה הַשָּׁמַיִם בִּתְבוּנָה
כִּי לְעוֹלָם חַסְדּוֹ	לְרֹקַע הָאָרֶץ עַל הַמָּיִם
כִּי לְעוֹלָם חַסְדּוֹ	לְעֹשֵׂה אוֹרִים גְּדֹלִים
כִּי לְעוֹלָם חַסְדּוֹ	אֶת הַשֶּׁמֶשׁ לְמֶמְשֶׁלֶת בַּיּוֹם
כִּי לְעוֹלָם חַסְדּוֹ	אֶת הַיָּרֵחַ וְכוֹכָבִים לְמֶמְשְׁלוֹת בַּלָּיְלָה
כִּי לְעוֹלָם חַסְדּוֹ	לְמַכֵּה מִצְרַיִם בִּבְכוֹרֵיהֶם
כִּי לְעוֹלָם חַסְדּוֹ	וַיּוֹצֵא יִשְׂרָאֵל מִתּוֹכָם
כִּי לְעוֹלָם חַסְדּוֹ	בְּיָד חֲזָקָה וּבִזְרוֹעַ נְטוּיָה
כִּי לְעוֹלָם חַסְדּוֹ	לְגֹזֵר יַם סוּף לִגְזָרִים
כִּי לְעוֹלָם חַסְדּוֹ	וְהֶעֱבִיר יִשְׂרָאֵל בְּתוֹכוֹ
כִּי לְעוֹלָם חַסְדּוֹ	וְנִעֵר פַּרְעֹה וְחֵילוֹ בְיַם סוּף
כִּי לְעוֹלָם חַסְדּוֹ	לְמוֹלִיךְ עַמּוֹ בַּמִּדְבָּר
כִּי לְעוֹלָם חַסְדּוֹ	לְמַכֵּה מְלָכִים גְּדֹלִים
כִּי לְעוֹלָם חַסְדּוֹ	וַיַּהֲרֹג מְלָכִים אַדִּירִים
כִּי לְעוֹלָם חַסְדּוֹ	לְסִיחוֹן מֶלֶךְ הָאֱמֹרִי
כִּי לְעוֹלָם חַסְדּוֹ	וּלְעוֹג מֶלֶךְ הַבָּשָׁן
כִּי לְעוֹלָם חַסְדּוֹ	וְנָתַן אַרְצָם לְנַחֲלָה
כִּי לְעוֹלָם חַסְדּוֹ	נַחֲלָה לְיִשְׂרָאֵל עַבְדּוֹ
כִּי לְעוֹלָם חַסְדּוֹ	שֶׁבְּשִׁפְלֵנוּ זָכַר לָנוּ
כִּי לְעוֹלָם חַסְדּוֹ	וַיִּפְרְקֵנוּ מִצָּרֵינוּ
כִּי לְעוֹלָם חַסְדּוֹ	נֹתֵן לֶחֶם לְכָל בָּשָׂר
כִּי לְעוֹלָם חַסְדּוֹ	הוֹדוּ לְאֵל הַשָּׁמָיִם

Give thanks to Adonai, for God is good;	**God's mercy endures forever!**
Give thanks to the Judge of judges;	**God's mercy endures forever!**
Give thanks to the Lord of lords;	**God's mercy endures forever!**
To the One alone who makes great wonders;	**God's mercy endures forever!**
To the One who made the heavens with understanding;	**God's mercy endures forever!**
To the One who spread out the earth over the waters;	**God's mercy endures forever!**
To the One who fashioned the great lights;	**God's mercy endures forever!**
The sun to rule by day;	**God's mercy endures forever!**
The moon and stars to govern the night;	**God's mercy endures forever!**
To the One who struck the first-born Egyptians;	**God's mercy endures forever!**
To the One who freed Israel from their grasp;	**God's mercy endures forever!**
With a strong hand and an outstretched arm;	**God's mercy endures forever!**
To the One who parted the Reed Sea;	**God's mercy endures forever!**
And ushered Israel through it;	**God's mercy endures forever!**
Who decimated Pharaoh and his troops in the Reed Sea;	**God's mercy endures forever!**
To the One who led the Israelites in the desert;	**God's mercy endures forever!**
To the One who punished great kings;	**God's mercy endures forever!**
And killed mighty kings;	**God's mercy endures forever!**
Sihon, the King of the Amorites;	**God's mercy endures forever!**
And Og, the King of Bashan;	**God's mercy endures forever!**
And gave their land to us as an inheritance;	**God's mercy endures forever!**
An inheritance for Israel, God's servant;	**God's mercy endures forever!**
Who remembered us when we were downtrodden;	**God's mercy endures forever!**
Who freed us from our enemies;	**God's mercy endures forever!**
Who gives sustenance to all;	**God's mercy endures forever!**
Give thanks to the God of the heavens;	**God's mercy endures forever!**

Psalms 136

Every Breath of Life

Plate 22

Even if our mouths were filled with song as water fills the sea,
And our tongues shouting joy like the multitude of waves,
And our lips as full of praise as the expanse of the heavens,
And our eyes as radiant as the sun and the moon,
And our hands spread wide as the wings of eagles in the sky,
And our legs as swift as gazelles,
We would still be unable to express even a fraction of the gratitude
That we owe to You, O Lord our God . . .
Nishmat Prayer recited on Shabbat and Yom Tov

The illumination is divided into six colorful bands framed top and bottom by the words, "every breath of life" and "will bless Your name." Each band depicts the abundant natural world, while the limited human features appear in bold Hebrew letters: the word "finu" (our mouths) sails on an aqua sea; "l'shoneinu" (our tongues) plays among the waves; "eineinu" (our eyes) basks in the light of the sun and the moon; "yadeinu" (our hands) reaches to the wings of soaring eagles; and "ragleinu" (our legs) prances in the fields with graceful gazelles.

GRATITUDE

In my father's house, we always finished the seder with a rousing rendition of "My Country 'Tis of Thee"
and "The Star Spangled Banner." It was his way of expressing gratitude to the land that had admitted him
and his family as immigrants from Germany in 1940. He knew the difference between tyranny and freedom first hand.
In America, Passover could be celebrated in unadulterated joy.

Ismar Schorsch

נִשְׁמַת כָּל חַי

תְּבָרֵךְ אֶת שִׁמְךָ יי אֱלֹהֵינוּ וְרוּחַ כָּל בָּשָׂר תְּפָאֵר וּתְרוֹמֵם זִכְרְךָ מַלְכֵּנוּ תָּמִיד מִן הָעוֹלָם וְעַד הָעוֹלָם אַתָּה אֵל, וּמִבַּלְעָדֶיךָ אֵין לָנוּ מֶלֶךְ גּוֹאֵל וּמוֹשִׁיעַ פּוֹדֶה וּמַצִּיל וּמְפַרְנֵס וּמְרַחֵם בְּכָל עֵת צָרָה וְצוּקָה אֵין לָנוּ מֶלֶךְ אֶלָּא אָתָּה. אֱלֹהֵי הָרִאשׁוֹנִים וְהָאַחֲרוֹנִים אֱלֹהַּ כָּל בְּרִיּוֹת אֲדוֹן כָּל תּוֹלָדוֹת הַמְהֻלָּל בְּרֹב הַתִּשְׁבָּחוֹת הַמְנַהֵג עוֹלָמוֹ בְּחֶסֶד וּבְרִיּוֹתָיו בְּרַחֲמִים. וַיי לֹא יָנוּם וְלֹא יִישָׁן הַמְּעוֹרֵר יְשֵׁנִים וְהַמֵּקִיץ נִרְדָּמִים וְהַמֵּשִׂיחַ אִלְּמִים, וְהַמַּתִּיר אֲסוּרִים, וְהַסּוֹמֵךְ נוֹפְלִים, וְהַזּוֹקֵף כְּפוּפִים לְךָ לְבַדְּךָ אֲנַחְנוּ מוֹדִים.

The breath of all life

will bless Your Name, Adonai, our God, and the soul of all flesh will laud and exalt Your remembrance, our Sovereign. From the beginning of time throughout eternity, You are God, and besides You, we have no sovereign who redeems, saves, supports, and shows mercy in times of sorrow and distress; You are our only Sovereign. God of the first and of the last, God of all creatures, Master of all generations, the One who is praised with many songs, the One who guides the world with kindness and God's creatures with mercy. Adonai neither slumbers nor sleeps; God wakes those who are sleeping and arouses those who are slumbering; God makes the mute speak and sets the shackled free; God raises those who fall and straightens those who are bowed down. To You alone we are grateful.

אִלּוּ פִינוּ מָלֵא שִׁירָה כַיָּם וּלְשׁוֹנֵנוּ רִנָּה כַּהֲמוֹן גַּלָּיו וְשִׂפְתוֹתֵינוּ שֶׁבַח כְּמֶרְחֲבֵי רָקִיעַ וְעֵינֵינוּ מְאִירוֹת כַּשֶּׁמֶשׁ וְכַיָּרֵחַ וְיָדֵינוּ פְרוּשׂוֹת כְּנִשְׁרֵי שָׁמַיִם וְרַגְלֵינוּ קַלּוֹת כָּאַיָּלוֹת, אֵין אֲנַחְנוּ מַסְפִּיקִים לְהוֹדוֹת לְךָ יי אֱלֹהֵינוּ וֵאלֹהֵי אֲבוֹתֵינוּ וּלְבָרֵךְ אֶת שִׁמְךָ עַל אַחַת מֵאֶלֶף אַלְפֵי אֲלָפִים וְרִבֵּי רְבָבוֹת פְּעָמִים הַטּוֹבוֹת שֶׁעָשִׂיתָ עִם אֲבוֹתֵינוּ וְעִמָּנוּ: מִמִּצְרַיִם גְּאַלְתָּנוּ יי אֱלֹהֵינוּ, וּמִבֵּית עֲבָדִים פְּדִיתָנוּ, בְּרָעָב זַנְתָּנוּ, וּבְשָׂבָע כִּלְכַּלְתָּנוּ, מֵחֶרֶב הִצַּלְתָּנוּ, וּמִדֶּבֶר מִלַּטְתָּנוּ, וּמֵחֳלָיִם רָעִים וְנֶאֱמָנִים דִּלִּיתָנוּ. עַד הֵנָּה עֲזָרוּנוּ רַחֲמֶיךָ וְלֹא עֲזָבוּנוּ חֲסָדֶיךָ וְאַל תִּטְּשֵׁנוּ יי אֱלֹהֵינוּ לָנֶצַח.

Even if our mouths were filled with song as water fills the sea, and our tongues shouting joy like the multitude of waves, and our lips as full of praise as the expanse of the heavens, and our eyes as radiant as the sun and the moon, and our hands spread as the wings of eagles in the sky, and our legs as swift as gazelles, we would still be unable to express even a fraction of the gratitude that we owe to You, O Lord our God and God of our ancestors, of blessing Your Name for even one thousandth or one ten thousandth for all the kindness that You did for our ancestors and for us. You redeemed us from Egypt, Adonai, our God; You freed us from the house of slavery. When we were hungry, You fed us and You provided us with plenty. You saved us from the sword and You rescued us from pestilence; You protected us from illness. Until now, Your mercy has assisted us and Your kindness has not abandoned us. Do not forsake us, Adonai, Our God, forever!

Participant:

This prayer expresses our inability to praise God sufficiently; ironically, this very declaration of inadequacy is itself an eloquent tribute.

Reflections

- What is the significance of the four squares at the corners of Plate 22?
- How do we experience God through nature?

Activity

- Sing *Kol ha-neshamah*. *Neshamah* is a soul, *neshimah* is a breath; by simply breathing (and singing!), we attest to the miracle of life.

Kol ha-neshamah

Kol ha-heshamah, tehallel Yah
Halleluyah.
Kol ha-heshamah, tehallel Yah
Halleluyah.

Every soul will praise God,
Halleluyah!
Every soul will praise God,
Halleluyah!
Psalms 150:6

כֹּל הַנְּשָׁמָה

כֹּל הַנְּשָׁמָה, תְּהַלֵּל יָהּ:
הַלְלוּ־יָהּ.
כֹּל הַנְּשָׁמָה, תְּהַלֵּל יָהּ:
הַלְלוּ־יָהּ.

עַל כֵּן אֵבָרִים שֶׁפִּלַּגְתָּ בָּנוּ וְרוּחַ וּנְשָׁמָה שֶׁנָּפַחְתָּ בְּאַפֵּינוּ, וְלָשׁוֹן אֲשֶׁר שַׂמְתָּ בְּפִינוּ, הֵן הֵם יוֹדוּ וִיבָרְכוּ וִישַׁבְּחוּ וִיפָאֲרוּ וִירוֹמְמוּ וְיַעֲרִיצוּ וְיַקְדִּישׁוּ וְיַמְלִיכוּ אֶת שִׁמְךָ מַלְכֵּנוּ. כִּי כָל פֶּה לְךָ יוֹדֶה וְכָל לָשׁוֹן לְךָ תִשָּׁבַע, וְכָל בֶּרֶךְ לְךָ תִכְרַע, וְכָל קוֹמָה לְפָנֶיךָ תִשְׁתַּחֲוֶה, וְכָל לְבָבוֹת יִירָאוּךָ, וְכָל קֶרֶב וּכְלָיוֹת יְזַמְּרוּ לִשְׁמֶךָ, כַּדָּבָר שֶׁכָּתוּב: כָּל עַצְמוֹתַי תֹּאמַרְנָה יי מִי כָמוֹךָ מַצִּיל עָנִי מֵחָזָק מִמֶּנּוּ וְעָנִי וְאֶבְיוֹן מִגֹּזְלוֹ.

Therefore the limbs You created in us, the spirit and breath which You placed within us, the language which You put in our mouths—these will thank You, bless You, praise You, laud You, exalt You, revere You and sanctify Your Name, our Sovereign. For every mouth will thank You, and every tongue will swear to You, and every knee will bend to You, and all who are upright will bow to You, and all hearts will fear You. All of our innermost parts will sing to Your Name, as it is written, "All of my bones will exclaim, 'Adonai, who is like unto You?'" *(Psalms 35:10)*. You rescue the poor from one who is stronger and the destitute from the one that would rob.

מִי יִדְמֶה לָּךְ וּמִי יִשְׁוֶה לָּךְ, וּמִי יַעֲרָךְ לָךְ, הָאֵל הַגָּדוֹל הַגִּבּוֹר וְהַנּוֹרָא אֵל עֶלְיוֹן קוֹנֵה שָׁמַיִם וָאָרֶץ, נְהַלֶּלְךָ וּנְשַׁבֵּחֲךָ וּנְפָאֶרְךָ וּנְבָרֵךְ אֶת שֵׁם קָדְשֶׁךָ כָּאָמוּר: לְדָוִד בָּרְכִי נַפְשִׁי אֶת יי וְכָל קְרָבַי אֶת שֵׁם קָדְשׁוֹ.

Who can compare to You? Who is Your equal? Who can match the worth of the God who is great, mighty, awesome, exalted on high, who created the heavens and the earth? We will praise You, laud You, glorify You, and bless Your Sacred Name, as it is said, "A Psalm of David. Bless Adonai, my soul, may my entire being bless God's Holy Name" *(Psalms 103:1)*.

הָאֵל בְּתַעֲצֻמוֹת עֻזֶּךָ, הַגָּדוֹל בִּכְבוֹד שְׁמֶךָ, הַגִּבּוֹר לָנֶצַח וְהַנּוֹרָא בְּנוֹרְאוֹתֶיךָ. הַמֶּלֶךְ הַיּוֹשֵׁב עַל כִּסֵּא רָם וְנִשָּׂא.

You are God in Your powerful might, the great one in Your honorable name, heroic forever and awe-filled in your awesomeness, the Sovereign who sits enthroned in a high and lofty place.

שׁוֹכֵן עַד מָרוֹם וְקָדוֹשׁ שְׁמוֹ, וְכָתוּב: רַנְּנוּ צַדִּיקִים בַּיי לַיְשָׁרִים נָאוָה תְהִלָּה, בְּפִי יְשָׁרִים תִּתְרוֹמָם, וּבְשִׂפְתֵי צַדִּיקִים תִּתְבָּרַךְ, וּבִלְשׁוֹן חֲסִידִים תִּתְקַדָּשׁ, וּבְקֶרֶב קְדוֹשִׁים תִּתְהַלָּל. וּבְמַקְהֲלוֹת רִבְבוֹת עַמְּךָ בֵּית יִשְׂרָאֵל, בְּרִנָּה יִתְפָּאַר שִׁמְךָ מַלְכֵּנוּ בְּכָל דּוֹר וָדוֹר, שֶׁכֵּן חוֹבַת כָּל הַיְצוּרִים לְפָנֶיךָ, יי אֱלֹהֵינוּ וֵאלֹהֵי אֲבוֹתֵינוּ, לְהוֹדוֹת, לְהַלֵּל, לְשַׁבֵּחַ, לְפָאֵר, לְרוֹמֵם, לְהַדֵּר, לְבָרֵךְ, לְעַלֵּה, וּלְקַלֵּס, עַל כָּל דִּבְרֵי שִׁירוֹת וְתִשְׁבְּחוֹת דָּוִד בֶּן יִשַׁי עַבְדְּךָ מְשִׁיחֶךָ.

The One who dwells in eternity, God's Name is exalted and holy, as it is written, "Righteous ones, rejoice in God! Praise is fitting for the upright" (Psalms 33:1). In the mouths of the upright, God will be praised, in the words of the righteous, God will be blessed, in the language of the pious ones God will be exalted, in the presence of those who are holy, God will be sanctified. In the midst of tens of thousands of Your people, the House of Israel, Your Name will be exalted with joy, our Sovereign, in every generation—for this is the obligation of all creatures before You, Adonai, our God and God of our ancestors, to thank, praise, laud, glorify, exalt, honor, bless, acclaim, and commend beyond all the words of song and praise of David, the son of Jesse, Your servant and Your anointed.

יִשְׁתַּבַּח שִׁמְךָ לָעַד מַלְכֵּנוּ, הָאֵל הַמֶּלֶךְ הַגָּדוֹל וְהַקָּדוֹשׁ בַּשָּׁמַיִם וּבָאָרֶץ. כִּי לְךָ נָאֶה יי אֱלֹהֵינוּ וֵאלֹהֵי אֲבוֹתֵינוּ שִׁיר וּשְׁבָחָה, הַלֵּל וְזִמְרָה, עֹז וּמֶמְשָׁלָה, נֶצַח, גְּדֻלָּה וּגְבוּרָה, תְּהִלָּה וְתִפְאֶרֶת, קְדֻשָּׁה וּמַלְכוּת, בְּרָכוֹת וְהוֹדָאוֹת מֵעַתָּה וְעַד־עוֹלָם.

May Your Name be praised forever, our Sovereign, the great and holy God who is Sovereign in the heavens and earth; to you, Adonai, our God and God of our ancestors, it is fitting to attribute song and praise, psalm and hymn, strength and majesty, victory, greatness and heroism, acclaim and glory, holiness and sovereignty, blessings and thanks now and forever.

בָּרוּךְ אַתָּה יי אֵל מֶלֶךְ גָּדוֹל בַּתִּשְׁבָּחוֹת,

אֵל הַהוֹדָאוֹת, אֲדוֹן הַנִּפְלָאוֹת, הַבּוֹחֵר בְּשִׁירֵי זִמְרָה,

מֶלֶךְ אֵל חֵי הָעוֹלָמִים.

Blessed are You, Adonai,
Sovereign, who is greatly praised, God of thanksgiving,
Lord of wonders, who chooses poetic songs,
Sovereign God of life forever and ever.

בָּרוּךְ אַתָּה יי
אֱלֹהֵינוּ מֶלֶךְ הָעוֹלָם
בּוֹרֵא פְּרִי הַגָּפֶן.

שׁוֹתִים בַּהֲסִבַּת שְׂמֹאל וּמְבָרְכִים בְּרָכָה אַחֲרוֹנָה:

בָּרוּךְ אַתָּה יי אֱלֹהֵינוּ מֶלֶךְ הָעוֹלָם עַל הַגֶּפֶן וְעַל פְּרִי הַגֶּפֶן, וְעַל תְּנוּבַת הַשָּׂדֶה וְעַל אֶרֶץ חֶמְדָּה, טוֹבָה, וּרְחָבָה שֶׁרָצִיתָ וְהִנְחַלְתָּ
לַאֲבוֹתֵינוּ, לֶאֱכֹל מִפִּרְיָהּ וְלִשְׂבֹּעַ מִטּוּבָהּ, רַחֶם נָא יי אֱלֹהֵינוּ עַל יִשְׂרָאֵל עַמֶּךָ וְעַל יְרוּשָׁלַיִם עִירֶךָ, וְעַל צִיּוֹן מִשְׁכַּן כְּבוֹדֶךָ
וְעַל מִזְבְּחֶךָ וְעַל הֵיכָלֶךָ, וּבְנֵה יְרוּשָׁלַיִם עִיר הַקֹּדֶשׁ בִּמְהֵרָה בְיָמֵינוּ וְהַעֲלֵנוּ לְתוֹכָהּ, וְשַׂמְּחֵנוּ בְּבִנְיָנָהּ, וְנֹאכַל מִפִּרְיָהּ וְנִשְׂבַּע
מִטּוּבָהּ וּנְבָרֶכְךָ עָלֶיהָ בִּקְדֻשָּׁה וּבְטָהֳרָה, (וּרְצֵה וְהַחֲלִיצֵנוּ בְּיוֹם הַשַּׁבָּת הַזֶּה,) וְשַׂמְּחֵנוּ בְּיוֹם חַג הַמַּצּוֹת הַזֶּה, כִּי אַתָּה יי טוֹב
וּמֵטִיב לַכֹּל, וְנוֹדֶה לְּךָ עַל הָאָרֶץ וְעַל פְּרִי הַגָּפֶן.

בָּרוּךְ אַתָּה יי
עַל הָאָרֶץ וְעַל פְּרִי הַגָּפֶן.

סְפִירַת הָעֹמֶר

בְּלֵיל שֵׁנִי שֶׁל פֶּסַח מְבָרְכִים עַל סְפִירַת הָעוֹמֶר:

בָּרוּךְ אַתָּה יי אֱלֹהֵינוּ מֶלֶךְ הָעוֹלָם, אֲשֶׁר קִדְּשָׁנוּ בְּמִצְוֹותָיו וְצִוָּנוּ עַל סְפִירַת הָעֹמֶר.

הַיּוֹם יוֹם אֶחָד לָעֹמֶר.
יְהִי רָצוֹן מִלְּפָנֶיךָ יי אֱלֹהֵינוּ וֵאלֹהֵי אֲבוֹתֵינוּ שֶׁיִּבָּנֶה בֵּית הַמִּקְדָּשׁ בִּמְהֵרָה בְיָמֵינוּ וְתֵן חֶלְקֵנוּ בְּתוֹרָתֶךָ.

Blessed are You, Adonai, our God, Sovereign of the Universe, who creates the fruit of the vine.

Drink the fourth cup of wine while reclining to the left; then say the blessing after drinking wine:

Blessed are You, Adonai, our God, Sovereign of the universe, for the vine and fruit of the vine, for the produce of the field, for the beloved, good and spacious land which You gave to our ancestors as an inheritance, to eat from its fruits and to be satisfied with its bounty; Please, Adonai, our God, show mercy to Israel, Your people; to Jerusalem, Your city; to Zion, the dwelling place of Your Glory; to Your altar, and Your shrine. Rebuild Jerusalem, the sacred city, speedily in our days, and bring us up to it, and allow us to rejoice in its rebuilding, and let us eat from its fruits and be satisfied by its bounty, and we will bless You for this privilege with holiness and purity. (*On Shabbat:* May You desire to strengthen us on this Shabbat day.) Make us happy on this day, the Festival of Unleavened Bread, for You Adonai, are good and You do good for all; we thank You for the land and the fruit of the vine.

Blessed are You, Adonai, for the land and the fruit of the vine.

Counting the Omer

On the second night of Passover, we begin counting the Omer, the period of forty-nine days between Pesaḥ and Shavuot.
Blessed are You, Adonai our God, Sovereign of the Universe, who has sanctified us with the commandments and commanded us to count the Omer.

Today is the first day of the Omer.

May it be your will, Adonai our God and God of our ancestors, that the Temple be rebuilt speedily in our days and that you give us a portion in your Torah.

Next Year in Jerusalem

Plate 23

One day, as Ḥoni the Circle-Maker was walking on the road, he saw a man planting a carob tree. Ḥoni asked him, "How long will it take for this tree to bear fruit?" The man replied, "Seventy years." Ḥoni asked, "Are you quite sure you will live another seventy years to eat its fruit?" The man replied, "I myself found fully grown carob trees in the world; as my ancestors planted for me, so am I planting for my children."

BT Ta'anit 23a

The illumination depicts an elderly gardener with his carob tree. Characteristic Jerusalem homes appear in the trunk of the tree; Jerusalem supports the carob tree—a plant which sustains us physically and spiritually. The background is suffused with more colorful dwellings. From a modest fruit, creativity and learning flourish. All of these contribute to a rebuilt Jerusalem.

• NIRTZAH • נִרְצָה •

REDEMPTION

Rabbi Yoḥanan ben Zakkai said,
"If you have a sapling in your hand and are told, 'Look, the Messiah is here,'
you should first plant the sapling and then go out to welcome the Messiah."
Avot d'Rabbi Nathan 31

All:

This Passover evening raises our consciousness of the world's imperfections and compels each of us to assume responsibility for *tikkun olam*, "repairing a broken world." Our actions today have an impact on the world tomorrow.

Leader:

The elderly gardener's act of planting (see Plate 23) is a selfless gesture of giving to future generations. May we too model such caring for others and concern for the future.

Sing together:

שָׁרִים בְּיַחַד:

The order of the Passover ritual according to its prescribed laws,
statutes, and ordinances is done.
Just as we merited to participate in the seder this year,
So may we have the opportunity to celebrate it in years to come.
May God who is pure, dwelling in the heavens, raise an innumerable throng.
Speedily return the offshoots of Your stock, redeemed, to Zion in song.

חֲסַל סִדּוּר פֶּסַח כְּהִלְכָתוֹ כְּכָל מִשְׁפָּטוֹ וְחֻקָּתוֹ.
כַּאֲשֶׁר זָכִינוּ לְסַדֵּר אוֹתוֹ כֵּן נִזְכֶּה לַעֲשׂוֹתוֹ.
זָךְ שׁוֹכֵן מְעוֹנָה, קוֹמֵם קְהַל מִי מָנָה,
בְּקָרוֹב נַהֵל נִטְעֵי כַנָּה, פְּדוּיִים לְצִיּוֹן בְּרִנָּה.

Next Year in a Rebuilt Jerusalem!

לְשָׁנָה הַבָּאָה
בִּירוּשָׁלַיִם הַבְּנוּיָה!

Reflections

- In what ways do we provide for our descendants (individually or collectively)?

- How do we express our hope in a Jewish future?

- What does "Jerusalem" represent for you, as a physical place and as a metaphor?

Once when I sat on the steps by a gate at David's Citadel, I placed my two heavy baskets by my side. A group of tourists was standing around their guide and I became their target marker. "You see that man with the baskets? Just right of his head there's an arch from the Roman Period. Just right of his head." "But he's moving, he's moving!" I said to myself: redemption will come only if their guide tells them, "You see that arch from the Roman Period? It's not important. But next to it, left and down a bit, there sits a man who bought fruit and vegetables for his family.
from "Tourists" by Yehuda Amiḥai

וַיְהִי בַּחֲצִי הַלַּיְלָה

אָז רֹב נִסִּים הִפְלֵאתָ בַּלַּיְלָה,
בְּרֹאשׁ אַשְׁמֹרֶת זֶה הַלַּיְלָה,
גֵּר צֶדֶק נִצַּחְתּוֹ כְּנֶחֱלַק לוֹ לַיְלָה,
וַיְהִי בַּחֲצִי הַלַּיְלָה.

דַּנְתָּ מֶלֶךְ גְּרָר בַּחֲלוֹם הַלַּיְלָה,
הִפְחַדְתָּ אֲרַמִּי בְּאֶמֶשׁ לַיְלָה,
וַיָּשַׂר יִשְׂרָאֵל לְמַלְאָךְ וַיּוּכַל לוֹ לַיְלָה,
וַיְהִי בַּחֲצִי הַלַּיְלָה.

זֶרַע בְּכוֹרֵי פַתְרוֹס מָחַצְתָּ בַּחֲצִי הַלַּיְלָה,
חֵילָם לֹא מָצְאוּ בְּקוּמָם בַּלַּיְלָה,
טִיסַת נְגִיד חֲרֹשֶׁת סִלִּיתָ בְּכוֹכְבֵי לַיְלָה,
וַיְהִי בַּחֲצִי הַלַּיְלָה.

יָעַץ מְחָרֵף לְנוֹפֵף אִוּוּי הוֹבַשְׁתָּ פְגָרָיו בַּלַּיְלָה,
כָּרַע בֵּל וּמַצָּבוֹ בְּאִישׁוֹן לַיְלָה,
לְאִישׁ חֲמוּדוֹת נִגְלָה רָז חֲזוֹת לַיְלָה,
וַיְהִי בַּחֲצִי הַלַּיְלָה.

מִשְׁתַּכֵּר בִּכְלֵי קֹדֶשׁ נֶהֱרַג בּוֹ בַּלַּיְלָה,
נוֹשַׁע מִבּוֹר אֲרָיוֹת פּוֹתֵר בְּעִתּוּתֵי לַיְלָה,
שִׂנְאָה נָטַר אֲגָגִי וְכָתַב סְפָרִים בַּלַּיְלָה,
וַיְהִי בַּחֲצִי הַלַּיְלָה.

עוֹרַרְתָּ נִצְחֲךָ עָלָיו בְּנֶדֶד שְׁנַת לַיְלָה,
פּוּרָה תִדְרוֹךְ לְשׁוֹמֵר מַה מִּלַּיְלָה,
צָרַח כַּשּׁוֹמֵר וְשָׂח אָתָא בֹקֶר וְגַם לַיְלָה,
וַיְהִי בַּחֲצִי הַלַּיְלָה.

קָרֵב יוֹם אֲשֶׁר הוּא לֹא יוֹם וְלֹא לַיְלָה,
רָם הוֹדַע כִּי לְךָ הַיּוֹם אַף לְךָ הַלַּיְלָה,
שׁוֹמְרִים הַפְקֵד לְעִירְךָ כָּל הַיּוֹם וְכָל הַלַּיְלָה,
תָּאִיר כְּאוֹר יוֹם חֶשְׁכַת לַיְלָה,
וַיְהִי בַּחֲצִי הַלַּיְלָה.

It Happened at Midnight

You performed many miracles at night,
At the beginning of the watches of this night,
The righteous convert, Abraham, prevailed when You divided the night for him.
It happened at midnight.

You judged the King of Gerar, Avimelekh, in a dream of the night,
You instilled fear in the Aramean, Lavan, in the dark of night,
And Israel wrestled and overcame his assailant at night.
It happened at midnight.

You decimated the first born of the Egyptians at midnight,
They could not find their soldiers when they rose at midnight,
You defeated the troops of Prince of Ḥaroshet, Sisera, by the stars of the night.
It happened at midnight.

The blasphemer, Sanḥeriv, sought to scatter My chosen people, You conquered him,
Crushing them to corpses in the night,
Bel and his pillar were overturned in the dark of the night,
To the man of delights, Daniel, was revealed the secret of visions at night.
It happened at midnight.

The one who became intoxicated by drinking from the sacred vessels, Belshazar, was killed at night,
The one who was redeemed from the lions' den, Daniel, revealed the awesome visions of the night,
Haman, the Agagite, who promoted hatred, wrote missives at night.
It happened at midnight.

You aroused Your victory over him when sleep was elusive at night,
The winepress You will tread for the one who queries the guard, "What of the night?"
Shout like the guard and declare, "Morning is coming and also the night."
It happened at midnight.

Bring near the day which is neither day nor night,
Exalted One, make known that the day is Yours as well as the night,
Station guards for Your city, all day and all night,
Make the darkness of the night shine like the light of day.
May it come to pass at midnight.

וַאֲמַרְתֶּם זֶבַח פֶּסַח

אֹמֶץ גְּבוּרוֹתֶיךָ הִפְלֵאתָ בַּפֶּסַח,
בְּרֹאשׁ כָּל מוֹעֲדוֹת נִשֵּׂאתָ פֶּסַח,
גִּלִּיתָ לְאֶזְרָחִי חֲצוֹת לֵיל פֶּסַח,
וַאֲמַרְתֶּם זֶבַח פֶּסַח.

דְּלָתָיו דָּפַקְתָּ כְּחוֹם הַיּוֹם בַּפֶּסַח,
הִסְעִיר נוֹצְצִים עֻגוֹת מַצּוֹת בַּפֶּסַח,
וְאֶל הַבָּקָר רָץ זֵכֶר לְשׁוֹר עֵרֶךְ פֶּסַח,
וַאֲמַרְתֶּם זֶבַח פֶּסַח.

זוֹעֲמוּ סְדוֹמִים וְלֹהֲטוּ בָּאֵשׁ בַּפֶּסַח,
חֻלַּץ לוֹט מֵהֶם וּמַצּוֹת אָפָה בְּקֵץ פֶּסַח,
טִאטֵאתָ אַדְמַת מוֹף וְנוֹף בְּעָבְרְךָ בַּפֶּסַח,
וַאֲמַרְתֶּם זֶבַח פֶּסַח.

יָהּ רֹאשׁ כָּל אוֹן מָחַצְתָּ בְּלֵיל שִׁמּוּר פֶּסַח,
כַּבִּיר עַל בֵּן בְּכוֹר פָּסַחְתָּ בְּדַם פֶּסַח,
לְבִלְתִּי תֵּת מַשְׁחִית לָבֹא בִּפְתָחַי בַּפֶּסַח,
וַאֲמַרְתֶּם זֶבַח פֶּסַח.

מְסֻגֶּרֶת סֻגָּרָה בְּעִתּוֹתֵי פֶּסַח,
נִשְׁמְדָה מִדְיָן בִּצְלִיל שְׂעוֹרֵי עֹמֶר פֶּסַח,
שׂוֹרְפוּ מִשְׁמַנֵּי פּוּל וְלוּד בִּיקַד יְקוֹד פֶּסַח,
וַאֲמַרְתֶּם זֶבַח פֶּסַח.

עוֹד הַיּוֹם בְּנוֹב לַעֲמוֹד עַד גָּעָה עוֹנַת פֶּסַח,
פַּס יָד כָּתְבָה לְקַעֲקֵעַ צוּל בַּפֶּסַח,
צָפֹה הַצָּפִית עָרוֹךְ הַשֻּׁלְחָן בַּפֶּסַח,
וַאֲמַרְתֶּם זֶבַח פֶּסַח.

קָהָל כִּנְּסָה הֲדַסָּה צוֹם לְשַׁלֵּשׁ בַּפֶּסַח,
רֹאשׁ מִבֵּית רָשָׁע מָחַצְתָּ בְּעֵץ חֲמִשִּׁים בַּפֶּסַח,
שְׁתֵּי אֵלֶּה רֶגַע תָּבִיא לְעוּצִית בַּפֶּסַח,
תָּעֹז יָדְךָ תָּרוּם יְמִינְךָ כְּלֵיל הִתְקַדֶּשׁ חַג פֶּסַח,
וַאֲמַרְתֶּם זֶבַח פֶּסַח.

And You Will Say,
"This is the Passover Sacrifice"

You wondrously displayed the strength of Your powers on Passover,
Above all of the festivals, You elevated Passover,
To Abraham You revealed the midnight occurrences of Passover night,
And you will say, "This is the Passover sacrifice."

Upon his door You knocked in the heat of the day of Passover,
He fed the angels unleavened bread on Passover,
And to the cattle he ran as a foreshadowing of the sacrifice of Passover,
And you will say, "This is the Passover sacrifice."

The Sodomites provoked God and were destroyed by fire on Passover,
Lot was saved from them and baked unleavened bread at the end of Passover,
You swept clear the Land of Egypt when You passed over on Passover,
And you will say, "This is the Passover sacrifice."

Mighty God! You crushed every first born on the night of watching, Passover,
You protected the first born of Israel through the blood of Passover,
You did not allow the slayer to enter my doors on Passover,
And you will say, "This is the Passover sacrifice."

Jericho was secured at the time of Passover,
Midian was destroyed by a cake of barley, the offering of Passover,
The fertile lands of Pul and Lud were burned on Passover,
And you will say, "This is the Passover sacrifice."

He was destined to stay at Nov until the time of Passover,
A hand wrote of the destruction of Babylon on Passover,
Station the guard and set the table on Passover,
And you will say, "This is the Passover sacrifice."

Hadassah assembled all for a three-day fast on Passover,
The head of a wicked house You crushed on fifty-cubit high gallows on Passover,
These two you will bring for Edom on Passover,
Your hand will be strong, and Your right hand You will raise as on the night that
You sanctified the Festival of Passover,
And you will say, "This is the Passover sacrifice."

It is Appropriate to Praise God, it is Fitting to Revere God!

כִּי לוֹ נָאֶה,
כִּי לוֹ יָאֶה!

Extraordinary in sovereignty, chosen appropriately,
God's troops declare,
"To You and to You; to You because of You;
To You, especially, to You; to You Adonai, is the kingdom."
It is appropriate to praise God, it is fitting to revere God!

אַדִּיר בִּמְלוּכָה, בָּחוּר כַּהֲלָכָה,
גְּדוּדָיו יֹאמְרוּ לוֹ:
לְךָ וּלְךָ, לְךָ כִּי לְךָ,
לְךָ אַף לְךָ, לְךָ יי הַמַּמְלָכָה.
כִּי לוֹ נָאֶה, כִּי לוֹ יָאֶה.

Distinguished in sovereignty, glorified appropriately,
God's loyal ones declare,
"To You and to You; to You because of You; to You, especially,
To You; to You Adonai, is the kingdom."
It is appropriate to praise God, it is fitting to revere God!

דָּגוּל בִּמְלוּכָה, הָדוּר כַּהֲלָכָה,
וָתִיקָיו יֹאמְרוּ לוֹ:
לְךָ וּלְךָ, לְךָ כִּי לְךָ,
לְךָ אַף לְךָ, לְךָ יי הַמַּמְלָכָה.
כִּי לוֹ נָאֶה, כִּי לוֹ יָאֶה.

Worthy in sovereignty, powerful accordingly,
God's angels declare,
"To You and to You; to You because of You; to You, especially,
To You; to You Adonai, is the kingdom."
It is appropriate to praise God, it is fitting to revere God!

זַכַּאי בִּמְלוּכָה, חָסִין כַּהֲלָכָה,
טַפְסְרָיו יֹאמְרוּ לוֹ:
לְךָ וּלְךָ, לְךָ כִּי לְךָ,
לְךָ אַף לְךָ, לְךָ יי הַמַּמְלָכָה.
כִּי לוֹ נָאֶה, כִּי לוֹ יָאֶה.

Unique in sovereignty, mighty accordingly,
God's learned ones declare,
"To You and to You; to You because of You; to You, especially,
To You; to You Adonai, is the kingdom."
It is appropriate to praise God, it is fitting to revere God!

יָחִיד בִּמְלוּכָה, כַּבִּיר כַּהֲלָכָה,
לִמּוּדָיו יֹאמְרוּ לוֹ:
לְךָ וּלְךָ, לְךָ כִּי לְךָ,
לְךָ אַף לְךָ, לְךָ יי הַמַּמְלָכָה.
כִּי לוֹ נָאֶה, כִּי לוֹ יָאֶה.

Exalted in sovereignty, rightfully awesome,
those around God declare,
"To You and to You; to You because of You; to You, especially,
To You; to You Adonai, is the kingdom."
It is appropriate to praise God, it is fitting to revere God!

מֶלֶךְ בִּמְלוּכָה, נוֹרָא כַּהֲלָכָה,
סְבִיבָיו יֹאמְרוּ לוֹ:
לְךָ וּלְךָ, לְךָ כִּי לְךָ,
לְךָ אַף לְךָ, לְךָ יי הַמַּמְלָכָה.
כִּי לוֹ נָאֶה, כִּי לוֹ יָאֶה.

Humble in sovereignty, redeemer accordingly,
God's righteous ones declare,
"To You and to You; to You because of You; to You, especially,
To You; to You Adonai, is the kingdom."
It is appropriate to praise God, it is fitting to revere God!

עָנָיו בִּמְלוּכָה, פּוֹדֶה כַּהֲלָכָה,
צַדִּיקָיו יֹאמְרוּ לוֹ:
לְךָ וּלְךָ, לְךָ כִּי לְךָ,
לְךָ אַף לְךָ, לְךָ יי הַמַּמְלָכָה.
כִּי לוֹ נָאֶה, כִּי לוֹ יָאֶה.

Sacred in sovereignty, merciful appropriately,
many in God's Presence declare,
"To You and to You; to You because of You; to You, especially,
To You; to You Adonai, is the kingdom."
It is appropriate to praise God, it is fitting to revere God!

קָדוֹשׁ בִּמְלוּכָה, רַחוּם כַּהֲלָכָה,
שִׁנְאַנָּיו יֹאמְרוּ לוֹ:
לְךָ וּלְךָ, לְךָ כִּי לְךָ,
לְךָ אַף לְךָ, לְךָ יי הַמַּמְלָכָה.
כִּי לוֹ נָאֶה, כִּי לוֹ יָאֶה.

Forceful in sovereignty, supportive accordingly,
God's innocent ones declare,
"To You and to You; to You because of You; to You, especially, to You;
To You Adonai, is the kingdom."
It is appropriate to praise God, it is fitting to revere God!

תַּקִּיף בִּמְלוּכָה, תּוֹמֵךְ כַּהֲלָכָה,
תְּמִימָיו יֹאמְרוּ לוֹ: לְךָ וּלְךָ, לְךָ כִּי לְךָ,
לְךָ אַף לְךָ, לְךָ יי הַמַּמְלָכָה.
כִּי לוֹ נָאֶה, כִּי לוֹ יָאֶה.

Adir Hu

Plate 24

Rabbi Ḥama son of Rabbi Ḥanina said, "After the Lord your God you will walk"
(Deuteronomy 13:5). The verse means that you are to follow the qualities of the Holy
Blessed One. God clothed the naked; so should you clothe the naked.
The Holy Blessed One visited the sick;
so should you visit the sick. The Holy Blessed One buried the dead;
so should you bury the dead.
The Holy Blessed One comforted mourners; so should you comfort mourners.
BT Sotah 14a

*Colorful letters are engraved against a black background. The darkness represents our world and the bright
letters allude to the rare, brilliant glimpses of God that inspire our lives. At such moments we are given the
gift of God's light. The Hebrew acrostic extols God's qualities: magnificent, chosen, great, exceptional,
glorified, eternal, perfect, righteous, pure, unique, powerful, learned, king, awesome, revered, mighty,
redeemer, just, holy, merciful, almighty, and strong.*

Awe

And now, Israel, what does God want of you?
Only that you remain in awe of the Lord your God, following God's path and loving God.

Deuteronomy 10:12

Leader:

Adir Hu began to appear in Ashkenazic (German) *haggadot* in the fourteenth century. The poet yearns for a rebuilt Temple, urging God, "Build, build Your House, again soon." The poet relies wholly on God to bring about his vision for the future. We may, however, prefer a partnership between humans and the Divine.

Magnificent is God

אַדִּיר הוּא

May God rebuild the Temple soon,

Speedily, quickly in our days and soon,

God, build! God, build! Build Your House again soon.

יִבְנֶה בֵיתוֹ בְּקָרוֹב.

בִּמְהֵרָה, בִּמְהֵרָה בְּיָמֵינוּ בְּקָרוֹב.

אֵל בְּנֵה, אֵל בְּנֵה, בְּנֵה בֵיתְךָ בְּקָרוֹב.

Chosen is God. Great is God. Distinguished is God.

May God rebuild the Temple soon,

Speedily, quickly in our days and soon,

God, build! God, build! Build Your House again soon.

בָּחוּר הוּא, גָּדוֹל הוּא, דָּגוּל הוּא,

יִבְנֶה בֵיתוֹ בְּקָרוֹב.

בִּמְהֵרָה, בִּמְהֵרָה בְּיָמֵינוּ בְּקָרוֹב.

אֵל בְּנֵה, אֵל בְּנֵה, בְּנֵה בֵיתְךָ בְּקָרוֹב.

Glorified is God. Eternal is God. Worthy is God. Pious is God.

May God rebuild the Temple soon,

Speedily, quickly in our days and soon,

God, build! God, build! Build Your House again soon.

הָדוּר הוּא, וָתִיק הוּא, זַכַּאי הוּא, חָסִיד הוּא,

יִבְנֶה בֵיתוֹ בְּקָרוֹב.

בִּמְהֵרָה, בִּמְהֵרָה בְּיָמֵינוּ בְּקָרוֹב.

אֵל בְּנֵה, אֵל בְּנֵה, בְּנֵה בֵיתְךָ בְּקָרוֹב.

Pure is God. Unique is God. Mighty is God. Learned is God.

Sovereign is God. Awesome is God. Exalted is God. Powerful is God.

Redeemer is God. Righteous is God.

May God rebuild the Temple soon,

Speedily, quickly in our days and soon,

God, build! God, build! Build Your House again soon.

טָהוֹר הוּא, יָחִיד הוּא, כַּבִּיר הוּא, לָמוּד הוּא,

מֶלֶךְ הוּא, נוֹרָא הוּא, סַגִּיב הוּא, עִזּוּז הוּא,

פּוֹדֶה הוּא, צַדִּיק הוּא

יִבְנֶה בֵיתוֹ בְּקָרוֹב.

בִּמְהֵרָה, בִּמְהֵרָה בְּיָמֵינוּ בְּקָרוֹב.

אֵל בְּנֵה, אֵל בְּנֵה, בְּנֵה בֵיתְךָ בְּקָרוֹב.

Holy is God. Merciful is God. Almighty is God. Resolute is God.

May God rebuild the Temple soon,

Speedily, quickly in our days and soon,

God, build! God, build! Build Your House again soon.

קָדוֹשׁ הוּא, רַחוּם הוּא, שַׁדַּי הוּא, תַּקִּיף הוּא,

יִבְנֶה בֵיתוֹ בְּקָרוֹב.

בִּמְהֵרָה, בִּמְהֵרָה בְּיָמֵינוּ בְּקָרוֹב.

אֵל בְּנֵה, אֵל בְּנֵה, בְּנֵה בֵיתְךָ בְּקָרוֹב.

Participant:

The poet conveys a sense of completion. Composed as an acrostic, it employs the entire *aleph-bet* to express God's attributes. Not only is God complete, but history will come full-circle too.

All:

In upholding the promise to Israel–rebuilding the Temple and leading the exiles to Israel–God reflects exceptional qualities. These attributes weave a tapestry of God and God's role in our world.

Reflections

- Why are the two songs that follow in similar modern block style?
- What are the results of focusing on God's attributes?
- How can we emulate these qualities in our own lives?

Who Knows One?

Plate 25

"Hear O Israel, the Lord our God, the Lord is One" (Deuteronomy 6:4). The Holy One said to Israel, "My children, note that all I created, I created in pairs: heaven and earth are a pair; Adam and Eve are a pair; this world and the world to come are a pair. But my glory is one and unique in the world."
Deuteronomy Rabbah 2:31

The graphic "bookends" located at the top and bottom of the illumination read, "Who Knows?" followed by the introductory response for each verse, "I Know." Vertical columns on either side of the painting list the letters of the Hebrew aleph-bet, each letter standing for its numerical equivalent (aleph=1, bet=2, gimmel=3, etc.). The narrative progression of the lyrics leads us through the corresponding images.

KNOWLEDGE

One's wisdom illuminates one's face.
Ecclesiastes 8:1

Leader:
Written during the Middle Ages, *Eḥad Mi Yodea* captures the spirit of the evening, alternating between questions and answers. It outlines the breadth of Jewish tradition and encourages us to delve deeper into its layers, exemplifying what we said at the beginning of the seder (page 53), "All who expand upon the story of the Exodus are to be praised."

Participant:
The *piyyut* (liturgical poem) begins and ends with God, opening with God as One and closing with the Thirteen Divine Attributes. In between these poles, are symbols of partnership between God and humans: the tablets of the covenant, the founders of the nation, Torah and Mishnah. The Divine message is handed to humans, heard, internalized, and retransmitted as Oral Torah.

All:
Knowledge is the path to the future.

Reflections

● See if you can identify any patterns or progressions in the song.

● How can the song be used as an educational tool?

Activity

● Based on the clues in the illumination (Plate 25), name each of the symbols associated with its proper number before singing *Eḥad Mi Yodea*.

אֶחָד מִי יוֹדֵעַ?

אֶחָד מִי יוֹדֵעַ? אֶחָד אֲנִי יוֹדֵעַ:
אֶחָד אֱלֹהֵינוּ שֶׁבַּשָּׁמַיִם וּבָאָרֶץ.

שְׁנַיִם מִי יוֹדֵעַ? שְׁנַיִם אֲנִי יוֹדֵעַ:
שְׁנֵי לוּחוֹת הַבְּרִית, אֶחָד אֱלֹהֵינוּ שֶׁבַּשָּׁמַיִם וּבָאָרֶץ.

שְׁלֹשָׁה מִי יוֹדֵעַ? שְׁלֹשָׁה אֲנִי יוֹדֵעַ:
שְׁלֹשָׁה אָבוֹת, שְׁנֵי לוּחוֹת הַבְּרִית, אֶחָד אֱלֹהֵינוּ שֶׁבַּשָּׁמַיִם וּבָאָרֶץ.

אַרְבַּע מִי יוֹדֵעַ? אַרְבַּע אֲנִי יוֹדֵעַ:
אַרְבַּע אִמָּהוֹת, שְׁלֹשָׁה אָבוֹת, שְׁנֵי לוּחוֹת הַבְּרִית, אֶחָד אֱלֹהֵינוּ שֶׁבַּשָּׁמַיִם וּבָאָרֶץ.

חֲמִשָּׁה מִי יוֹדֵעַ? חֲמִשָּׁה אֲנִי יוֹדֵעַ:
חֲמִשָּׁה חֻמְשֵׁי תוֹרָה, אַרְבַּע אִמָּהוֹת, שְׁלֹשָׁה אָבוֹת, שְׁנֵי לוּחוֹת הַבְּרִית, אֶחָד אֱלֹהֵינוּ שֶׁבַּשָּׁמַיִם וּבָאָרֶץ.

שִׁשָּׁה מִי יוֹדֵעַ? שִׁשָּׁה אֲנִי יוֹדֵעַ:
שִׁשָּׁה סִדְרֵי מִשְׁנָה, חֲמִשָּׁה חֻמְשֵׁי תוֹרָה, אַרְבַּע אִמָּהוֹת, שְׁלֹשָׁה אָבוֹת, שְׁנֵי לוּחוֹת הַבְּרִית, אֶחָד אֱלֹהֵינוּ שֶׁבַּשָּׁמַיִם וּבָאָרֶץ.

שִׁבְעָה מִי יוֹדֵעַ? שִׁבְעָה אֲנִי יוֹדֵעַ:
שִׁבְעָה יְמֵי שַׁבַּתָּא, שִׁשָּׁה סִדְרֵי מִשְׁנָה, חֲמִשָּׁה חֻמְשֵׁי תוֹרָה, אַרְבַּע אִמָּהוֹת, שְׁלֹשָׁה אָבוֹת, שְׁנֵי לוּחוֹת הַבְּרִית, אֶחָד אֱלֹהֵינוּ שֶׁבַּשָּׁמַיִם וּבָאָרֶץ.

שְׁמוֹנָה מִי יוֹדֵעַ? שְׁמוֹנָה אֲנִי יוֹדֵעַ:
שְׁמוֹנָה יְמֵי מִילָה, שִׁבְעָה יְמֵי שַׁבַּתָּא, שִׁשָּׁה סִדְרֵי מִשְׁנָה, חֲמִשָּׁה חֻמְשֵׁי תוֹרָה, אַרְבַּע אִמָּהוֹת, שְׁלֹשָׁה אָבוֹת, שְׁנֵי לוּחוֹת הַבְּרִית, אֶחָד אֱלֹהֵינוּ שֶׁבַּשָּׁמַיִם וּבָאָרֶץ.

תִּשְׁעָה מִי יוֹדֵעַ? תִּשְׁעָה אֲנִי יוֹדֵעַ:
תִּשְׁעָה יַרְחֵי לֵידָה, שְׁמוֹנָה יְמֵי מִילָה, שִׁבְעָה יְמֵי שַׁבַּתָּא, שִׁשָּׁה סִדְרֵי מִשְׁנָה, חֲמִשָּׁה חֻמְשֵׁי תוֹרָה, אַרְבַּע אִמָּהוֹת, שְׁלֹשָׁה אָבוֹת, שְׁנֵי לוּחוֹת הַבְּרִית, אֶחָד אֱלֹהֵינוּ שֶׁבַּשָּׁמַיִם וּבָאָרֶץ.

Who Knows One?

Who knows one? I know one.
One is our God in the heavens and on earth.

Who knows two? I know two.
Two are the tablets of the covenant. One is our God in the heavens and on earth.

Who knows three? I know three.
Three are the patriarchs. Two are the tablets of the covenant. One is our God in the heavens and on earth.

Who knows four? I know four.
Four are the matriarchs. Three are the patriarchs. Two are the tablets of the covenant. One is our God in the heavens and on earth.

Who knows five? I know five.
Five are the books of Torah. Four are the matriarchs. Three are the patriarchs. Two are the tablets of the covenant. One is our God in the heavens and on earth.

Who knows six? I know six.
Six are the orders of Mishnah. Five are the books of Torah. Four are the matriarchs. Three are the patriarchs. Two are the tablets of the covenant. One is our God in the heavens and on earth.

Who knows seven? I know seven.
Seven are the days of the week. Six are the orders of Mishnah. Five are the books of Torah. Four are the matriarchs. Three are the patriarchs. Two are the tablets of the covenant. One is our God in the heavens and on earth.

Who knows eight? I know eight.
Eight are the days until circumcision. Seven are the days of the week. Six are the orders of Mishnah. Five are the books of Torah. Four are the matriarchs. Three are the patriarchs. Two are the tablets of the covenant. One is our God in the heavens and on earth.

Who knows nine? I know nine.
Nine are the months of pregnancy. Eight are the days until circumcision. Seven are the days of the week. Six are the orders of Mishnah. Five are the books of Torah. Four are the matriarchs. Three are the patriarchs. Two are the tablets of the covenant. One is our God in the heavens and on earth.

עֲשָׂרָה מִי יוֹדֵעַ? עֲשָׂרָה אֲנִי יוֹדֵעַ:

עֲשָׂרָה דִבְּרַיָּא, תִּשְׁעָה יַרְחֵי לֵידָה, שְׁמוֹנָה יְמֵי מִילָה, שִׁבְעָה יְמֵי שַׁבַּתָּא, שִׁשָּׁה סִדְרֵי מִשְׁנָה, חֲמִשָּׁה חֻמְשֵׁי תוֹרָה, אַרְבַּע אִמָּהוֹת, שְׁלֹשָׁה אָבוֹת, שְׁנֵי לוּחוֹת הַבְּרִית, אֶחָד אֱלֹהֵינוּ שֶׁבַּשָּׁמַיִם וּבָאָרֶץ.

אַחַד עָשָׂר מִי יוֹדֵעַ? אַחַד עָשָׂר אֲנִי יוֹדֵעַ:

אַחַד עָשָׂר כּוֹכְבַיָּא, עֲשָׂרָה דִבְּרַיָּא, תִּשְׁעָה יַרְחֵי לֵידָה, שְׁמוֹנָה יְמֵי מִילָה, שִׁבְעָה יְמֵי שַׁבַּתָּא, שִׁשָּׁה סִדְרֵי מִשְׁנָה, חֲמִשָּׁה חֻמְשֵׁי תוֹרָה, אַרְבַּע אִמָּהוֹת, שְׁלֹשָׁה אָבוֹת, שְׁנֵי לוּחוֹת הַבְּרִית, אֶחָד אֱלֹהֵינוּ שֶׁבַּשָּׁמַיִם וּבָאָרֶץ.

שְׁנֵים עָשָׂר מִי יוֹדֵעַ? שְׁנֵים עָשָׂר אֲנִי יוֹדֵעַ:

שְׁנֵים עָשָׂר שִׁבְטַיָּא, אַחַד עָשָׂר כּוֹכְבַיָּא, עֲשָׂרָה דִבְּרַיָּא, תִּשְׁעָה יַרְחֵי לֵידָה, שְׁמוֹנָה יְמֵי מִילָה, שִׁבְעָה יְמֵי שַׁבַּתָּא, שִׁשָּׁה סִדְרֵי מִשְׁנָה, חֲמִשָּׁה חֻמְשֵׁי תוֹרָה, אַרְבַּע אִמָּהוֹת, שְׁלֹשָׁה אָבוֹת, שְׁנֵי לוּחוֹת הַבְּרִית, אֶחָד אֱלֹהֵינוּ שֶׁבַּשָּׁמַיִם וּבָאָרֶץ.

שְׁלֹשָׁה עָשָׂר מִי יוֹדֵעַ? שְׁלֹשָׁה עָשָׂר אֲנִי יוֹדֵעַ:

שְׁלֹשָׁה עָשָׂר מִדַּיָּא, שְׁנֵים עָשָׂר שִׁבְטַיָּא, אַחַד עָשָׂר כּוֹכְבַיָּא, עֲשָׂרָה דִבְּרַיָּא, תִּשְׁעָה יַרְחֵי לֵידָה, שְׁמוֹנָה יְמֵי מִילָה, שִׁבְעָה יְמֵי שַׁבַּתָּא, שִׁשָּׁה סִדְרֵי מִשְׁנָה, חֲמִשָּׁה חֻמְשֵׁי תוֹרָה, אַרְבַּע אִמָּהוֹת, שְׁלֹשָׁה אָבוֹת, שְׁנֵי לוּחוֹת הַבְּרִית, אֶחָד אֱלֹהֵינוּ שֶׁבַּשָּׁמַיִם וּבָאָרֶץ.

Who knows ten? I know ten.

Ten are the Commandments. Nine are the months of pregnancy. Eight are the days until circumcision. Seven are the days of the week. Six are the orders of Mishnah. Five are the books of Torah. Four are the matriarchs. Three are the patriarchs. Two are the tablets of the covenant. One is our God in the heavens and on earth.

Who knows eleven? I know eleven.

Eleven are the stars in Joseph's dream. Ten are the Commandments. Nine are the months of pregnancy. Eight are the days until circumcision. Seven are the days of the week. Six are the orders of Mishnah. Five are the books of Torah. Four are the matriarchs. Three are the patriarchs. Two are the tablets of the covenant. One is our God in the heavens and on earth.

Who knows twelve? I know twelve.

Twelve are the Tribes of Israel. Eleven are the stars in Joseph's dream. Ten are the Commandments. Nine are the months of pregnancy. Eight are the days until circumcision. Seven are the days of the week. Six are the orders of Mishnah. Five are the books of Torah. Four are the matriarchs. Three are the patriarchs. Two are the tablets of the covenant. One is our God in the heavens and on earth.

Who knows thirteen? I know thirteen.

Thirteen are God's attributes. Twelve are the Tribes of Israel. Eleven are the stars in Joseph's dream. Ten are the Commandments. Nine are the months of pregnancy. Eight are the days until circumcision. Seven are the days of the week. Six are the orders of Mishnah. Five are the books of Torah. Four are the matriarchs. Three are the patriarchs. Two are the tablets of the covenant. One is our God in the heavens and on earth.

One Goat

Plate 26

Rabbi Joshua ben Levi said, "Scripture teaches, 'I have spread you abroad as the four winds of heaven, says the Lord' *(Zekhariah 2:10)*. As the world cannot endure without winds, so the world cannot endure without Israel."
BT Ta'anit 3b

This illumination continues the modern style employed in Adir Hu and Eḥad Mi Yodea. White space conveys a sense of God's intangible Presence. The center of the colorfully graphic rendition contains the song's chorus: "One goat that my father bought for two zuzim, one goat." Each character is depicted, from the top right hand corner clockwise: the goat purchased for two zuzim, the cat eating the kid, the dog biting the cat, the stick hitting the dog, the fire burning the stick, the water extinguishing the fire, the ox drinking the water, the slaughterer slaughtering the ox, the Angel of Death striking the slaughterer, and, finally, the Holy Blessed One overpowering the Angel of Death.

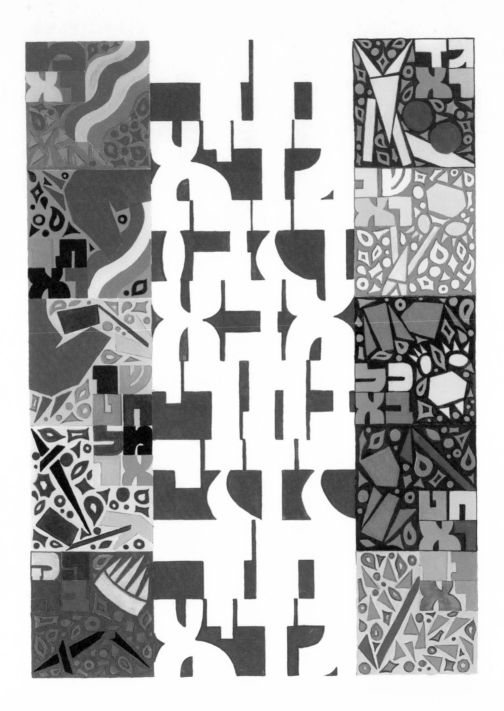

HISTORICAL CONSCIOUSNESS

We are composites of our past experiences.
Self-understanding will forever elude us as long as we remain in the dark about the details of whence we came.

Ismar Schorsch

Leader:

Ḥad Gadya, "One Goat," entered the Ashkenazic Passover Haggadah around the fifteenth century. It has its roots in the Talmud (*BT Bava Batra 10a*) and Midrash (*Genesis Rabbah 38:28*), but it is based stylistically on German folk songs. While on its surface it seems to be a childish and nonsensical song, it reveals a sophisticated theology. The song creates a pyramid of oppressors; although each believes that he has the upper hand, he quickly realizes that he is but a link in a chain which culminates with the Holy Blessed One.

Participant:

Perhaps "One Goat" is a metaphor for Israel, who was acquired by God with two Tablets of the Law. Each successive character represents another occupier of Israel: Assyrians, Babylonians, Persians, Greeks, Romans, Byzantines, Arabs, Crusaders, and Ottomans.

All:

Despite them all, God's plan has triumphed and the people Israel have returned to their homeland—an appropriate bridge to the singing of *Hatikvah*.

Reflections

- Is this simply a playful song or does it have deeper meaning? What might that meaning be?

- What might the "two *zuzim*" represent?

- Why is this song the last one?

- Can future generations add to the haggadah?

Activity

- Imitate the sound of each actor in *Ḥad Gadya* (sound of a goat, cat, etc.). Everyone around the table is assigned a different "voice." Then the leader of the seder orchestrates the entire song pointing to the different players to make their sounds as their roles appear in the song.

חַד גַּדְיָא

חַד גַּדְיָא. דְּזַבֵּן אַבָּא בִּתְרֵי זוּזֵי, חַד גַּדְיָא, חַד גַּדְיָא.

וַאֲתָא שׁוּנְרָא וְאָכְלָה לְגַדְיָא, דְּזַבֵּן אַבָּא בִּתְרֵי זוּזֵי, חַד גַּדְיָא, חַד גַּדְיָא.

וַאֲתָא כַלְבָּא וְנָשַׁךְ לְשׁוּנְרָא, דְּאָכְלָה לְגַדְיָא, דְּזַבֵּן אַבָּא בִּתְרֵי זוּזֵי, חַד גַּדְיָא, חַד גַּדְיָא.

וַאֲתָא חוּטְרָא וְהִכָּה לְכַלְבָּא, דְּנָשַׁךְ לְשׁוּנְרָא, דְּאָכְלָה לְגַדְיָא, דְּזַבֵּן אַבָּא בִּתְרֵי זוּזֵי, חַד גַּדְיָא, חַד גַּדְיָא.

וַאֲתָא נוּרָא וְשָׂרַף לְחוּטְרָא, דְּהִכָּה לְכַלְבָּא, דְּנָשַׁךְ לְשׁוּנְרָא, דְּאָכְלָה לְגַדְיָא, דְּזַבֵּן אַבָּא בִּתְרֵי זוּזֵי, חַד גַּדְיָא, חַד גַּדְיָא.

וַאֲתָא מַיָּא וְכָבָה לְנוּרָא, דְּשָׂרַף לְחוּטְרָא, דְּהִכָּה לְכַלְבָּא, דְּנָשַׁךְ לְשׁוּנְרָא, דְּאָכְלָה לְגַדְיָא, דְּזַבֵּן אַבָּא בִּתְרֵי זוּזֵי, חַד גַּדְיָא, חַד גַּדְיָא.

וַאֲתָא תוֹרָא וְשָׁתָא לְמַיָּא, דְּכָבָה לְנוּרָא, דְּשָׂרַף לְחוּטְרָא, דְּהִכָּה לְכַלְבָּא, דְּנָשַׁךְ לְשׁוּנְרָא, דְּאָכְלָה לְגַדְיָא, דְּזַבֵּן אַבָּא בִּתְרֵי זוּזֵי, חַד גַּדְיָא, חַד גַּדְיָא.

וַאֲתָא הַשּׁוֹחֵט וְשָׁחַט לְתוֹרָא, דְּשָׁתָא לְמַיָּא, דְּכָבָה לְנוּרָא, דְּשָׂרַף לְחוּטְרָא, דְּהִכָּה לְכַלְבָּא, דְּנָשַׁךְ לְשׁוּנְרָא, דְּאָכְלָה לְגַדְיָא, דְּזַבֵּן אַבָּא בִּתְרֵי זוּזֵי, חַד גַּדְיָא, חַד גַּדְיָא.

וַאֲתָא מַלְאַךְ הַמָּוֶת וְשָׁחַט לְשׁוֹחֵט, דְּשָׁחַט לְתוֹרָא, דְּשָׁתָא לְמַיָּא, דְּכָבָה לְנוּרָא, דְּשָׂרַף לְחוּטְרָא, דְּהִכָּה לְכַלְבָּא, דְּנָשַׁךְ לְשׁוּנְרָא, דְּאָכְלָה לְגַדְיָא, דְּזַבֵּן אַבָּא בִּתְרֵי זוּזֵי, חַד גַּדְיָא, חַד גַּדְיָא.

וַאֲתָא הַקָּדוֹשׁ בָּרוּךְ הוּא וְשָׁחַט לְמַלְאַךְ הַמָּוֶת, דְּשָׁחַט לְשׁוֹחֵט, דְּשָׁחַט לְתוֹרָא, דְּשָׁתָא לְמַיָּא, דְּכָבָה לְנוּרָא, דְּשָׂרַף לְחוּטְרָא, דְּהִכָּה לְכַלְבָּא, דְּנָשַׁךְ לְשׁוּנְרָא, דְּאָכְלָה לְגַדְיָא, דְּזַבֵּן אַבָּא בִּתְרֵי זוּזֵי, חַד גַּדְיָא, חַד גַּדְיָא.

One Goat

One goat that my father bought for two *zuzim*. One goat, one goat.

Then came a cat and ate the goat that my father bought for two *zuzim*. One goat, one goat.

Then came a dog and bit the cat that ate the goat that my father bought for two *zuzim*. One goat, one goat.

Then came a stick and beat the dog that bit the cat that ate the goat that my father bought for two *zuzim*. One goat, one goat.

Then came a fire and burned the stick that beat the dog that bit the cat that ate the goat that my father bought for two *zuzim*. One goat, one goat.

Then came water and extinguished the fire that burned the stick that beat the dog that bit the cat that ate the goat that my father bought for two *zuzim*. One goat, one goat.

Then came an ox and drank the water that extinguished the fire that burned the stick that beat the dog that bit the cat that ate the goat that my father bought for two *zuzim*. One goat, one goat.

Then came a slaughterer and slaughtered the ox that drank the water that extinguished the fire that burned the stick that beat the dog that bit the cat that ate the goat that my father bought for two *zuzim*. One goat, one goat.

Then came the Angel of Death and slaughtered the slaughterer who slaughtered the ox that drank the water that extinguished the fire that burned the stick that beat the dog that bit the cat that ate the goat that my father bought for two *zuzim*. One goat, one goat.

Then came the Holy Blessed One and slaughtered the Angel of Death who slaughtered the slaughterer who slaughtered the ox that drank the water that extinguished the fire that burned the stick that beat the dog that bit the cat that ate the goat that my father bought for two *zuzim*. One goat, one goat.

Hatikvah

Plate 27

As long as deep in the heart   *Kol od baleivav p'nimah*
A Jewish soul yearns,   *Nefesh Yehudi homiyah*
And toward the east   *Ulfa'atei mizrah kadimah*
An eye gazes toward Zion,   *Ayin l'Tziyon tzofiyah*

The Hope has still not been lost, *Od lo avda tikvateinu*
A Hope two thousand years old, *Hatikvah bat shnot alpayim*
To be a free people in our Land *Lihyot am hofshi b'artzeinu*
the Land of Zion, Jerusalem.   *Eretz Tzion Viyerushalayim.*

The floral design surrounding the Israeli national anthem is based on a ketubbah (marriage contract) from 1822. The ketubbah is an appropriate connection to Hatikvah and the conclusion of the seder. Just as the ketubbah attests to the covenant between a bride and groom, so is the seder experience a reminder of the lasting relationship between God and the Jewish people. Just as a couple expresses their love by telling and retelling their story of finding each other, so too do God and the Israelites relate yearly their narrative of discovery and love. Moreover, Hatikvah means hope. Over the course of this special evening, we have expressed many hopes for ourselves, our communities, our nation, and our world. Now our hearts and minds turn to the Jewish homeland as we recognize and celebrate the miracle of modern-day Israel.

הַתִּקְוָה

כֹּל עוֹד בַּלֵּבָב פְּנִימָה
נֶפֶשׁ יְהוּדִי הוֹמִיָּה
וּלְפַאֲתֵי מִזְרָח קָדִימָה
עַיִן לְצִיּוֹן צוֹפִיָּה·

עוֹד לֹא אָבְדָה תִּקְוָתֵנוּ
הַתִּקְוָה בַּת שְׁנוֹת אַלְפַּיִם
לִהְיוֹת עַם חָפְשִׁי בְּאַרְצֵנוּ
אֶרֶץ צִיּוֹן וִירוּשָׁלַיִם·

ISRAEL

The Land of Israel is not something apart from the soul of the Jewish people . . .
it is part of the very essence of our nationhood; it is bound organically to its very life and inner being.
Abraham Isaac Kook

Participant:

As we look forward, we nevertheless acknowledge that redemption is rooted in the past. Knowing our story, especially a narrative born of oppression, allows us to envision a dream and a hope. History is the fertile ground in which a landscape of redemption takes root. Only then can we move ahead, mindful of whence we have come and where we are headed.

All:

The word *kadimah* has three meanings: "backward," "eastward," and "forward."
Israel is at the center of our story—past, present, and future.

Sing Hatikvah (pages 178–179).

Reflections

- Why is the border for *Hatikvah* modeled on an Italian *ketubbah*?
- How do we define Zionism? Is it possible to be a Zionist without living in Israel? How do we show our attachment to Israel, and how will this commitment grow in the coming year?
- Why is *Hatikvah* a fitting conclusion to the seder?

...The real task, the most difficult task,
has still to be commenced.

Pharaoh is gone, but the work remains;

The master has ceased to be master,
but the slaves have not ceased to be slaves...

Aḥad Ha'am (1856–1927)

Sources

Dedication page: Abraham Joshua Heschel in Susannah Heschel, ed. *Moral Grandeur and Spiritual Audacity*, (Farrar, Straus and Giroux, NY, 1996), 373.

Pages 14–15: Friedrich Nietzsche, *Daybreak: Thoughts on the Prejudices of Morality*, trans. R.J. Hollingdale (Cambridge University Press, 1982), 5.

Page 15: Nahum Sarna, *Exploring Exodus: The Origins of Biblical Israel*, (Schocken Books, NY, 1996), 87.

Pages 15–16: Samson Raphael Hirsch, *Hirsch Commentary on the Torah: Exodus*, (The Judaica Press, Inc., 1966), 138.

Page 24: "Decorate the seder table with jewelry! . . ." David Golinkin, *Insight Israel: Reflections on Israel, Jewish Law, and the Jewish Calendar*, Second Series, (Schechter Institute of Jewish Studies, 2006), 79.

Page 24: "the kittel . . ." Edward Greenstein in Michael Strassfeld, ed. *The Jewish Holidays*, (Harper & Row, Publishers, NY 1985), 19.

Page 24: "Leave the door open . . ." and "Give candy . . ." David Golinkin, *loc.cit.*

Page 30: Frank Herbert, *Chapterhouse Dune*, (G.P. Putnam's Sons, 1985), 344.

Page 30: "The order of Jewish living . . ." Abraham Joshua Heschel, *op. cit.*, 133.

Page 34: "Human beings are the source . . ." Abraham Joshua Heschel, *ibid.*, 60.

Page 38: Excerpt by Sheila Peltz Weinberg is from *The Women's Seder Sourcebook: Rituals and Readings for Use at the Seder*, ed. by Sharon Cohen Anisfeld, Tara Mohr and Catherine Spector, (Jewish Lights Publishing, 2003), 45–46.

Page 39: "There is more madness . . ." Abraham Joshua Heschel, *op. cit.*, 8.

Page 40: "Replete is the world with spiritual radiance . . ." Abraham Joshua Heschel, *ibid.*, 8.

Page 42: Michael Walzer, *Exodus and Revolution*, (Basic Books, 1985), 24.

Page 44: Isabel Allende in *This I Believe*, (Henry Holt and Company, LLC, 2006), 14.

Page 45: "Reenact the Exodus . . ." David Golinkin, *op. cit.*, 81.

Page 53: Michael Walzer, *op. cit.*, 74.

Page 62: Ismar Schorsch, *Canon Without Closure*, (Aviv Press, NY, 2007), 695.

Page 72: Cologne inscription in *The Judaic Tradition*, (Beacon Press, 1972), 623.

Page 75: Anne Frank, *The Diary of a Young Girl*, (Pocket Books, NY, 1972), 237.

Page 85: Wendell Phillips, speech in Boston, MA, January 28, 1852, in *Speeches Before the Massachusetts Anti-Slavery Society*, (1853), 13.

Page 102: Michael Walzer, *op. cit.*, 115.

Page 104: Avivah Gottlieb Zornberg, *The Particulars of Rapture: Reflections on Exodus*, (Doubleday, 2001), 16.

Page 106: "What is at stake . . ." Abraham Joshua Heschel, *op. cit.*, 3.

Page 114: Arnold Eisen in Michael Strassfeld, ed. *The Jewish Holidays*, (Harper & Row, NY, 1985), 6.

Page 116: "A haggadah printed in Spanish . . ." David Golinkin, *op. cit.*, 87.

Page 117: "The *afikoman* . . ." David Golinkin, *ibid.*, 88–89.

Page 129: "Pour out your love . . ." in *Hatza'ah L'seder*, Tel Aviv, 2000 quoted by David Golinkin, *ibid.*, 92.

Page 130: Martin Luther King, Jr. in his acceptance of the Nobel Peace Prize, Oslo, Norway, December 11, 1964.

Page 144: Ismar Schorsch, *op. cit.*, 698.

Page 153: "Tourists" by Yehuda Amihai in his *Poems of Jerusalem and Love Poems*, (The Sheep Meadow Press, NY, 1988), 134–135.

Page 175: Ismar Schorsch, *op. cit.*, 568.

Page 175: "Imitate the sound . . ." Shula Laderman, Lecturer in Jewish Art, Schechter Institute of Jewish Studies in her editorial notes on *The Lovell Haggadah*.

Page 181: Abraham Isaac Kook in *Contemporary Jewish Thought: A Reader*, ed. Simon Noveck (The Colonial Press, Inc., Clinton, MA, 1963), 112.

Page 183: Aḥad Ha'am *ibid.*, 42.

Page 214: Ilana Pardes in David Biale, ed., *Cultures of the Jews*, (Schocken Books, NY, 2002), 17–18.

Bibliography

Sharon Cohen Anisfeld, Tara Mohr and Catherine Spector, *The Women's Seder Sourcebook: Rituals and Readings for Use at the Seder*, (Jewish Lights Publishing, 2003).

Ḥayyim Naḥman Bialik and Y.H. Ravnitzky, *The Book of Legends*, (Schocken Books Inc., NY, 1992).

Baruch M. Bokser, *The Origins of the Seder*, (Jewish Theological Seminary Press, 2002).

Daniel Goldschmidt, *The Passover Haggadah: Its Sources and History* (Hebrew), (Mossad Bialik, Jerusalem, 1960).

David Golinkin, *Insight Israel: Reflections on Israel, Jewish Law, and the Jewish Calendar*, Second Series, (Schechter Institute of Jewish Studies, 2006), pp. 77–96

Samson Raphael Hirsch, *Hirsch Commentary on the Torah: Exodus*, (The Judaica Press, Inc, 1966).

Menaḥem Kasher, *Haggadah Shleimah* (Hebrew), (*Torah Shleimah*, Jerusalem, 1961).

Naḥum Sarna, *Exploring Exodus: The Origins of Biblical Israel*, (Schocken Books, NY, 1996).

Michael Strassfeld, ed. *The Jewish Holidays*, (Harper & Row Publishers, NY, 1985).

Michael Walzer, *Exodus and Revolution*, (Basic Books, 1985).

Avivah Gottlieb Zornberg, *The Particulars of Rapture: Reflections on Exodus*, (Doubleday, 2001).

Rabbi Matthew L. Berkowitz

is the Senior Rabbinic Fellow in The Jewish Theological Seminary's KOLLOT: Voices of Learning Program. Ordained by JTS in 1999, Rabbi Berkowitz conducts private and group study for lay people.

Completing his undergraduate degree in International Relations and Middle East Studies, he graduated *summa cum laude* from Colgate University. A Wexner Fellow, he studied at The Pardes Institute and The Schechter Institute of Jewish Studies in Jerusalem. Formally trained in scribal arts in Jerusalem, he wrote *Megillat Esther*, illuminated several *ketubbot*, and created many fusions of art and Hebrew calligraphy before embarking on this haggadah.

Rabbi Berkowitz is married to Rabbi Miriam Berkowitz. Rabbis Berkowitz are the proud parents of Adir Pinḥas, Rachel Naama, and Shira Lilach.

The Schechter Institute of Jewish Studies, Inc.

a tax-exempt organization, supports four *amutot* (non-profits) based in Jerusalem, which teach Jewish studies to over 35,000 Jews throughout Israel and Europe. At the Schechter Institute of Jewish Studies, a Graduate School for Israeli educators, over 550 students learn Jewish studies within a pluralistic environment. It includes Applied Research Institutes in Halakhah, Women in Jewish Law, and Judaism and the Arts. The Schechter Rabbinical Seminary, affiliated with the Jewish Theological Seminary and the Masorti/Conservative movement in Israel, trains rabbis for Israel and the Diaspora. The TALI Education Fund provides enriched Jewish studies for over 31,000 Israeli children in 170 state schools and kindergartens. *Midreshet Yerushalayim* runs outreach activities for Russian immigrants in Israel and for Jewish communities in the Ukraine and Hungary. All of these programs advance the struggle for Jewish knowledge and religious pluralism in Israel and throughout the world.

Publications of the Schechter Institute of Jewish Studies

Collected Articles

David Golinkin, Moshe Benovitz, Mordechai Akiva Friedman, Menahem Schmelzer, Daniel Sperber, eds., *Torah Lishmah: Essays in Jewish Studies in Honor of Professor Shamma Friedman*, Jerusalem, 2007, cxvi + 561 pp. (Hebrew and English; co-published by Bar Ilan University Press and The Jewish Theological Seminary)

David Golinkin, *Insight Israel - The View from Schechter*, Jerusalem, 2003, 175 pp.

David Golinkin, *Insight Israel - The View from Schechter*, Second Series, Jerusalem, 2006, 297 pp.

Michael Corinaldi, Moshe David Herr, Rivka Horowitz, Yohanan Sillman, eds., *Professor Ze'ev Falk Memorial Volume*, Jerusalem, 2005, xxxix + 400 pp. (Hebrew and English; co-published by Meisharim)

The Individual, the Collective and Kelal Yisrael: Israel as a Multi-Cultural Society, Jerusalem, no date, 63 pp. (Hebrew)

Common Values – Different Sources: Jewish, Christian and Muslim Reflections, Jerusalem, 1994, 194 pp. (Hebrew; co-published by ICCI)

Theodore Friedman, *Be'er Tuvia: From the Writings of Rabbi Theodore Friedman*, edited by David Golinkin, The Masorti Movement, Jerusalem, 1991, 317 + 106 pp. (English, Hebrew and Spanish)

Alice Shalvi and Linda Price, eds., *Israel as a Pluralist State: Achievements and Goals*, Jerusalem, 2006, 49 + 50 pp. (English and Hebrew)

Bible

Ze'ev Falk, *Torah Words "To the Very End"*, Jerusalem, 1998, 500 pp. (Hebrew)

Halakhah

David Golinkin, *Halakhah for Our Time: The Approach of the Masorti Movement to Halakhah*, Jerusalem 5758 / 1998 (Hebrew version: 40 pp.; Russian version: 47 pp.; English version: 49 pp.)

Isaac Klein and David Golinkin, *A Time to Be Born and a Time to Die*, Jerusalem, 1991, 80 pp. (Hebrew); Russian version translated and edited by Mikhael Kovsan, Jerusalem, 2004, 95 pp.

Shmuel Glick, *Education in Light of Israeli Law and Halakhic Literature*, Volume 1, Jerusalem, 5759; Volume 2, Jerusalem, 5760, 926 pp. (Hebrew)

Ze'ev Falk, *Introduction to Jewish Law in the Second Temple Period*, Jerusalem, 1983, 388 pp. (Hebrew)

Ze'ev Falk, *Law and Religion: The Jewish Experience*, Jerusalem, 1981, 238 pp.

Ze'ev Falk, *Legal Values and Judaism: Towards a Philosophy of Halakhah*, Jerusalem, 1980, 193 pp.

Responsa

David Golinkin, ed. *Responsa of the Va'ad Halakhah of the Rabbinical Assembly of Israel*, Volume 6 (5755–5758 / 1995–1998), Jerusalem, 1998, 358 + xxxiii pp. (Hebrew; co-published by The Rabbinical Assembly of Israel and the Masorti Movement)

David Golinkin, *Responsa in a Moment*, Jerusalem, 2000, 103 pp.

Isaac Klein, *Responsa and Halakhic Studies*, second revised and expanded edition, edited by David Golinkin and Monique Susskind Goldberg, Jerusalem, 2005, xxiv + 239 pp.

Shmuel Glick, ed., *Kuntress Hateshuvot Hehadash: A Bibliographic Thesaurus of Responsa Literature published from ca.* 1470–2000, Vol. I (א-ל) , Jerusalem and Ramat-Gan, 2006, xxiv + 106 + 524 pp.; Vol. II (מ-ק), Jerusalem and Ramat-Gan, 2007, 11 + 483 pp. (Hebrew; co-published by Bar-Ilan University Law Faculty and the Schocken Institute)

Hayyim Hirschensohn, *Malki Bakodesh*, edited by David Zohar, Volume 1, Jerusalem, 2006, xxii + 56 + 234 pp. (Hebrew; co-published by Bar-Ilan University and The Shalom Hartman Institute)

Women in Judaism

Miriam Berkowitz, *Taking the Plunge: A Practical and Spiritual Guide to the Mikveh*, edited by David Golinkin, Jerusalem, 2007, xvii + 187 pp.

David Golinkin, *The Status of Women in Jewish Law: Responsa*, Jerusalem, 2001, liv + 250 pp. (Hebrew with English summaries)

Monique Susskind Goldberg and Diana Villa, *Za'akat Dalot: Halakhic Solutions for the Agunot of Our Time*, edited by David Golinkin, Moshe Benovitz and Richard Lewis, Jerusalem, 2006, 16 + 426 + xxxii pp. (Hebrew with English summaries)

Monique Susskind Goldberg and Diana Villa, *Jewish Law Watch: The Agunah Dilemma*, edited by David Golinkin, Nos. 1–7, January 2000–July 2003 (Hebrew and English)

Monique Susskind Goldberg and Diana Villa, *To Learn and To Teach: Study Booklets Regarding Women in Jewish Law*, edited by David Golinkin, Nos. 1–5, April 2004–January 2008 (Hebrew, English, French, Spanish, Russian)

Ze'ev Falk, *The Laws of Marriage*, Jerusalem, 1983, 178 pp. (Hebrew)

Renée Levine Melammed, editor, *"Lift Up Your Voice": Women's Voices and Feminist Interpretation in Jewish Studies*, Tel Aviv, 2001, 205 pp. (Hebrew; Yediyot Aharonot, Sifrei Hemed)

Bat-Sheva Margalit Stern, *Redemption in Bondage: The Women Workers' Movement in Eretz Israel 1920–1939*, Jerusalem, 2006, 451 pp. (Hebrew; co-published by Yad Ben-Zvi)

Nashim: *A Journal of Jewish Women's Studies and Gender Issues*, Vols. 1–13, 1998–2007, (co-published by Brandeis University and Indiana University Press)

Prayer and Liturgy

Matthew Berkowitz, *The Lovell Haggadah*, Jerusalem, 2008, 225 pp. (co-published by Nirtzah Editions)

Hayyim Herman Kieval, *The High Holy Days: A Commentary on the Prayerbook of Rosh Hashanah and Yom Kippur*, second edition edited by David Golinkin and Monique Susskind Goldberg, Jerusalem, 2004, xii + 359 pp.

Megillat Hashoah, The Shoah Scroll, by Avigdor Shinan, translated by Jules Harlow, edited by David Golinkin and Philip Scheim, Jerusalem, 2003, 68 pp. (co-published by the Rabbinical Assembly); also published in Hebrew, Hebrew-French, Hebrew-Russian and Hebrew-Spanish editions and as a *Tikkun* for copying by Scribes

David Golinkin, *Rediscovering the Art of Jewish Prayer*, The United Synagogue, New York, 1996, 34 pp.

Jewish Thought

Alexander Even-Chen, *A Voice from the Darkness: Abraham Joshua Heschel - Phenomenology and Mysticism*, Tel Aviv, 1999, 253 pp. (Hebrew; co-published by Am Oved)

Joseph Turner, *Faith and Humanism: A Study in Franz Rosenzweig's Religious Philosophy*, Tel-Aviv, 2001, 252 pp. (Hebrew; Hakibbutz Hameuhad)

Ze'ev Falk, *Torah and Philosophy: Towards a Philosophy of Torah*, Jerusalem, 2001, 281 pp. (Hebrew)

Eliezer Schweid, *A History of Modern Jewish Religious Philosophy*, 5 volumes, Tel Aviv, 2001–2006 (Hebrew; co-published by Am Oved)

Jewish History

David Levine, *Communal Fasts and Rabbinic Sermons — Theory and Practice in the Talmudic Period*, Tel Aviv, 2001, 269 pp. (Hebrew; Hakibbutz Hameuhad),

Robert Bonfil, *The Rabbinate in Renaissance Italy*, second edition, Jerusalem, 2005, 327 pp., (Hebrew; co-published by the Bialik Institute and the Schocken Institute)

Bat-Sheva Margalit Stern, *Redemption in Bondage: The Women Workers' Movement in Eretz Israel 1920–1939*, Jerusalem, 2006, 451 pp. (co-published by Yad Ben-Zvi)

Books in Russian

David Golinkin, *Halakhah for Our Time: The Approach of the Masorti Movement to Halakhah*, Jerusalem 5758 / 1998, 47 pp.

Noah Golinkin, *Ein Keloheinu*, Jerusalem, 1994, 127 pp.

Megillat Hashoah, The Shoah Scroll, by Avigdor Shinan, translated by Michael Kovsan, edited by David Golinkin and Philip Scheim, Jerusalem, 2006, 72 pp. (co-published by the Rabbinical Assembly)

Mikhael Kovsan, *Names in the Bible: Philosophical, Religious and Literary Meanings*, Jerusalem, 1996, 203 pp.

Mikhael Kovsan, *Jerusalem in the Jewish Tradition*, Jerusalem, 1999, 192 pp.

Mikhael Kovsan, *The Birth and Death of Rabbi Akiva*, Jerusalem, 2002, 200 pp.

Isaac Klein, David Golinkin and Mikhael Kovsan, *A Time to Be Born and a Time to Die*, Jerusalem, 2004, 95 pp.

David Golinkin, ed., *To Learn and To Teach: Study Booklets Regarding Women in Jewish Law*, Nos. 1–5, April 2004–January 2008

The Lovell Haggadah

Appendix:
The Illuminations Illuminated

Matthew L. Berkowitz

Plate 1

When You Enter the Land   וְהָיָה כִּי תָבוֹא אֶל הָאָרֶץ

Passover evening is a threshold for the Jewish people, a moment of transition suspended in time and space. Indeed, it marks two milestones in our national life: the Israelite journey through the desert and our eventual entry into the Land of Israel. While the first Passover in Israel occurs several years after the initial observance in Egypt, in the words of the liturgical poem *Lekha Dodi*, סוֹף מַעֲשֶׂה בְּמַחֲשָׁבָה תְחִלָּה (*sof ma'aseh b'maḥshavah t'ḥilah*), "the concluding deed is [contained] within the initial thought." In the telescoped time of seder night we journey to redemption in one evening; here fulfillment of the dream is represented by the Land of Israel.

Coming into the land is realized in the Book of Joshua. There, we see the first Passover celebration in the Land of Israel:

> Today I have rolled away from you the disgrace of Egypt... Encamped at Gilgal... the Israelites offered the Passover sacrifice on the fourteenth day of the month toward evening... (Joshua 5: 9–10).

Once the Israelites became rooted in the land, the manna ceased and "they eat of the yield of the land of Canaan" (Joshua 5:12). What was the "yield of the land of Canaan"? *Parashat Ekev* details the seven species, שִׁבְעַת הַמִּינִים (*shivat ha'minim*), with which the Land of Israel is especially blessed: "a land of wheat and barley, of grapes, figs, and pomegranates, a land of olive trees and [date] honey" (Deuteronomy 8:8).

This illumination centers on a verse from *Parashat Ki Tavo*:

> When you enter the land that the Lord your God is giving you as a heritage, and you possess it and settle it, you will take from the first fruits of the ground that you harvest from your land that the Lord is giving you, put it in a basket and go to the place where the Lord your God will choose to establish God's Name. You shall go to the priest in charge at that time and say to him, "I acknowledge this day before the Lord your God that I have entered the land that the Lord swore to our ancestors to assign to us" (Deuteronomy 26:1–3).

What better way to mark arrival in the Promised Land than to express appreciation to the One who enabled the journey! This is a moment not to be taken for granted. So too on Passover eve, as we gather with family and friends, we savor, show gratitude, and sanctify. Another excerpt from Deuteronomy 26 (*Ki Tavo*) shapes the *Maggid* section of the haggadah. The text relates how the priest receives the basket from the hand of the pilgrim and sets it down before the altar. Then the pilgrim declares:

> My ancestor was a wandering Aramean. He went down to Egypt and sojourned there few in number, and there too he became a nation—great, mighty, and numerous. The Egyptians dealt harshly with us... (Deuteronomy 26:5–10).

Other themes in *Parashat Ki Tavo* complement the seder evening. Both the Biblical narrative and Passover ritual focus on reflection and gratitude. Having reached the Promised Land,

> You may say in your heart, "My own power and the might of my own hand have won this wealth for me." Remember that it is Adonai your God who gives you the power to acquire wealth, in fulfillment of the covenant that God made an oath with your ancestors, as is still the case today" (Deuteronomy 8: 17–18).

Being mindful of the journey allows one to appreciate more fully the destination.

Accordingly, this design weaves together the two *parshiyot* of *Ekev* and *Ki Tavo*. Etched into the illuminated window is a decorative frame comprised of the seven species. The center of the page features the Hebrew verse, "You will take from the first fruits of the ground that you harvest from your land," hovering over a pilgrim's basket. That woven basket is filled with the pilgrim's first fruits, overflowing with the bounty of the seven species. Gazelles, just above the basket, symbolize the gracefulness and beauty of Israel, which is referred to as ארץ הצבי (*eretz ha'tzvi*), "the Land of the Gazelle," in Daniel 11:16, 41.

Plate 2
Saturating its Furrows תְּלָמֶיהָ רַוֵּה

Preciousness and fragility indelibly mark the land. Not irrigated by a river cutting through the length of the country like Egypt, Israel is almost entirely dependent on the heavens. The need to transform one's concept of irrigation from the Nile below to the heavens above represents not only a physical shift, but more significantly a spiritual one. To illustrate, note the produce of Egypt. In Numbers 11:5, the Israelites yearn for "the cucumbers, melons, leeks, onions, and garlic" of Egypt. All are harvested with posture and focus toward the ground. The signature fruits of Israel—dates, figs, pomegranates, olives, and grapes—require a radically different posture. One must reach heavenward, physically and spiritually, in order to harvest these fruits. Seder evening is about such change in orientation. We transform ourselves from the downtrodden slave to the uplifted dreamer. As the Psalmist declares,

> I raise my eyes to the mountains; whence will my help come? From God, the Creator of the heavens and the earth (Psalms 121:1–2).

This perspective came to life for me on a hike through Neot Kedumim, the Biblical Landscape Reserve in Israel. Accompanied by a group of thirty-eight adult students and led by guide Batya Uval, we walked through the agricultural cycle of the Jewish year. Just as the month of Nisan heralds the rebirth of the natural world after a winter of dormancy, the flora and fauna of Israel are signs of the rebirth of the land and the Jewish people.

Psalm 65 acknowledges that it is God who ultimately tends the earth, "saturating its furrows, leveling its ridges, softening it with showers, and blessing its growth" (Psalms 65:11). The psalm concludes with rich imagery:

> You crown the year with Your bounty; fatness is distilled in Your paths; the pasturelands distill it; the hills are girded with joy. The meadows are clothed with flocks, the valleys mantled with grain; they raise a shout, they break into song (Psalms 65:11–14).

The painting encapsulates the words of this psalm.

Plate 3

Order of the Seder   סֵדֶר הַסֵּדֶר

Some haggadah manuscripts begin with an illustration of מעשה בראשית (*ma'aseh bereshit*), the Creation. Though the narrative of יציאת מצרים (*yetziat mitzrayim*), the Exodus, begins with Israel's slavery in Egypt, the illuminators of these *haggadot* felt that descent into slavery and subsequent liberation were part of God's overall blueprint in creating the world. This concept is especially prominent in *The Sarajevo Haggadah*. Acquired by The Sarajevo Museum in 1894, this work was commissioned in Spain around 1350. It opens with the creation of the world. Why is this so powerful? *The Sarajevo Haggadah*, which accompanied the Jews into exile in 1492, affirms order and direction, returning readers to the moment when God carefully and thoughtfully created the world. In darkness, light emanates, connecting the experience of גירוש ספרד (*gerush Sefarad*), the expulsion from Spain, to יציאת מצרים, the Exodus from Egypt. Both "leavings" may be seen as part of God's plan.

This page adopts the theme of creation, progressing through the seven days of the week, with the steps of the seder on either side. Sequential Hebrew letters (*aleph* to *zayin*) are integrated into the drawing. The right side details *Kadesh* (a Kiddush cup and three stars representing the beginning of nightfall), *Urḥatz* (a jug washing hands, without a blessing), *Karpas* (leafy parsley adorning the background), *Yaḥatz* (the "yud" dividing the middle matzah), *Maggid* (a thumbnail map representing the journey from Egypt to Israel), *Raḥtzah* (a stream of water flowing from the word *barukh*, this time with a blessing), and *Motzi Matzah* (a stalk of wheat bounded by the broken *matzah*). The left-hand column portrays *Maror* (the bitter herb in various shades of green), *Korekh* (assembling the Hillel sandwich), *Shulḥan Orekh* (sharing the festive meal with guests), *Tzafun* (fruits of Israel for dessert, followed by the *afikoman*), *Barekh* (blessing after the meal, symbolized by hands offering the Priestly Blessing), *Hallel* (psalms of song with letters ascending as musical notation), and *Nirtzah* (conclusion, represented by a sunrise over Jerusalem).

The center column, depicting the six days of creation, culminates in Shabbat. Each horizontal band captures the essential act of creation on that day, and notes its corresponding letter of the *aleph-bet*. The letter *zayin* for the seventh day forms part of the Hebrew word, Shabbat. Thus, the ritual order of the evening reflects a larger order of creation.

As we set out in search of redemption, the haggadah encourages us to think about what role order plays in our lives. How disciplined are we? What constructive boundaries do we set for ourselves? How have we affirmed order and light even in moments of absolute chaos this past year? Like Rosh Hashanah, this evening begins a new year, marking the birth of the Jewish people (*Mishnah Rosh Hashanah* 1:1). The journey from *Kadesh* to *Nirtzah* is an opportunity for personal and communal transformation.

Plate 4

Bread of Affliction   הָא לַחְמָא עַנְיָא

On Passover eve we declare:

> This is the bread of affliction which our ancestors ate in the Land of Egypt. All who are hungry, come and eat! All who are in need, come and join this Passover gathering. Now we are here; next year may we be in the Land of Israel! Now we are slaves; next year may we be a free people!

Why does the Passover recitation begin with an offer of hospitality? One of the greatest *mitzvot* we can fulfill as Jews is הכנסת אורחים (*hakhnasat orḥim*)—inviting guests into our homes. The Talmud provides us with an exemplar of הכנסת אורחים: Rav Huna of Babylonia. Before sitting down to any meal, Rav Huna would open his door and declare: "Let all who are in need come and eat" (*BT Ta'anit 20b*). In the original Aramaic of the Talmud, this phrase contains a double entendre. It reads הוה פתח לבביה (*hava pataḥ l'vavei*), literally, "he would open his door". But the Aramaic לבביה (*l'vavei*) resembles the Hebrew לב (*lev*), heart. Rav Huna opened both his door and his heart.

Indeed, Maimonides makes Rav Huna's sensitive largesse a Jewish obligation:

> When a person eats and drinks at a festive meal, s/he is obligated to provide food for the stranger, the orphan, and the widow, along with the rest of the poor and despondent. And whoever locks the doors of the courtyard, and eats and drinks with family and does not provide food and drink for the poor or suffering people, this is not a *mitzvah* celebration, but a celebration of the stomach, and this kind of celebration is a disgrace (Maimonides, *Mishneh Torah, Yom Tov 6:18*).

Freedom is truly sanctified only when mindful of the needs of others.

This illustration underscores several messages. First, the festive meal of Rav Huna is bounded by history—slavery and redemption. Moving from bottom to top, we stylistically transition from the slavery of Egypt to the freedom of Jerusalem. How do we journey from slavery to redemption? Freedom is realized by taking care of the needs of the poor and inviting guests; we broaden our definition of family to include community. Note the welcoming gestures and countenance of Rav Huna, his wife, and their children, pointing to the matzah. Of what consequence is this matzah, indeed of this entire ritual, if it does not transform our behavior, if it does not encourage us to truly act in the image of God?

The seder provides for a potential experience on two levels: the real and the abstract. As we recount the story, we are given the opportunity to experience freedom with friends and family and those who are in need. It is both through the abstract storytelling and the deeds performed on the evening of Passover itself that we redeem ourselves. Bridging the gap between the real and the ideal is the sacred call of the evening.

Design influences for this illustration include a haggadah from Budapest, Hungary (1942), found in the collection of Harvard University (Yerushalmi, *Haggadah and History*, Plates 163 & 164), a haggadah from Augsburg, Germany (1534) found in the collection of The Jewish Theological Seminary (Yerushalmi, Plate 14), a haggadah from Mantua, Italy (1560) also from the JTS collection (Yerushalmi, Plate 22), and *Mashal HaKadmoni* (1491), JTS collection.

Plate 5

How Different is This Night! מַה נִּשְׁתַּנָּה הַלַּיְלָה הַזֶּה

The Four Questions are the much anticipated centerpiece of the Passover seder. These "questions" have become canonized by normative Judaism; who would consider a seder without "The Four Questions"? Yet, the original Mishnaic source (see page 46) of these queries yields surprising discoveries. First, "The Four Questions" are not even questions. Secondly, our version is a departure from the original rabbinic script.

The ideal is for children to ask their own questions. Only if a child is insufficiently curious does the parent open the discussion with the four observations. The Mishnah's script can initiate the evening's conversation, but the goal is to be inspired by the seder atmosphere to ask questions and offer one's own comments.

Furthermore, the original version of the fourth "question" differs from the text we read today. The Mishnah returns us to the Biblical observance of Passover. Exodus 12:1–13 mandates the sacrifice and consumption of the Paschal Lamb. It further commands Israelites to join family and friends in consuming the Paschal Lamb by dawn. The rules of how to cook and eat the lamb were crucial to the celebration. With the destruction of the Second Temple (70 C.E.), however, the Torah's mandated observance of Passover came to an abrupt end. How were the rabbis to envision Passover without a Temple?

The development of the seder coincides with the development of Rabbinic Judaism, a radical revolution that coped with the end of Temple worship by creating the Judaism we know today. The ritual of the seder came to replace the slaughter of the Paschal Lamb; the question relating to roasted meat came to be replaced by a question related to reclining on seder night. Early generations after the destruction of the Temple retained the original question, perhaps to encourage memory, or to prepare for a renewal of Temple ritual. Soon, however, the rabbis made a virtue out of necessity and embraced the seder as a legitimate surrogate for the sacrifice, replacing the fourth "question" with one relevant to the new reality.

The visual design reflects this history and the original version of "The Four Questions." A lamb lies at the center of the illumination, recalling the original *Pesah* observance. Each column of this design is devoted to one of "The Four Questions" of today, with the original statement regarding the Paschal Lamb subtly inscribed in the background.

"On all other nights" stands boldly calligraphed at the top of the page and "on this night" at the bottom of the page. Both the habitual and special rituals are woven into the columns of each design. In the right vertical panel, leavened bread transforms into matzah. Next, a cluster of vegetables becomes *maror*. The third design is set against a background of rushing waters, moving from a typical evening in which there is no dipping of foods, to seder evening in which we dip vegetables twice. The fourth panel juxtaposes sitting upright to reclining, for the latter is clearly a symbol of freedom. Shackles of slavery dangling from the corner disappear as three crowns emerge. We are all aristocracy this evening, not only because we recline like royalty, but because tonight we learn Torah. This idea is echoed by the crowns which typically adorn certain Hebrew letters in the Torah. True aristocracy in Judaism is not the human aristocrat, but the Divine word.

Plate 6

We Were Slaves to Pharaoh in Egypt   עֲבָדִים הָיִינוּ

In order to celebrate freedom, why do we need first to relive slavery? Michael Walzer explains, "slavery is begun and sustained by coercion, while service is begun and sustained by covenant" (*Exodus and Revolution*, 74). Only by re-engaging the covenant through active remembrance may the Israelites become a Holy Nation. The graphic design conveys these messages. Mount Sinai and a pyramid mirror each other, two halves of a whole. The pyramid is upside down, demonstrating that slavery is an unnatural and inverted state. Mount Sinai is upright, indicating that learning Torah is natural, the very purpose for which we were created.

The lower image of the pyramid is inspired by a midrashic commentary:

> Rav Ḥanin[a] expounded: The Holy Blessed One said to the tribes, "You have sold Joseph into slavery. By your lives, every year will you recite, 'We were slaves to Pharaoh,' and thereby atone for the sin of selling Joseph." And just as Joseph went forth from imprisonment to royalty, so we too have gone forth from slavery to freedom... (*Midrash Tehillim, Mizmor 10*).

This midrash is inscribed in the background of the pyramid. The lower design of the pyramid is rendered as a pit of shackles and/or snakes (according to Rashi's commentary that Joseph's brothers threw him into "a pit that had no water" but that was brimming with scorpions and snakes). The serpentine shackles become the roots of a small tree, a symbol of hope and resilience in its parched surroundings.

Rav Ḥanina's midrash is particularly compelling given the state of intra-Jewish relations in both Israel and the Diaspora. Joseph's fate, a product of brotherly enmity, is based partially on justifiable grievances (Joseph's haughtiness and their father's favoritism). However, the brothers' inability to express their frustration or to restrain their impulses leads to violence instead of healing words. Accordingly, the pyramid is draped with the כתונת פסים (ketonet passim), Joseph's striped or multicolored coat which was torn and dipped into lamb's blood as "evidence" to his father that Joseph had been killed. The colors of the כתונת פסים carry over into the border, a mosaic of shattered multicolored glass, reflecting the shattered love of a family torn apart by jealousy.

Still, there is always the hope for repair. We become redeemed individuals (and a redeemed people) by repenting for our misdeeds. אהבת ישראל (ahavat Yisrael), the absolute love of fellow Jews, is desperately needed today. Perhaps this is the way back to Sinai and ultimately to redemption. As Rav Kook said, the repair of שנאת חינם (sinat ḥinam), causeless hatred, is אהבת חינם (ahavat ḥinam), love motivated by no other reason than Jewish kinship. Differences are real, but they can be negotiated with respect and an understanding that what unites us is greater than that which divides. We are siblings, engaged in building a Jewish nation. By learning from the past, we can journey toward a more hopeful future.

Plate 7

The Morning Shema   קְרִיאַת שְׁמַע

The illumination, inspired by the rabbis seated in *B'nei Berak* (see page 57), reflects rabbinic attempts to define the precise time when one becomes obligated to recite the morning *Shema*. This issue is extensively addressed in the opening tractate of the Talmud, *Berakhot*. The text that frames this illumination is *Mishnah Berakhot 1:2*:

> From when may one read the *Shema* in the morning? From [the moment that] one may distinguish between blue and white. Rabbi Eliezer says, "[From the moment we can distinguish] between blue and green; and one may finish reading the *Shema* until the sun peers over the ridge of the mountains." Rabbi Yehoshua teaches, [we may read it] "until the third hour of the morning."

Five images connected to the recitation of the *Shema* appear within a decorative frame. The first is based on a *baraita* (tannaitic teaching) which rules that we are permitted to begin reading only when "we see a fellow human being from a distance of four arms' lengths and recognize that individual" (*BT Berakhot 9b*). What is the import of this definition? Before we can read the *Shema* and declare our belief in and allegiance to God, we must recognize our relationship to our fellow humans. We affirm what Martin Buber calls an *I–Thou* encounter. Relationships between humans give us a glimpse of the Eternal and allow us to enter God's presence. In the top left hand image, the silhouettes of two individuals face each other with "four *amot*" inscribed in Hebrew letters between them. This is the most compelling definition determining our obligation to recite the *Shema*. One may approach God only after having approached humanity. Encountering our fellow human, then meditating on God's presence, grounds us in this world, helping us realize the purpose of leading a God-inspired life: to better our own lives and the lives of those around us, to effect *tikkun olam*, the repair of a broken world.

The second image is that of a *ḥilazon* or field snail. Numbers 15:38 teaches the *mitzvah* of including a thread of blue in each group of the white *tzizit* that hang from the four corners of a *tallit*. The blue dye employed for the *tzitzit* is derived from a snail found on Israel's northern coast (*BT Menahot 44a*). According to the anonymous view of our mishnah, once we are able to distinguish between this blue and the white of the other threads, we can recite the *Shema*. This definition affirms both the *mitzvah* of *tzitzit* and the purpose of the act, namely, to look upon the *tzitzit* and remember the *mitzvot*. To fulfill the *mitzvah* of *tzitzit* is to feel commandedness—to pray, to engage in a life of learning and good deeds, and to recognize distinctions and boundaries in the human and natural worlds.

In the third image, a band of green and blue hues represents Rabbi Eliezer's opinion. He calls for a recitation time that is later in the morning, since more light is required to distinguish between green and blue than between blue and white. There is greater subtlety in Rabbi Eliezer's definition. Not only does one require more patience in waiting for the appropriate time to say the *Shema*, but also one must be more discerning and perceptive, more nuanced, to make the distinction that Rabbi Eliezer demands. His is a world requiring careful attention to detail.

Next, the lower left cartouche, composed of layers of blues (representing the sea, the sky, and the firmament) and a gold band (alluding to Divine Sovereignty) reflects a rabbinic teaching:

> *Tekhelet* (the blue dye of the snail) resembles the sea, and the sea resembles the firmament, and the firmament resembles the sapir stone, and the sapir stone resembles the throne of glory (*BT Menahot 43b*).

Recitation of the *Shema* bridges the earthly and heavenly realms. Such movement is reflected both in this teaching as well as in the arrangement of the three Biblical paragraphs that comprise the *Shema*—albeit in opposite directions. While the paragraphs of the *Shema* journey from God to the land to the individual, this midrash transitions from the land to the throne of God, encouraging us to aspire heavenward.

Finally, four strands of colorful *tzitziot* dance playfully down the right panel. The strands are woven tightly together at the top and project outward at the base of the *tzitzit*. The tied parts are shorter than the free-flowing strands; commitment to the *mitzvot* is not only compatible with freedom, it defines freedom. The knots (totaling six hundred thirteen by numerological calculations) remind us of the commandments.

The most significant connection between the *Shema* and the haggadah is the precision with which we read both texts. Every word, indeed every letter of the *Shema*, must be enunciated, and the paragraphs of the *Shema* must be recited in their proper order. The thought and attention with which we read the *Shema* define how we read a text Jewishly. As *Pirkei Avot* teaches, "turn it over and over, for everything is in it" (*Pirkei Avot 5:24*). Similarly, we pore over every word of the haggadah, drawing new insights with every reading.

Plate 8

The Four Children　אַרְבָּעָה בָנִים

Haggadot showcase many creative interpretations of The Four Children. They appear, among other representations, as characters on a deck of cards, abstract designs, and immigrants to the United States or to the Land of Israel. In this illustration, The Four Children appear as personalities from the *Tanakh*, the Hebrew Bible; for just as *Tanakh* is meant to be internalized, so are The Four Children a part of each of us, part of what we must contend with in order to mature in our freedom. The challenge is to be mindful of who we are today, and more importantly to envision whom we wish to be at next year's seder.

Deborah the Wise

The prophetess Deborah represents knowledge and understanding. The Book of Judges states that the Israelites went up to seek judgment from this great leader: "and the Israelites would come to her for decisions" (Judges 4:5). A judge must gather information, plumb its depths, and understand its applications. Deborah was courageous, discerning, and insightful. The image portrays Deborah seated gracefully under her palm tree. A tentative Barak consults with her before waging war against Sisera on Mount Tavor.

King Aḥav the Wicked

King Aḥav of Samaria is a fitting model of the one who acts selfishly without regard for "the other." During his reign, Aḥav turns to his neighbor, Navot, who owns a vineyard adjacent to the royal palace, and offers to purchase the property. Aḥav desires this land to plant a garden. However, loyally attached to his family's estate, Navot politely refuses Aḥav's offer. Navot's unwillingness to part with his vineyard inflames the king, who returns to his palace angry and agitated. Acting like a spoiled child, Aḥav refuses food and sulks in the presence of his manipulative wife, Jezebel. Jezebel schemes and finds two townspeople to testify falsely against Navot, saying that he had cursed both God and the king. Navot is then stoned to death and Aḥav triumphantly takes possession of the vineyard.

In response, God sends Elijah the Tishbite—for whom we open the door at the seder—to rebuke Aḥav (I Kings 21), for he and Jezebel have abused their power, profanely disregarding God, justice, and human dignity. This episode of "eminent domain" gone awry reminds us to wrestle with envy and deceit, passions which we must all struggle to restrain. Graphically, the design focuses on Aḥav and Jezebel. Aḥav rises out of a cluster of colorful grapes. The colors evoke jealousy and rage. Jezebel stands on the sidelines, instigating and orchestrating the intrigue which leads ultimately to her husband's demise.

Lot the Simple

Lot, the nephew of Avram, plays the role of the simple, innocent character. In a dramatic encounter between Lot and Avram, Genesis 13 relates that their flocks have become so numerous, that the men can no longer dwell in close proximity. In his wisdom, Avram turns to Lot and suggests a resolution to avoid conflict, "Let there be no strife between you and me, between my herdsmen and yours, for we are kinsmen. Is not the whole land before you? Let us separate: if you go north, I will go south; and if you go south, I will go north." Avram magnanimously places the choice in Lot's hands. The narrative continues,

Lot looked about him and saw how well-watered was the whole plain of the Jordan, all of it—this was before the Lord had destroyed Sodom and Gomorrah—all the way to Zoar, like the garden of the Lord, like the land of Egypt. So Lot chose for himself the whole plain of the Jordan, and Lot journeyed eastward (Genesis 13:10–11).

While a more mature individual would weigh other factors in a decision to relocate, Lot makes his decision based solely on appearances. Numbers 15:39 cautions us not to be seduced by our eyes nor by our impulses. Lot, on the other hand, acts like a child, a slave to visual temptation. He lacks judgment and sophistication and ends up in the corrupt Sodom and Gemorrah, facing the consequences of his naïve choice.

The image portrays a naïve Lot scanning the well-watered plain of Jordan in his eagerness to take possession. Lot has turned away from אשל אברהם (eshel Avraham), the tamarisk tree that our patriarch planted in Beersheva—also in the Hebrew taken as an acronym for hospitality: אכילה (akhilah), food; שתיה (shtiyah), drink; לינה (linah), lodging. This turning alludes to Rashi's commentary on Lot's journey, namely that he journeys literally, not *to* the east (mikedem), as the context of the story would suggest, but *from* the east, where God's presence dwelt in Eden: "Lot traveled away *from* the presence of God saying, 'I want neither Avram nor his God.'" His decision was not just a turning toward fertile land, but a turning away from God and from Avram's vision.

Adam and Eve, Who Know Not How to Ask

Finally, for the child who knows not how to ask, the illustration renders Adam and Eve. Representative of the first generation of humans, they are childlike in their innocence. "The two of them were naked, the man and his wife, yet they felt no shame" (Genesis 2:25). Questioning and self-reflection were not part of their vocabulary. If they had sought to understand God's rules or question the serpent's motives, they might have avoided their eviction from Eden.

Questions nurture identity and open the door for answers. Inquiry brings the power to understand and to challenge. Adam and Eve are depicted without mouths to show their inability, at this early stage of human development, to formulate questions. The fig tree, also prominent in the narrative and design, suggests a powerful midrash:

Why is Torah compared to a fig tree? Because most trees are harvested at once, but not so the fig tree. Its fruit ripens slowly and is harvested over a lifetime. So too, Torah; for Torah is not learned in a year or two, but over a lifetime (*Bemidbar Rabbah 12:9*).

Mishnah Pesaḥim 10:4 encourages parents to engage a child in an appropriate manner. Each child must receive the information that he or she can absorb, presented in a manner that he or she can comprehend. If the child is too young, unable to speak, or distant from the tradition, it is the parents' responsibility to take the initiative and to begin the discussion.

Plate 9

The Roots of the Nation שָׁרְשֵׁי הָעָם

When Jonah identifies himself to the sailors bound for Tarshish (Jonah 1:9), he announces, עִבְרִי אָנֹכִי (*Ivri anokhi*)—"I am a Hebrew!" What is the derivation of the word עִבְרִי (*Ivri*), and what does it teach us about our identity?

Based on the root *ayin-vet-resh* (עבר), *Ivri* means "the one who crosses over." It is an allusion to the first עִבְרִי, Avram, who crossed over the Euphrates River as he journeyed to the Land of Canaan. The frame of this illumination is a web of tributaries—the many tributaries that our ancestors crossed as they searched for new homes. Though often involuntary, these migrations were powerful reenactments of Avram's journey of *lekh lekha*—both a journey of a whole nation and a journey of the self.

While Avram's odyssey begins as he leaves homeland, town, and family and sets out across the river, the national journey begins definitively at Sinai, where the people receive the tools they will need to live as an independent nation. The linguistic progression in the illumination begins with God's declaration at Mount Sinai, "Behold I come to you in the עַב (*av*), thickness [or darkness] of the cloud" (Exodus 19:9). It is out of darkness that God reveals the Divine presence to the Israelites. This starting point is fitting, given the connection between עַב, darkness, and עבר (*ever*), "crossing over"—literally crossing from darkness into light. The transformation of the nation at this point in its history reminds us of Avram's personal transition from the darkness of idolatrous belief in his homeland, to the light of the knowledge of one God.

The illumination alludes to Joshua 24:2–3 in which Joshua declares to the assembled Israelites,

> Your ancestors were settled on the other side בְּעֵבֶר (*b'ever*) of the river [the Euphrates in Ur of the Chaldees], from long ago—Teraḥ, the father of Abraham and Naḥor—and they served other gods. And I took your ancestor Abraham from the other side of the river and guided him through the Land of Canaan...

The latter part of the verse raises the question, why does God choose Avram? Though God initially reaches out to Avram, our sages believe that Avram also chooses God. *Genesis Rabbah 39:1* teaches:

> Rabbi Isaac told the story of a man who was traveling from place to place when he saw a mansion ablaze. He wondered, "Is it possible that the mansion is without someone to look after it?" At that moment the owner of the mansion peered out at him and said, "I am the owner of this mansion!" So too Avram was wondering, "Is it possible that the world should be without someone to look after it?" The Holy Blessed One peered down at him and said, "I am the world's Owner!"

God embraces Avram, but Avram certainly reciprocates. Avram becomes the first Jew because he is willing to respond to God's call. If, as Arthur Hertzberg says, "To be a Jew is to be commanded," it is also true that to be a Jew is to respond to God's command, crossing into a place of faith governed by God's plan for the future. Still, even after he becomes the father of a great nation, we remember Avram's humble roots on the other side of the river, acknowledging what he had to sacrifice in order to embrace the new.

From the embryonic roots of the Jewish people, the piece turns the reader's attention to the Hebrew midwives or the [Egyptian] midwives of the Hebrews, (הַמְיַלְּדֹת הָעִבְרִיֹּת *ha-meyaldot ha-ivriot*, Exodus 1:15). In their courage, lovingkindness, and wisdom, they defy Pharaoh's orders and save the Hebrew males whom Pharaoh had condemned to death. By virtue of their collective conscience, they become a vehicle for national survival.

The narrative in Exodus continues, as Moses witnesses an Egyptian taskmaster brutally beating a slave whom he recognizes as a Hebrew and considers a brother (אִישׁ עִבְרִי מֵאֶחָיו *ish ivri me'eḥav*, Exodus 2:11). Moses takes justice into his own hands as he deals a murderous blow to the Egyptian. He looks "this way and that" (Exodus 2:12), not only for others who may have witnessed the act, but also seeks internally, deciding how to react. As the sage Hillel teaches, "In a place that is lacking in leaders, make every effort to be a leader" (*Pirkei Avot 2:6*). This incident awakens Moses' identification as a Hebrew and marks the start of his career as a leader.

The design concludes with the expression וְהַעֲבַרְתָּ שׁוֹפַר תְּרוּעָה (*v'ha'avarta shofar teruah*), "and you shall sound the shofar blast" (Leviticus 25:9), heralding the Jubilee Year in which all property and slaves are returned to God. Creating a transition from darkness to light, from slavery to freedom, the entire visual composition reflects the Biblical verses found in the centerpiece, as well as the hopeful direction of the seder narrative.

Each of us can illuminate the darkness; we are commanded to sound the shofar of freedom. Every day, as Jews and as human beings, we are obligated to think how we can truly become עִבְרִים (*Ivrim*)—ones who actively cross over from being self-centered to being God-directed. We must also strive to emulate the midwives, putting our consciences above political expediency, doing what is right in God's eyes, and helping the Jewish people thrive.

Plate 10

The Covenant Between the Parts   בְּרִית בֵּין הַבְּתָרִים

At a moment of extreme darkness for Avram, as he is caught in a war between Canaanite kings, his nephew Lot taken captive, and he and his wife bereft of children, the word of God comes to Avram in a vision. God tells Avram, "Look heavenward and count the stars—if you are able to count them, so will your seed be" (Genesis 15:5). The first panel on the left illustrates this scene.

The next panel is split between two images. From above, Avram smashes the idols belonging to his father Terah (a midrash, *Genesis Rabbah 38:13*), marking the first stage in his journey toward monotheism. Once Avram realizes how alienated he is from his cultural milieu, he is ready to hear the call of לֶךְ לְךָ (*lekh lekha*), go forth to become an עִבְרִי (*Ivri*) Hebrew, and to cross over into Canaan. The lower section of the panel shows the produce of the Land of Canaan in full bloom as it offers the promise of abundance and fertility to Avram.

The third panel reflects God's instructions to the nascent patriarch in the Covenant Between the Parts, to take a heifer, goat, ram, turtle dove, and pigeon and divide them (Genesis 15:9–10). Birds of prey swoop down upon the offerings but Avram scatters them. Darkness descends and God declares, "Know well that your descendants will be strangers in a land not theirs; they will serve them, and [this nation] will afflict them for four hundred years. But I will judge that nation, and afterward they [the Israelites] will go forth with great wealth" (Genesis 15:13–14).

The fourth and final panel depicts the inevitable slavery predicted in the Covenant Between the Parts. At the top, the Israelites cry out to God—their cry setting into motion God's empathetic response and the beginning of the deliverance (Exodus 2:23–25). Ever hopeful, resourceful, and optimistic, Jews manage to turn periods of oppression into opportunities for growth. The taskmaster's whip—a dry, lifeless image of violence and pain, turns into the roots of a tree—alive, growing, full of potential, reaching heavenward. Some nations have their eyes to the ground, thinking only of the past and material success, venting their anger on the easiest victim. As Israelites, we seek to train our gaze upward, imagining a better future, remembering without blaming, judging success by education, arts, civil rights, and social services as well as economic and technological development, and seeking partners in *tikkun olam*.

Plate 11

And "She" Stood by Us וְהִיא שֶׁעָמְדָה

A riddle: who or what has stood by us throughout Jewish history? Some maintain that the indefinite feminine article "She" must be God, even though God is usually referred to in the masculine. Others insist that "She" refers to Torah or God's Promise הבטחתו (*havtaḥato*). The question demands theological wrestling.

Three Biblical episodes and one later historical one provoke these related questions: Who or what stood by us in the past? What stands by us, unwavering, in both our personal and national lives today? If "She" refers to God, do we constantly feel God's active presence or do we experience God's absence at certain moments? How can we live with such perceived "absence" and still continue to have faith in God's goodness, power, and empathy?

The top left corner portrays a vignette of Jacob, Rachel, and Leah standing before Jacob's notorious uncle, Lavan. The haggadah understands this as a dark moment in the biography of the Jewish people: by subtle deceit, Lavan tried to destroy our ancestor's morale. Jacob worked seven years for Lavan without wages, believing that this would enable him to marry his beloved Rachel. However, Lavan substituted Rachel's older sister Leah for Jacob's intended. Jacob married Rachel but was compelled to work for Lavan for another seven years.

Lavan's name means "white", an allusion to his *modus operandi*. Overtly, Lavan was gracious and hospitable; his crafty side emerged only later. The slavery Jacob experienced was unrecognizable until it was too late. Such bondage is worse than the easily identifiable slavery. What gave Jacob hope through these years of loneliness and estrangement from family? What stood by him? Indeed, it was God's promise:

> Your descendants will be as the dust of the earth; you will spread out to the west and east, to the north and to the south. All the families of the earth will be blessed through you and your descendants. Remember, I am with you: I will protect you wherever you go and will bring you back to this land. I will not leave you until I have done what I have promised you (Genesis 28:14–15).

The top right corner depicts Amalek's slaughter of the Israelites as they depart Egypt:

> Remember what Amalek did to you on your journey after you left Egypt—how, undeterred by fear of God, he surprised you on the march when you were famished and weary, and cut down all the stragglers in your rear... (Deuteronomy 25:17–18).

Amalek descends on the weakest of the Israelites, mercilessly annihilating them as they take their first steps toward freedom. Amalek's blatant lack of fear of God makes him a symbol of unrestrained evil. Here again, God's promise to Avram gives the people strength to continue on their journey.

It is fitting to move from Amalek to his descendant, Haman. In the lower left corner of the illumination, King Ahasuerus and Queen Esther ponder the noose of Haman, the villain of the Purim narrative, who sought to annihilate the Jewish people in the Persian empire. God's presence is felt behind the scenes in this tale of tragedy and deliverance, but God's name is absent from the text. Still, the earlier covenantal promise empowers Esther to approach the king and lends the people courage to confront Haman. Indeed, the rabbinic reading understands the Purim story as the Jews' confirmation of the covenant at Sinai.

The image in the lower right corner recalls the Shoah, which strained the Jewish people's trust in Divine Promise as never before. Barbed wire, yellow badges, and flames of Kristallnacht bear witness to the devastation of a people. In small golden letters, the word התקוה (*hatikvah*), "the hope" is inscribed, alluding to the hope that enabled people to survive, and foreshadowing the birth of the modern State of Israel.

The center of the page contains a floral motif. The oval egg shape suggests the fragility of the Divine Promise, while the center of the page contains a floral motif. Sprouting shoots testify to life reborn after destruction. Inside, the words והיא שעמדה (*v'hi she'amda*) declare boldly, "She [all of these promises] indeed stood by us!"

Plate 12

Abundant as the Plants of the Field וְרָבְבָה כְּצֶמַח הַשָּׂדֶה

Abundance and fertility form the heart of the promise made to our ancestors, as in God's assurance to Abraham, "I will bestow my blessing on you and make your descendants as numerous as the stars of heaven and the sands on the seashore..." (Genesis 22:17). *Genesis Rabbah*, a classic midrash on Genesis, cites a verse from Hosea:

> "I found Israel like grapes in the wilderness; I saw your fathers as the first ripened fruits on the fig tree at her first season" (Hosea 9:10). Rabbi Yudan said, "At first a fig tree's fruit is picked one by one, then two by two, then three by three until the figs ripen so abundantly that baskets must be used to gather them." So, too, at the beginning, "Abraham was one and he inherited the Land" (Ezekiel 33:24). Then two: Abraham and Isaac. And after that, three: Abraham, Isaac, and Jacob. Until finally, "The children of Israel were fruitful and increased abundantly and multiplied and waxed exceedingly mighty" (Exodus 1:7) (*Genesis Rabbah 46:1*).

Similarly, Rabbi Menahem Kasher (editor of *Torah Shleimah*) quotes a teaching of the *Rishonim* (the medieval rabbis): "Israel is likened to the plants of the field. Why? The more you prune them back, the more vigorously they grow." Indeed, the trials of Israel have made us a stronger, more resilient people.

Rich colors illuminate this page, alluding to Ezekiel 16:10, which speaks of God enrobing the Israelites in garments of "linen, silk, and embroidery." The floral design at each corner represents ארבע כנפות הארץ (*arbah kanfot ha'aretz*), "the four corners of the world" to which the Israelites were dispersed with the destruction of the Temple.

This piece is inspired by *The Nuremberg Maḥzor*, an illuminated manuscript on vellum dating from 1330–1331. The *maḥzor* is significant for its origins as well as its artwork: just as Jacob's descendants integrated quickly into Egypt and lived for some time in relative calm and prosperity, so did Jews settle and prosper in Germany for centuries. But just as the sweet blessings of Egypt gradually turned sour, so did the promise of acceptance and prosperity in Germany prove ephemeral.

Plate 13

Maror: The Subtle Descent יְרִידָה לְעַבְדוּת

The painting conveys the subtle descent into bondage. A graphic timeline reads from top to bottom, as the lives of the Israelites gradually become embittered. The narrative begins with Joseph and his brothers. Sold into slavery, Joseph is brought to Egypt where he rises to become second-in-command to Pharaoh. Due to famine, his brothers go down to Egypt to secure provisions for the family. Unbeknownst to them, the viceroy whom they beg for grain is really their brother Joseph. Eventually, the entire family descends to Egypt and is welcomed by Pharaoh and given land in Goshen. There they become numerous, and a pivotal moment in their history occurs: "A new king arose over Egypt who did not know Joseph" (Exodus 1:8). Joseph, who saved Egypt from famine, is forgotten. His descendants, once quite comfortable in the land of their sojourn, slowly become marginalized. They are viewed as a fifth column, a source of suspicion and fear. Pharaoh declares to his people, "Let us deal shrewdly with them, so that they may not increase; otherwise in the event of war they may join our enemies in fighting against us and gain ascendancy over the country" (Exodus 1:10).

Pictured in his ruthlessness, Pharaoh decrees that first born males must be drowned in the Nile. At the headwaters of the flowing river, Egyptians cast Israelite children into the river.

Next, Yocheved gently, reluctantly places her son Moses into a basket. She hopes this will save him from Egyptian persecution, but she knows the chances for survival are slim.

Further downstream, Pharaoh's daughter (known in the midrash as Batya, "daughter of God," for her compassion and empathy) removes Moses from the water and raises him, foreshadowing how she will raise him to adulthood. She earns the honor of naming Moses, declaring כי מן המים משיתהו (ki min ha-mayim mishitihu), "for I drew him out of the water" (Exodus 2:10).

At the base of the picture, faceless Israelites slide into an abyss. Now fully enslaved, they have lost their individuality. Naked, powerless, bowed by burdens and abused by taskmasters, they risk losing their humanity as well. Chillingly familiar, Pharaoh's twin strategies of propaganda and dehumanization have characterized persecution and enslavement throughout history.

Inscribed in the background of the page is the critical excerpt from the opening chapter of Exodus:

> And [Pharaoh] said to his people... "let us deal shrewdly with them, so that they may not increase; otherwise in the event of war they may join our enemies in fighting against us and gain ascendancy over the country." So [the Egyptians] set taskmasters over them to oppress them with forced labor. And they built garrison cities for Pharaoh, Pithom and Raamses. But the more they were oppressed, the more they increased and spread out, so that the Egyptians came to dread the Israelites. The Egyptians ruthlessly imposed hard labor upon the Israelites... (Exodus 1:9–13).

The calligraphed text transitions from light to dark, conveying the experience of the Israelites in Egypt. The sequence of events transpires inside a *maror* leaf, echoing the teaching of Rabbi Shmuel bar Naḥmani (see page 82).

Plate 14

And We Cried Out   וַנִּצְעַק

And we cried out to Adonai, the God of our ancestors, and God heard our voices and saw our suffering, our toil, and our oppression (Deuteronomy 26:7).

Emil Fackenheim, the great Jewish philosopher of the past century, remarked, "The response from below calls forth a response from above." Here a human act, the crying out of the Israelites, triggers successive actions from God: God hears, God remembers, God looks, and God takes notice.

I have always been moved by Fackenheim's theology, particularly by the extent to which he places responsibility on human beings. We are endowed with much more power than we are often willing to admit. We must take steps toward our goals and dreams, not sit passively expecting God to do all the work. We see this expressed in Deuteronomy 4:29, "But if you search there for the Lord your God, you will find God, if only you seek God with all your heart and soul…" The rabbis expressed the same concept in another way: אין סומכין על הנס (*ain somkhin al ha'nes*)—"one ought not to rely on miracles." The Divine acts in partnership with us; sometimes human action is a necessary precursor to a Divine response.

This plate conveys the message underlying this narrative in Exodus. "And we cried out" appears repeatedly in various Hebrew styles. Elsewhere in Tanakh "crying out" is interpreted by later commentators to mean prayer (for example, when the Israelites are trapped between the Reed Sea ahead of them and Pharaoh's chariots approaching from the rear, Exodus 14:10, and Moses in Exodus 4:15; see *Midrash Tanḥuma, Parashat Beshalaḥ* 9). The variety of lettering styles mirrors the many different ways in which individual Israelites cried out—or prayed—personally and collectively, to elicit a response from above.

"And we cried out to Adonai, the God of our ancestors," as it is said:

> After a long time, the king of Egypt died. The Children of Israel were groaning under their bondage and they cried out. And their outcry because of the bondage went up to God. God heard their moaning, and God remembered the covenant with Abraham, with Isaac, and with Jacob. God looked upon the Children of Israel and God knew (Exodus 2:23–25).

Interspersed among the cries appear the responses: וישמע (*vayishma'*), "and God heard"; ויזכור (*vayizkor*), "and God remembered"; וירא (*vayar*), "and God saw"; and וידע (*vayeda'*), "and God knew." Sometimes it takes much crying out to God before we hear a response, sometimes we cannot discern a response, and sometimes the heavenly response is not to interfere. But in the Passover story at least, the human act—calling God's attention to the plight of God's people through heartfelt prayer and communication—ultimately leads God to intervene and deliver the Israelites.

Plates 15 & 16

Plagues עֶשֶׂר מַכּוֹת

Today, the recitation of the Ten Plagues is often accompanied by humorous plague bags and gimmicks. It is, however, a moment for serious reflection. Rabbinic explanations seek to multiply the plagues: Rabbi Yosse the Galiliean says God brought ten plagues in Egypt and fifty at the Reed Sea; Rabbi Eliezer says forty in Egypt and two hundred at the sea; Rabbi Akiva says fifty in Egypt and two hundred fifty at the sea. While each year we may express our impatience with this midrashic math, we can learn from their message through metaphor. Why are the rabbis so intent on increasing the number of plagues? Such exegesis is employed to increase the grandeur of God. The miracle of redemption becomes even greater than previously imagined.

Yet our joy is restrained, for the Israelites' freedom was attained through the suffering of others. The tradition teaches that wine is a symbol of joy:

> ...as it is written, "And you will rejoice on your festival" (Deuteronomy 16:14). How should a man cause his household to rejoice? With wine... we have learned in a *baraita*, Rabbi Yehudah ben Bateira said: "When the Temple was still in existence, there was no better mode of rejoicing, than with (the eating of) meat, as it is written, "And you will slay peace-offerings, and eat them there; and you will rejoice before the Lord your God" (Deuteronomy 27:7) but now, in the absence of the Temple, wine is the principle means of rejoicing, as it is written (Psalms 104:15): "Wine gladdens the heart of man" (*BT Pesaḥim 109a*).

A full cup of wine represents joy overflowing. On seder night, we diminish the cup of wine. Dr. Eduard Baneth, a German-Jewish scholar, explains this custom, "There are those who teach that the tradition to remove drops of wine from the cup is for the sake of acknowledging that our joy is diminished and incomplete because our redemption came through the suffering of other human beings"(*Der Sederabend, Berlin, 1904, p. 29*). Baneth's teaching dovetails well with Proverbs 24:17: "Do not rejoice at the downfall of your enemy...".

Similarly, we learn from *Yalkut, Emor 654*:

> Another answer to the question of why Scripture gives no command to rejoice even once during Passover: because the Egyptians died during Passover. Therefore, you find that though we read the entire *Hallel* on each of the seven days of Sukkot [an entirely joyful feast], on Passover we read the entire *Hallel* only on the first day and the night preceding it. Why not on the other days of the festival? It is taught: "Do not rejoice at the downfall of your enemy, nor let your heart be glad when he stumbles" (Proverbs 24:17).

Our actions reflect a moment of deep humanity and sensitivity. All people are God's creatures, even when they are not on "our side." The suffering of others, even of our enemies, is no cause for joy. It is not uncommon to gloat at the suffering of one's enemies. But, as a freed people, the Jewish people should always aspire to a higher morality. We are told explicitly not to oppress others. Here, we go further and recognize the other's pain. Egyptian oppression sensitizes us—even to the suffering of the oppressors.

The design reflects Rabbi Akiva's teaching (on page 97) that each plague in Egypt was actually five separate plagues:

> Rabbi Akiva says, "How do we know that each plague was actually five plagues? Scripture teaches, 'God sent anger, wrath, retribution, sorrow, and a cabal of evil messengers' (Psalms 78:49). Anger—one. Wrath—two. Retribution—three. Sorrow—four. A cabal of evil messengers—five. So one may conclude that in Egypt they were stricken by fifty plagues..."

The colors reflect the nature of each plague: a band of reds for blood, greens for the frogs, pale colors for the lice, a mixed spectrum for the horde of beasts, shades of brown for the cattle pestilence, yellows for the boils, blues for hail, progressively darker grays for locusts gradually covering the skies, blackened tones for darkness, and reds again for the death of the first born. The design eschews a realistic depiction of the plagues, creating a visual equivalent of Rabbi Yehudah's allusive acronyms, *D'tzakh*, *Adash*, and *Be'aḥav* (on page 92).

The passage scrolled around the border derives from Baneth's commentary (see previous page). Burgundy and blue stippling recalls the drops of wine removed from the cup.

Plate 17

The Teaching of Rabban Gamliel   רַבָּן גַּמְלִיאֵל הָיָה אוֹמֵר

What is the essence of the seder? In the tenth chapter of *Pesaḥim*, Rabban Gamliel distills the seder down to three core elements:

> Rabban Gamliel used to say: Whoever does not mention these three symbols on Passover has not fulfilled the obligation for seder evening: the Paschal Lamb, Unleavened Bread, and the Bitter Herb.

Why *speak* about these three foods? The requirement for discussing them derives from both Exodus 12:27 and 13:8. In response to children asking, "What does this service mean to you?" the Torah commands, "You will say, 'It is the Passover sacrifice to the Lord, because God protected the homes of the Israelites in Egypt when God smote the Egyptians.'" Since the verse opens, "You will say," Rabban Gamliel understands an obligation to speak specifically about the Passover sacrifice (*Pesaḥ*). Since matzah and *maror* were eaten with the *Pesaḥ* in Biblical and Temple times, later even replacing the actual *Pesaḥ*, rabbinic logic extends the obligation to speaking about these items as well.

The illumination is divided into three horizontal bands, echoing the tripartite structure of the mishnah: *Pesaḥ*, *Matzah*, and *Maror*.

Rabban Gamliel's teaching wraps around the entire frame. It is built of square, brick-colored letters, as it forms the foundation of the seder experience. The name of each segment appears, divided between the right and left margins.

Pesaḥ—because God protected the homes of our ancestors in Egypt...

The uppermost window is devoted to the *Pesaḥ* or Paschal Lamb and the pilgrimage which preceded its slaughter at twilight on the fourteenth of Nisan. The pilgrimage and the eating of the Paschal Lamb together comprised the essential Biblical observance of Passover: "Take a lamb to a family, a lamb for each household... the Israelites will slaughter it at twilight... they will eat the flesh that same night; they will eat it roasted over the fire, with unleavened bread and with bitter herbs" (Exodus 12:3–8). A household too small to consume an entire lamb invited others to join, so that the lamb could be eaten by daybreak. This home-based ritual applied from the very first year the Israelites left Egypt, through their wanderings in the desert and their settling in Israel. Once the Temple was built, the Paschal Lamb had to be slaughtered within its precincts.

The lamb takes a prominent place in the illumination. A hyssop plant, used by the Israelites to brush the blood of the lamb on their lintels, blooms near the lamb. Pilgrims approach Jerusalem from all sides and prepare to enter the city.

The three major festivals in the Torah—*Pesaḥ, Shavuot,* and *Sukkot*—are referred to as שלוש רגלים (*shalosh regalim*), the three pilgrimage festivals. On each of these occasions, male Israelites were required to make a pilgrimage to the devotional site of Israel's God. (Women and children were welcome though not obligated.) From the time of Solomon (965 B.C.E.) through the destruction of the Second Temple (70 C.E.)—with a brief interruption between the two Temples—that site was the Temple Mount in Jerusalem. It must have been dramatic to see Jews streaming into Jerusalem from all directions, by mule or on foot, farmers and artisans, wealthy and poor, from as close as Lod or as far as Alexandria. The Tractate of *Bikkurim*, related to the holiday of Shavuot, describes the visitors' festive approach into the city, and the warm welcome they received from its inhabitants:

> Those who lived close by brought figs and grapes, and those who lived far away brought dried figs and raisins. And an ox went before them with its horns overlaid with gold and a crown of olive leaves on its head. The flute played before them until they drew near to Jerusalem. As they came close to Jerusalem, they sent messengers before them, and they adorned their first fruits (*bikkurim*). The governors, the chiefs, and the treasurers went out to meet them. According to the rank of those coming in, they used to go forth. And all the craftsmen in Jerusalem stood before them and greeted them, "Brethren of such-and-such a place, be welcome!" (*Mishnah Bikkurim 3:3*).

The spirit of such pilgrimage festivals resonates today in modern Jerusalem as the day breaks on *Shavuot*. After a full night of learning, Jews from all over the world—both Israelis and holiday visitors—stream through the streets to gather at the Western Wall.

Matzah—because their dough did not rise until God revealed God's Self and redeemed them immediately...

It is especially praiseworthy to eat special matzah, known as מצה שמורה (*matzah shmurah*), "guarded matzah," at both *sedarim*. Seder night is called ליל שימורים (*leyl shimurim*), "a night of watching," because God watched over the houses of the Israelites as the Angel of Death was unleashed. We recall God's watchful eye by our own act of watching. *Shmurah matzah's* wheat is guarded continuously from the time it is harvested in the field until its baking.

The baking of matzah is an intricate and involved process, requiring special care and attention. The center painting outlines many of the steps involved: growing the wheat, harvesting the sheaves, kneading the dough, serating the matzah with a special instrument, and finally the baking. Dough for matzah must be baked within eighteen minutes of mixing the flour with water. Once this time threshold has been crossed, the dough becomes *ḥametz*, leavened bread, and as such is proscribed during the entire festival. Therefore the number eighteen appears in gold in its Hebrew letter equivalent—*yud ḥet*. The pink and blue lettering forms the phrase "and they could not tarry… and they baked" (Exodus 12:39), recalling the matzah of the first Passover night in Egypt.

Maror—because the Egyptians embittered the lives of our ancestors…

The *maror* or bitter herb illustration alludes to another classical rabbinic quandary: What is the bitter herb to which the Torah refers? The canonical legal text of normative Judaism, the *Shulḥan Arukh*, relates, "these vegetables fulfill one's obligation to eat the bitter herb: *ḥazeret, ulshin, tamkha, ḥarḥavina,* and *maror*" (*Oraḥ Ḥayyim, Hilkhot Pesaḥ 473:5*). The many choices listed here tell us either that our ancestors were uncertain of the exact nature of the Biblical *maror*, or whether any bitter vegetable would do. They listed romaine lettuce, endives, chervil, ivy, and marrubium. Lettuce and endives become more bitter as they are chewed, simulating the gradual descent into slavery (see "*Maror: The Subtle Descent*"). An early twentieth century commentary, the *Mishnah Berurah*, suggests that *tamkha* is *ḥrain*, grated horseradish root rather than chervil, and this opinion forms the basis for the widespread practice of using horseradish as *maror*. However, it is preferable to use *ḥazeret* which is romaine lettuce.

The third window, "The Evolution of *Maror*," showcases the multiple answers to this rabbinic conundrum. It begins in actual servitude, with an Israelite straining under the burden of his labors, and continues with the varied menu of bitter herbs: chervil, horseradish root, endives, and marrubium—culminating in a well-known American variety, Gold's Horseradish.

Plate 18

In Every Generation   בְּכָל דּוֹר וָדוֹר

In every generation each person is obligated to relate to the Exodus as if it had been a personal journey, as it said, "You will tell your child on that day saying, 'It is because of what Adonai did for me when I went free from Egypt…' " (Exodus 13:8). It was not our ancestors alone whom God redeemed, but we who are present here today also were redeemed with them, as it is written, "God brought us out of there for the sake of giving us the land which God had promised to our ancestors" (Deuteronomy 6:23).

"In every generation" is a brilliant expression of our conception of Jewish history. It is insufficient to understand history as merely past events unrelated to our present and future. The many unexpected turns, the maze of history, have shaped us as individuals and as a people, and will continue to influence the direction and destination of our future journeys. The holidays are meant to reactualize past events as present experience, so that national history becomes personal memory. This notion fashions a more empathetic charge, for the experience of one generation becomes the memory of another. With Abraham, we are torn between family and duty; with Rachel, we experience the pain of childlessness; we descend to Egypt with Jacob and his sons; we jump into the waters of the Reed Sea with Naḥshon ben Aminadav; we dance with Miriam and her timbrel; we cross into the Land with Joshua. To be a Jew is to define ourselves from each of these memories, across the generations.

"In every generation" heightens our awareness of living in the image of God. Having been slaves, we are obligated to care for the weak and needy of society, seeing each person as a world worth cultivating. For "whoever rescues a single soul, Scripture credits with saving an entire world" (*Mishnah Sanhedrin 4:5*).

The relevant text of the haggadah is hollowed over a map of the journey from Egypt to Israel.

While it is difficult for us to imagine living in slavery, the more we are able to empathize with our ancestors, the sweeter our celebration becomes on seder night.

Plate 19

Israel's Departure   בְּצֵאת יִשְׂרָאֵל מִמִּצְרָיִם

Prior to drinking the second cup of wine, we sing the first half of *Hallel*, which will be completed after the meal. Psalm 114, the second psalm in the *Hallel* service, celebrates the redemption from Egypt. This liminal moment marks the Israelites' coalescence as a group even before the covenant at Sinai. Ilana Pardes writes,

> The Israelites are delivered collectively out of the womb of Egypt. National birth, much like individual births, takes place on a delicate border between life and death. It involves the transformation of blood from a signifier of death to a signifier of life... Then comes the climactic moment of delivery, which includes the ultimate revenge: the scene by the Reed Sea. Moses parts the waters at God's command. The Israelites walk upon land in the midst of the sea, and the Egyptian soldiers, who are pursuing them, drown as the waters return. The downfall of the parent nation seems total. Pharaoh, who wished to cast the Hebrew babies into the Nile, now finds his soldiers and fancy chariots sinking "like a stone" in the waters of the Reed Sea.

Just as the leaving of Egypt conjures up birth imagery, so does this episode mirror the creation of the world. Creation is accompanied by an act of separation, dividing light from darkness, heavens from earth, sea from dry land. Here, in shaping a nation, God removes the Israelites from their Egyptian surroundings.

While the imagery of Psalm 114 describes the Exodus, another stream of exegesis believes the author is alluding to Revelation. Liturgical allusions to Sinai declare, "The whole world trembled at Your presence and Your works of creation were in awe of You" (*Rosh Hashanah Musaf, Shofarot*). Whether the psalm evokes Exodus or Sinaitic Revelation, it echoes the three significant moments of Judaism: Creation, Revelation, and Redemption (Rosenzweig). A nation is born. The natural world trembles and retreats as Divine revelation issues forth. Objects defy their limitations: the inanimate flint is transformed into a spring of water. Weary souls become fertile ground for the building of a nation. Each Israelite acquires identity and responsibility in the experience of freedom. Indeed, they regain the individuality they had when they came to Egypt.

Like the psalm, the illustration is filled with movement: hills dance like gazelles and young lambs. Below, the waves part as the Israelites pass through on the sandy sea bed. *Midrashim* offer various opinions about exactly how the water parted; this rendering follows the literal text from Exodus 14:29, והמים להם חומה מימינם ומשמאלם "The waters were like a wall for them, to their right and to their left." The transition from sea to hills to sky simultaneously evokes the themes of creation and of separation.

Plate 20

Pour Out Your Wrath שְׁפֹךְ חֲמָתְךָ

The most difficult passage of the haggadah for many modern Jews is the request for God to unleash Divine retribution on those who have persecuted the Jewish people. We pour the wine of Elijah's cup, open the door and call out,

> Pour out Your wrath on the nations which do not know You, and upon governments which have not called upon Your Name. For the enemy has consumed Jacob and destroyed his refuge. Pour out Your wrath upon them, and let Your rage overpower them. Angrily pursue them and erase them from under God's sky.

Although many modern *haggadot* or seder leaders have excised this passage, I prefer understanding the text in context. Born of a history of suffering, the passage reflects emotional responses to physical, spiritual, political, and national persecution. שפוך חמתך (*shfokh ḥamatkha*) reveals a theology of הסתר פנים (*hester panim*), the hiding of the Divine presence. We hear the author of this cry knocking on the door of the Holy of Holies, demanding that God notice the suffering of the Jewish people. We call out to God in the words of the Psalmist,

> God of retribution, Lord, God of retribution appear! Rise up, judge of the earth, give the arrogant what they are due! How long will the wicked exult, will they utter insolent speech, will all evildoers vaunt themselves? They crush your people, O Lord, they afflict Your very own... (Psalms 94:1–5).

Since the declaration "Pour out Your wrath..." is juxtaposed in the seder with the Cup of Elijah, a symbol of redemption, this design depicts an inverted wine goblet. The wine is the text. A mirror image of "Pour out Your wrath," expresses the ambivalence in our recitation. This upside down kiddush cup also forms a doorway into a Jewish home. We are both inside the doorway shouting *shfokh ḥamatkha*, and outside with God and Elijah the prophet, looking in. How might God respond to our plea for retribution? Perhaps rather than vengeance, God offers to stand with us in our suffering. In the words of Isaiah,

> "Comfort, oh comfort My people," says your God. Speak tenderly to Jerusalem, and declare to her that her term of service is over, that her iniquity is expiated; for she has received at the hand of the Lord double for all her sins (Isaiah 40:1–2).

While it may be natural to wish for revenge, a sensitive soul restrains this urge. A desire for vengeance, even if justified, too often brings further destruction, making us callous to suffering and returning the world to chaos. We were redeemed from Egypt not to carry the burden of bitterness toward our oppressors, but to be more attuned to the needs of the oppressed.

In our own times, Israeli Jews and Palestinians have wasted many years with anger, recriminations, and hardened hearts. Many doors have been opened, and through them both sides can glimpse the potential for new partnerships, for economic and cultural flourishing. It is easy to shout for vengeance—much harder to patiently build. שפוך חמתך acknowledges history, pain, and loss. But the desire for retaliative action or for excessive self-pity must be contained and quelled. Future generations need to focus on mutual respect and peaceful coexistence.

Just as we inverted our experience in Egypt into a positive construct to redeem the world, so too must that anger of today be transformed. Venting our feelings enables us to remain human in relation to our enemies and to move forward instead of becoming fixated on "getting even". This passage acknowledges anger in words, hoping this will avert the wish to act on our impulses. Self-control becomes the flowering of our redemption, depicted in the design framing our doorway-kiddush cup.

Plate 21

Miriam the Prophetess   מִרְיָם הַנְּבִיאָה

Joy is the theme of the hour as God's praises are sung during the completion of *Hallel*. The image that dances forth is that of Miriam the prophetess and the women celebrating their newly found freedom on the banks of the Reed Sea, "For the horses of Pharaoh, with his chariots and horsemen, went into the sea; and the Lord turned back the waters of the sea on them; but the Israelites marched on dry ground in the midst of the sea" (Exodus 15:19). While the moment is solemn, it is also one of intense elation. And so the word "halleluyah," the refrain of many *Hallel* psalms, floats boldly at the top of the design. A mosaic of blues evokes the sea.

Vivid, glowing colors distinguish this illumination. Miriam stands prominently in the crowd of women, musical instruments in hand, dancing to celebrate their salvation. Scrolled around the frame is the Hebrew excerpt from *Parashat Beshalaḥ*:

> Then Miriam the prophetess, Aaron's sister, took a timbrel in her hand, and all the women went out after her in a dance with timbrels. And Miriam chanted for them, "Sing to the Lord, for God has triumphed gloriously; horse and driver God has hurled into the sea" (Exodus 15:20–21).

Miriam figures prominently in the story of redemption. According to a midrash (*BT Sotah 12a*), after her parents divorced to avoid Pharaoh's decree, she convinced them to remarry and have more children. Miriam watched over Moses in the basket and arranged for Yokheved, Moses' own mother, to be his wet nurse until he was weaned. Since babies were nursed for several years in ancient cultures, Yokheved is able to transmit core values to Moses in his formative years, planting the seeds of his identity as a man of ethics and as a Hebrew.

Here, Miriam takes the foreground, leading the women in song and dance and showing by personal example that these are appropriate expressions of gratitude and joy. Thirty-six women surround our prophetess. This number is significant. Abbaye, a Babylonian scholar of the Talmudic period, teaches, "There are not fewer than thirty-six righteous individuals in the world [at any given time] who receive the Divine presence" (*Sanhedrin 97b* and *Sukkah 45b*). These individuals are credited with God's daily decision to sustain the world; their righteousness tilts the scale in our favor.

However, celebration without limits leads to chaos. Delight must occur within a context, connected somehow to the betterment of humanity. These *lamed-vavnikot*, thirty-six righteous women, convey this message. They are dancing for a cause, not only for their present deliverance, but also for the redemption to come. Later tradition teaches us that the identities of the thirty-six righteous individuals in every generation are not revealed to others or even to themselves. Only the Heavens know who they are. Let each of us aspire to their ideal, acting as if the world's survival depended on our righteousness. And let us treat others with respect and deference, knowing that "the other" might be one of the thirty-six.

Plate 22

Breath of All Life   נִשְׁמַת כָּל חַי תְּבָרֵךְ אֶת שְׁמֶךָ

This prayer, at the heart of the *Hallel* section, expresses our inability to praise God sufficiently:

> Even if our mouths were filled with song as water fills the sea,
> And our tongues shouting joy like the multitude of waves,
> And our lips as full of praise as the expanse of the heavens,

And our eyes as radiant as the sun and the moon,
And our hands spread as the wings of eagles in the sky,
And our legs as swift as gazelles,
We would still be unable to express even a fraction of the gratitude that we owe to You, O Lord our God...

Ironically, this very declaration of inadequacy is itself an eloquent tribute. And though we are limited by our human capacities, we know that נשמת כל חי (nishmat kol ḥai), the soul of every living creature, declares God's eternal praise. נשמה (neshamah) is a soul, נשימה (neshimah) is a breath; by simply breathing, not to mention making use of our higher functions, we attest to the miracle of life. The illumination is divided into six colorful bands bordered by the words, "the breath of all life," at the top, and "will bless Your name," at the base.

Each band depicts the abundant natural world, while the limited human features appear in bold Hebrew letters: the word פינו (finu) "our mouths" sails on an aqua sea; לשוננו (l'shoneinu) "our tongues" plays among the waves; עינינו (eineinu) "our eyes" basks in the light of the sun and the moon; ידינו (yadeinu) "our hands" reaches to the wings of soaring eagles; and רגלינו (ragleinu) "our legs" prances in the fields with graceful gazelles.

Four colorful squares grace the corners of the design, recalling the four corners of the earth which all play their role in declaring the magnificence of God's works. The orientation of the piece is horizontal, and the repeating horizontal lines hint at a sheet of music, since *Hallel* is sung.

Plate 23

Next Year in Jerusalem   לְשָׁנָה הַבָּאָה בִּירוּשָׁלָיִם

What is the meaning of this conclusion to the Passover festivities? Is it simply a hope to be present in the sacred city of Jerusalem in the coming year, or is the wish more spiritual and existential? Indeed, our dream is for a future punctuated by human-Divine partnership. This Passover evening raises our consciousness of the world's imperfections. Awareness leads to a greater sense of responsibility and, hopefully, to caring actions. The narrative of Ḥoni the Circle-Maker (see page 150) conveys this message.

This story is more than a fable about the altruistic generosity of one (presumably elderly) man. The gardener and the tree are important symbols. First, this gardener represents selflessness. His act of planting is חסד של אמת (ḥesed shel emet), an unconditional gesture of giving to future generations. He will not derive any benefit from the sapling he plants and nurtures today. He is an unselfish individual who recognizes the needs of generations beyond himself and of the larger world. His ḥesed brings to mind the stirring poem of Rabbi Avraham Yitzḥak Kook, שיר מרובע (The Fourfold Song):

There is one who ascends with all these songs in unison—the song of the soul, the song of the nation, the song of humanity, the song of the cosmos—resounding together, blending in harmony, circulating the sap of life, the sound of holy joy.

Second, it is no coincidence that our gardener plants a carob tree. What is the carob's significance? First, it is linked to physical survival. We know from Talmudic sources that the carob was the least expensive fruit of the Land of Israel, a dietary staple. "In years of scarcity," say the Sages, "one may not hoard even one *kav* of carobs, because such hoarding results in scarcity for Israel" (*BT Bava Batra 90b*). Rabbi Aḥa also taught that since carob is the sustenance of the poor, "it is what Israel requires to put them on the road to repentance" (*Pesikta DeRav Kahana 14:3*).

Perhaps for this reason, too, carob is considered the fruit of the sages. *BT Berakhot 17b* relates, "Rabbi Judah said in the name of Rav: Each and every day a Divine voice issues forth from Mount Ḥoreb and proclaims, 'The entire world is sustained on account of My son Ḥanina. But as for my son Ḥanina, he sustains himself on a *kav* of carobs from Sabbath to Sabbath.' " Similarly, Rabbi Shimon bar Yoḥai and his son are sustained by a carob tree when they learn Torah in a cave, secluded from Roman authorities (*BT Shabbat 33b*). Carob is a fruit of humility and wisdom; both are essential as we dwell on the message of Passover. Even as we celebrate our physical deliverance and continuity as a people, we do so with learning and discussion, showing gratitude and deference to the Holy One. Thus the carob is a fitting symbol for both aspects of the seder experience.

The illumination depicts our elderly gardener steadying his carob tree; characteristic Jerusalem homes appear blended in the trunk of the tree. Indeed, Jerusalem supports the carob tree—a plant that sustains us physically and spiritually. The background is suffused with more colorful dwellings of the sacred city. From a modest fruit, creativity and learning flourish. All of these contribute to a rebuilt Jerusalem. While the closing message of the haggadah may ostensibly be about the physical Jerusalem, its deeper message is related to ירושלים של מעלה (*Yerushalayim shel ma'alah*), "heavenly Jerusalem"—Jerusalem above and Jerusalem inside each of us.

Plate 24

Magnificent is God   אַדִּיר הוּא

The song *Adir Hu* began to appear in Ashkenazic (German) *haggadot* in the fourteenth century. In form and in content, this poem conveys three themes: building, God's praiseworthy qualities, and completion. First and most importantly, the poet yearns for a rebuilt Temple, urging God, "Build, build Your House again soon." The poet relies wholly on God to bring about his vision for the future.

Secondly, in order to uphold the promises made to Israel (namely, to rebuild the Temple and to lead the exiles back to Israel), God must exhibit exceptional qualities. These attributes weave a tapestry of God and God's role in our world.

Thirdly, the poet conveys totality and completion. The poem is written as an acrostic, employing the entire aleph-bet to express God's attributes. Not only is God complete, but the historical circle will be brought to completion.

Whereas the poetic vision centers on the physical rebuilding of the Temple and God's primary role in that task, the poet's words challenge us to wrestle with our own understanding of the Messianic Era and God's role in that ultimate redemption. This *piyyut* encapsulates "restorative messianism," a return to a golden age, symbolized by the Temple. We, on the other hand, may prefer "utopian messianism," a time of peace and harmony for people and the natural world, brought about by a partnership between humans and the Divine attributes which they seek to emulate (see midrash on page 160).

Colorful letters are engraved against a black background. The darkness represents our world, and the bright letters allude to the rare, vivid glimpses of God that inspire our lives. At such moments, we are given the gift of God's light. The Hebrew acrostic delineates God's qualities: magnificent, chosen, great, exceptional, glorified, eternal, perfect, righteous, pure, unique, powerful, learned, king, awesome, revered, mighty, redeemer, just, holy, merciful, almighty, and strong. When we are at our best, we internalize these divine attributes.

Isaiah offers yet another description of Messianic times:

> And the many peoples will go and say, "Come let us go up to the Mount of the Lord, to the House of the God of Jacob; that God may instruct us in God's ways, and that we may walk in God's path." For instruction will go forth from Zion, the word of the Lord from Jerusalem (Isaiah 2:3).

In Isaiah's vision, Israel and God will become teachers to the world, and the house that will be built will be a *Beit Midrash*, a House of Learning. The poet of *Adir Hu* waits for God to redeem; the midrash (page 160) expects humans to make the effort; Isaiah relies on the Torah to mediate between God and humans.

Plate 25

Who Knows One?   אֶחָד מִי יוֹדֵעַ?

Written during the Middle Ages, *Eḥad Mi Yodea* is a frenetic quiz of numerical associations in Jewish tradition. The song captures the spirit of the evening, alternating between questions and answers. It attests to the ongoing creativity of the tradition, exemplifying the dictum, "all who embellish the story of the Exodus are to be praised." Highlighting the breadth of Jewish tradition, the song encourages us to delve deeper into its layers.

The graphic "bookends" located at the top and bottom of the illumination read, "Who Knows?" followed by the introductory response for each verse, "I Know." Vertical columns on either side of the painting list the letters of the Hebrew aleph-bet, each letter standing for its numerical equivalent. The narrative progression of the lyrics leads us through a rich set of images:

One is God; Two are the Tablets of the Covenant; Three are the patriarchs (Abraham, Isaac, and Jacob); Four are the matriarchs (Sarah, Rebecca, Rachel, and Leah); Five are the books of Torah (Genesis, Exodus, Leviticus, Numbers, and Deuteronomy); Six are the orders of the Mishnah (Seeds, Festivals, Women, Damages, Holy Things, and Laws of Ritual Purity); Seven are the days of the week; Eight are the days until circumcision; Nine are the months of pregnancy; Ten are the Commandments (1. Do not have any other gods beside The One; 2. Do not worship idols; 3. Do not swear by the Divine Name or use God's Name in vain; 4. Remember the Sabbath and keep it holy; 5. Honor your father and your mother; 6. Do not murder; 7. Do not commit adultery; 8. Do not steal; 9. Do not testify falsely; 10. Do not covet). Eleven are the stars in Joseph's dream; Twelve are the Tribes of Israel (Reuven, Shimon, Levi, Judah, Dan, Naftali, Gad, Asher, Issachar, Zevulun, Joseph, and Benjamin); Thirteen are the atributes of God (1. merciful before a person sins, 2. merciful after the sin, 3. powerful, 4. compassionate, 5. gracious even to the undeserving, 6. slow to anger, 7. abundant in kindness and 8. abundant in truth, 9. preserving kindness for thousands of generations, 10. forgiving of iniquity, 11. forgiving of willful sin, 12. forgiving of error, and 13. willing to cleanse the sins of those who repent).

The structure of *Eḥad Mi Yodea* contains a potent theological message. The *piyyut* begins and ends with God—opening with God as *Eḥad* (One) and closing with the thirteen Divine attributes. In between these poles are symbols of partnership between God and humans: the Tablets of the Covenant, our ancestors, Torah, and Mishnah. The Divine message is handed to humans—heard, internalized, reworked, and retransmitted as Oral Torah.

Plate 26

One Goat   חַד גַּדְיָא

Ḥad Gadya, "One Goat," entered the Ashkenazic Passover haggadah around the fifteenth century. It is based stylistically on German ballad songs. While on its surface it seems to be a childish or nonsensical song, upon deeper examination it reveals a sophisticated theology. The song creates a pyramid of oppressed and oppressors. And though each oppressor believes that he has the upper hand, he quickly realizes that he is but a link in a chain which culminates with the Holy Blessed One. Power is elusive, and even the Angel of Death comes to realize where true strength resides.

This illumination continues the modern style employed in *Adir Hu* and *Eḥad Mi Yodea*. Negative (white) space conveys a sense of God's intangible presence. The center of the colorfully graphic rendition contains the song's chorus: "One goat which father bought for two *zuzim*, one goat." Beginning on the right side of the piece, the chronology of the song unfolds. Each protagonist or antagonist is identified in its own box, from the top right corner continuing clockwise: the goat purchased for two *zuzim*, the cat eating the goat, the dog biting the cat, the stick hitting the dog, the fire burning the stick, the water extinguishing the fire, the ox drinking the water, the slaughterer slaughtering the ox, the Angel of Death striking the slaughterer, and finally the Holy

Blessed One conquering the Angel of Death.

Perhaps "One Goat" is a metaphor for the people Israel, who were acquired by God with two Tablets of the Law. Each successive character represents another occupier of Israel: Assyrians, Babylonians, Persians, Greeks, Romans, Byzantines, Arabs, Crusaders, and Ottomans. Despite them all, God's plan has triumphed and the people Israel have been brought back to their homeland—an appropriate bridge to the singing of *Hatikvah*.

Plate 27

The Hope   הַתִּקְוָה

Inspired by the founding of the settlement of *Petaḥ Tikvah*, Galician-born poet Naphtali Herz Imber authored *Hatikvah* in 1878. More than the anthem of the Zionist Movement and later the modern State of Israel, this song is a paean to redemption, the *leitmotif* of seder eve. Redemption orients itself expansively. Although forward-looking, redemption is rooted in the past. Knowing our story, especially a narrative born of oppression, allows us to envision a dream and a hope. History is the fertile ground in which a landscape of redemption takes root. Only then can we move ahead.

Hatikvah reflects this multivalent orientation. In his insightful essay, "Locus and Language: Hebrew Culture in Israel 1890–1990," Ariel Hirschfeld (Professor of Hebrew Literature at The Hebrew University of Jerusalem) focuses on the line, "And toward the East קדימה (*kadimah*) an eye gazes toward Zion." With the sensitivity of a skilled philologist, Hirschfeld writes of the ambiguity latent in the root of the Hebrew word, קדימה. Three potent meanings emerge: backward as in "days of old" קדם (*kedem*), eastward קדים (*kadim*), and forward קדימה (*kadimah*). For Hirschfeld, these three directions reflect the redemptive yearning of the Jewish people. Having unearthed the narrative of Israelite history this seder night, we are now ready to gaze forward.

The decorative frame around *Hatikvah* is inspired by an illuminated *ketubbah* from Ferrara, Italy, 1822 (from the collection of Mr. Richard Levy of Boca Raton, Florida). Italian illuminated *ketubbot* are among the most exquisite and decorative in the history of *ketubbah* illumination. Moreover, the *ketubbah* is an appropriate connection to *Hatikvah* and to the conclusion of the seder for three reasons:

First, just as the *ketubbah* attests to the covenant between the bride and bridegroom, so the seder experience is a tangible reminder of the lasting relationship between God and the Jewish people. Similarly, *Hatikvah*, with its emotional connection to the Land of Israel, represents ראשית צמיחת גאולתנו (*reshit tzmiḥat geulateinu*), "the first flowering of our redemption." The *ketubbah* is an expression of hope and protection; the modern State of Israel symbolizes cautious optimism for a new generation of Jews. And finally, one way that a couple expresses their love for each other is through the telling and retelling of their own story. Just as a couple repeatedly tells their story of finding each other, so too do God and the Israelites come together yearly to relate their narrative of discovering each other.

דוֹר לְדוֹר יְשַׁבַּח מַעֲשֶׂיךָ וּגְבוּרֹתֶיךָ יַגִּידוּ

Generation to generation will praise Your deeds,
and they will tell of Your great works.

Psalms 145:4